FRUIT OF KNOWLEDGE

THE VULVA
VS.
THE PATRIARCHY

LIV STRÖMQUIST

FANTAGRAPHICS BOOKS

Supervising Editor: Gary Groth
Translator: Melissa Bowers
Editor: Kristy Valenti
Designer: Keeli McCarthy
Cover designer: Josefine Edenvik and Keeli McCarthy
Production: Paul Baresh
Editorial Assistants: Gareth Bentall, RJ Casey,
Conrad Groth, Manon Hume, Avi Kool, Minna Lee
Associate Publisher: Eric Reynolds
Publisher: Gary Groth

Fantagraphics Books, Inc.
7563 Lake City Way NE,
Seattle, WA 98115
(800) 657-1100

www.fantagraphics.com

Follow us on Twitter @fantagraphics and on
Facebook at Facebook.com/Fantagraphics.

ISBN: 978-1-68396-110-9
Library of Congress Control Number: 2017957137

First Printing: August 2018
Printed in Hong Kong

Thanks to Sara Hansson, Sara Granér,
and Livia Rostovanyi

1. MEN WHO HAVE BEEN TOO INTERESTED IN THE FEMALE GENITALIA

2. UPSIDE-DOWN ROOSTER COMB

3. AAH HAA

4. FEELING EVE

5. BLOOD MOUNTAIN

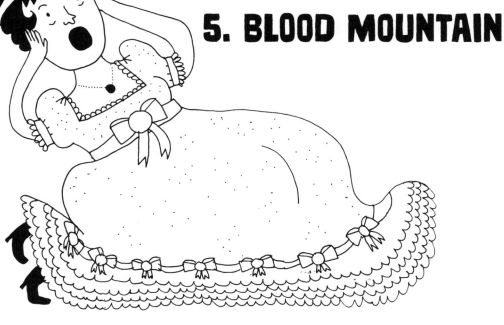

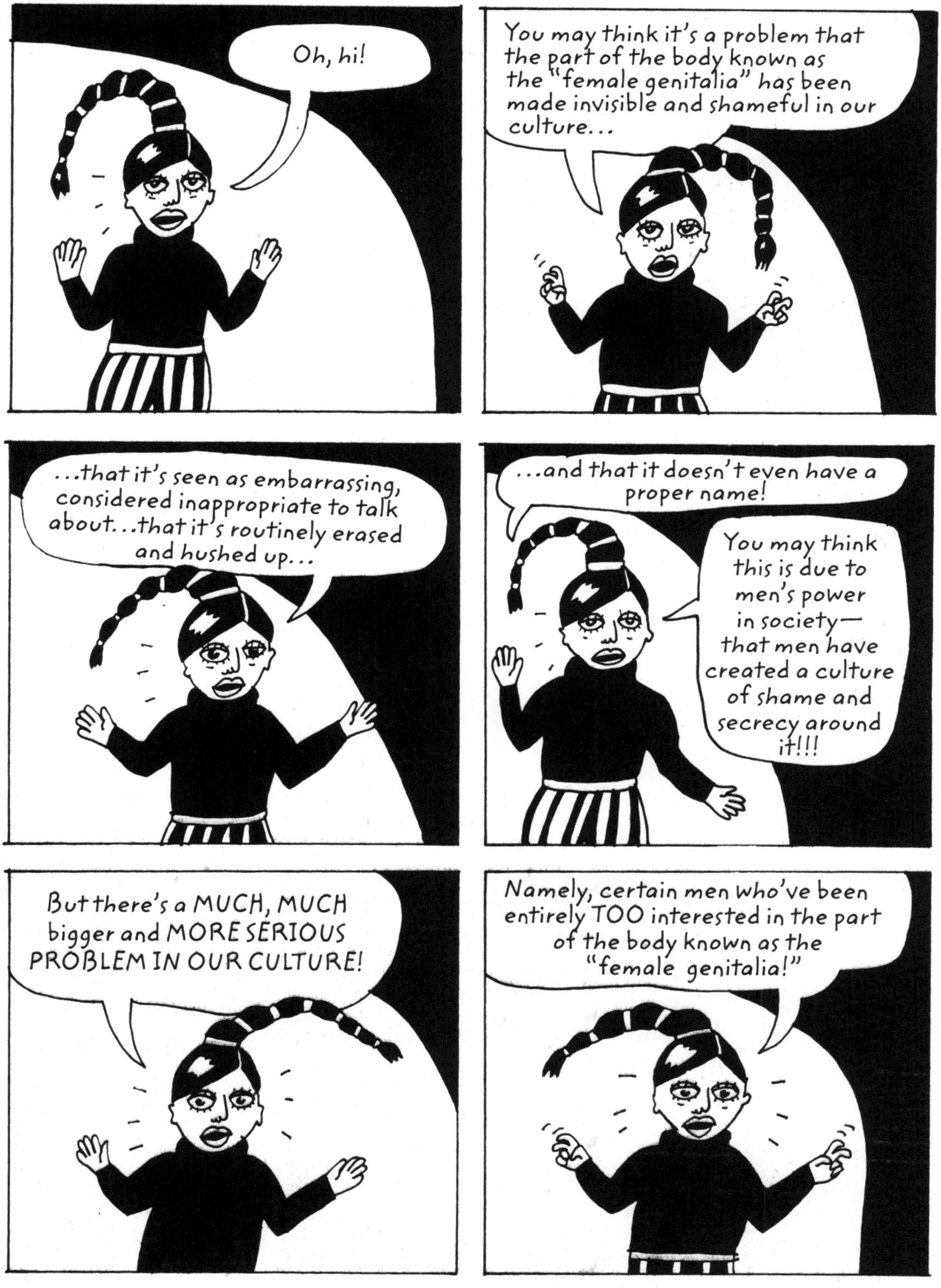
Oh, hi!
You may think it's a problem that the part of the body known as the "female genitalia" has been made invisible and shameful in our culture...
...that it's seen as embarrassing, considered inappropriate to talk about...that it's routinely erased and hushed up...
...and that it doesn't even have a proper name!
You may think this is due to men's power in society— that men have created a culture of shame and secrecy around it!!!
But there's a MUCH, MUCH bigger and MORE SERIOUS PROBLEM IN OUR CULTURE!
Namely, certain men who've been entirely TOO interested in the part of the body known as the "female genitalia!"

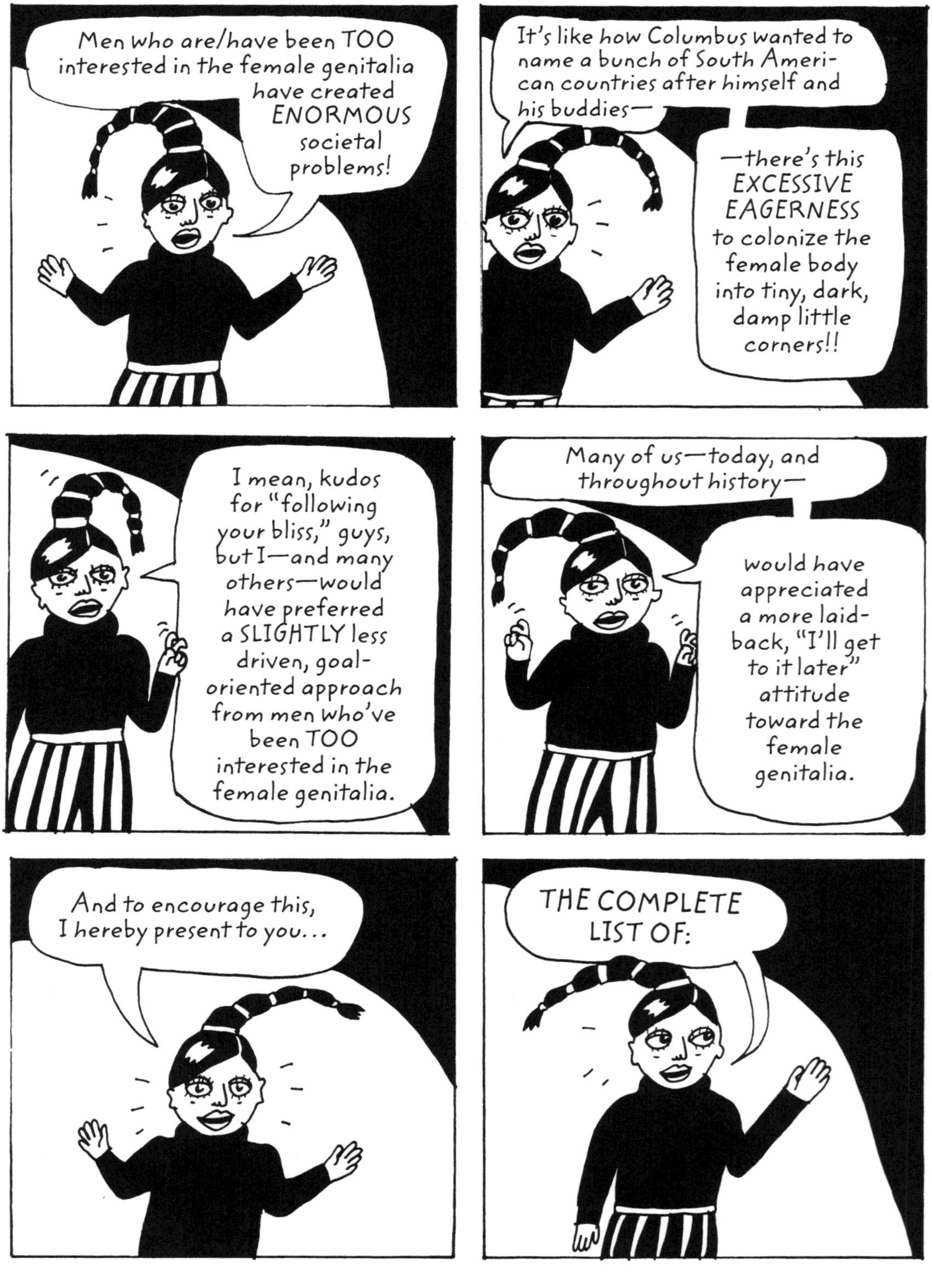
Men who are/have been TOO interested in the female genitalia have created ENORMOUS societal problems!
It's like how Columbus wanted to name a bunch of South American countries after himself and his buddies—
—there's this EXCESSIVE EAGERNESS to colonize the female body into tiny, dark, damp little corners!!
I mean, kudos for "following your bliss," guys, but I—and many others—would have preferred a SLIGHTLY less driven, goal-oriented approach from men who've been TOO interested in the female genitalia.
Many of us—today, and throughout history—
would have appreciated a more laid-back, "I'll get to it later" attitude toward the female genitalia.
And to encourage this, I hereby present to you...
THE COMPLETE LIST OF:

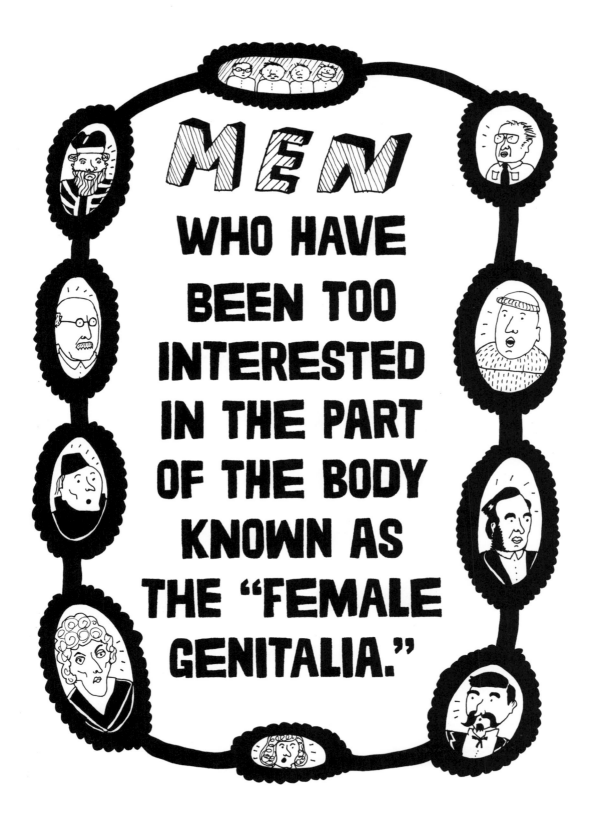

MEN WHO HAVE BEEN TOO INTERESTED IN THE PART OF THE BODY KNOWN AS THE "FEMALE GENITALIA."

And in 7th place, we have JOHN HARVEY KELLOGG (1852–1943).

Now, you might think that all John Harvey Kellogg did was invent cornflakes.

BUT JOHN HARVEY KELLOGG HAD OTHER IRONS IN THE FIRE!!!

He was also a doctor, and one of his major areas of focus was women's genitals— more specifically, PREVENTING women from TOUCHING their genitals.

I'm not just a doctor—I also invented cornflakes!

And that's not all—in my spare time, I prevent women from touching their genitals!

John Harvey Kellogg was PASSIONATE about preventing women from touching their genitals! The anti-masturbation movement was all the rage in medical circles at the time.

ONANIA; OR THE HEINOUS SIN OF Self=Pollution.

AND

All its Frightful Consequences, in both Sexes, Consider'd.

WITH

Spiritual and Physical Advice to those, who have already injur'd themselves by this abominable Practice.

And seasonable Admonition to the Youth of the Nation, (of both Sexes) and those whose

Kellogg wrote health education books in which he claimed that masturbation caused uterine cancer, epilepsy, insanity, and general mental and physical weakness.

Why do I have cancer?

Too much clitoral stimulation.

Why am I mentally ill?

Too much clitoral stimulation.

Why does my leg hurt?

Too much clitoral stimulation.

ETC ETC!

As luck would have it, Kellogg himself had discovered a cure for the scourge of masturbation! In his book *Plain Facts for Old and Young* he writes:

In females, the author has found that the application of pure carbolic acid to the clitoris...

...is an excellent means of allaying the abnormal excitement.

So if you think the worst thing Kellogg's has ever done to women is to churn out a zillion commercials featuring the aspirational tableau of an anorexic woman stretching poolside and ruminating on a bowl of grayish breakfast flakes...
Carpe diem.
...IT'S TIME TO REASSESS—or at least add to your assessment the fact that the company's founder loved pouring corrosive acid on clitorises!
AND THAT BRINGS US TO NUMBER 6 ON THE LIST OF MEN WHO'VE BEEN TOO INTERESTED IN THE "FEMALE GENITALIA," NAMELY...
DR. ISAAC BAKER BROWN (1811–1873).
Dr. Isaac Baker Brown was another fervent opponent of female masturbation. His preferred prevention technique was simply to SURGICALLY REMOVE the clitoris.
Dilatateurs du col.
A. Dilatateur de Sims. — B. Dilatateur d'Ellinger. — C. Dilatateur de Collin.
This operation—radical clitoridectomy—was fully accepted at the time and was performed by many doctors.*
*See, e.g., Ulrika Nilsson, Kampen om Kvinnan (Uppsala: Universitetstryckeriet, 2003).

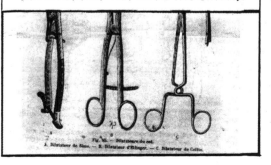

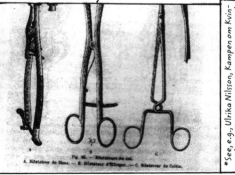

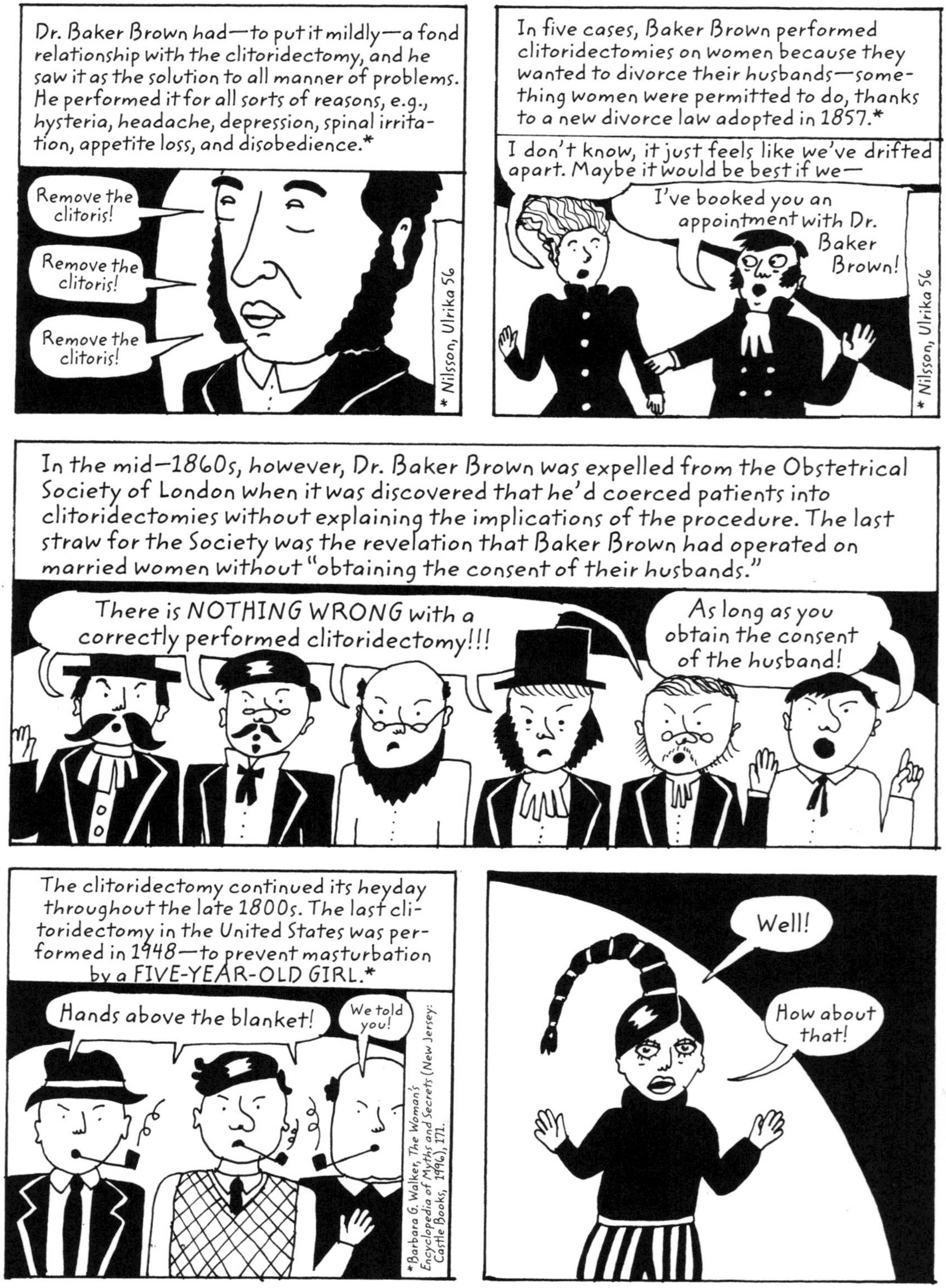
Dr. Baker Brown had—to put it mildly—a fond relationship with the clitoridectomy, and he saw it as the solution to all manner of problems. He performed it for all sorts of reasons, e.g., hysteria, headache, depression, spinal irritation, appetite loss, and disobedience.*
Remove the clitoris!
Remove the clitoris!
Remove the clitoris!
* Nilsson, Ulrika 56
In five cases, Baker Brown performed clitoridectomies on women because they wanted to divorce their husbands—something women were permitted to do, thanks to a new divorce law adopted in 1857.*
I don't know, it just feels like we've drifted apart. Maybe it would be best if we—
I've booked you an appointment with Dr. Baker Brown!
* Nilsson, Ulrika 56
In the mid-1860s, however, Dr. Baker Brown was expelled from the Obstetrical Society of London when it was discovered that he'd coerced patients into clitoridectomies without explaining the implications of the procedure. The last straw for the Society was the revelation that Baker Brown had operated on married women without "obtaining the consent of their husbands."
There is NOTHING WRONG with a correctly performed clitoridectomy!!!
As long as you obtain the consent of the husband!
The clitoridectomy continued its heyday throughout the late 1800s. The last clitoridectomy in the United States was performed in 1948—to prevent masturbation by a FIVE-YEAR-OLD GIRL.*
Hands above the blanket!
We told you!
*Barbara G. Walker, The Woman's Encyclopedia of Myths and Secrets (New Jersey: Castle Books, 1996), 171.
Well!
How about that!

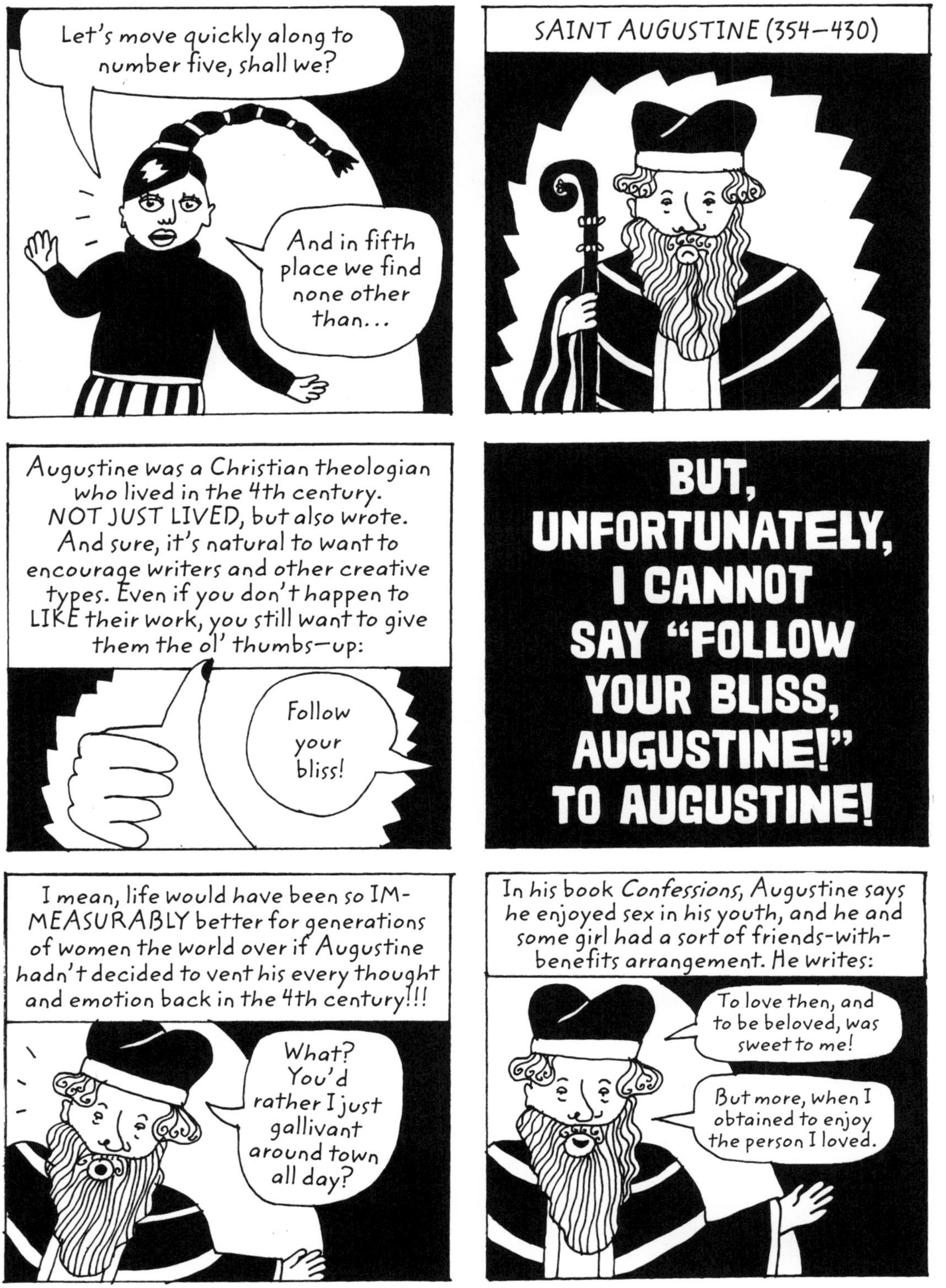
Let's move quickly along to number five, shall we?
And in fifth place we find none other than...
SAINT AUGUSTINE (354–430)
Augustine was a Christian theologian who lived in the 4th century. NOT JUST LIVED, but also wrote. And sure, it's natural to want to encourage writers and other creative types. Even if you don't happen to LIKE their work, you still want to give them the ol' thumbs-up:
Follow your bliss!
BUT, UNFORTUNATELY, I CANNOT SAY "FOLLOW YOUR BLISS, AUGUSTINE!" TO AUGUSTINE!
I mean, life would have been so IMMEASURABLY better for generations of women the world over if Augustine hadn't decided to vent his every thought and emotion back in the 4th century!!!
What? You'd rather I just gallivant around town all day?
In his book *Confessions*, Augustine says he enjoyed sex in his youth, and he and some girl had a sort of friends-with-benefits arrangement. He writes:
To love then, and to be beloved, was sweet to me!
But more, when I obtained to enjoy the person I loved.

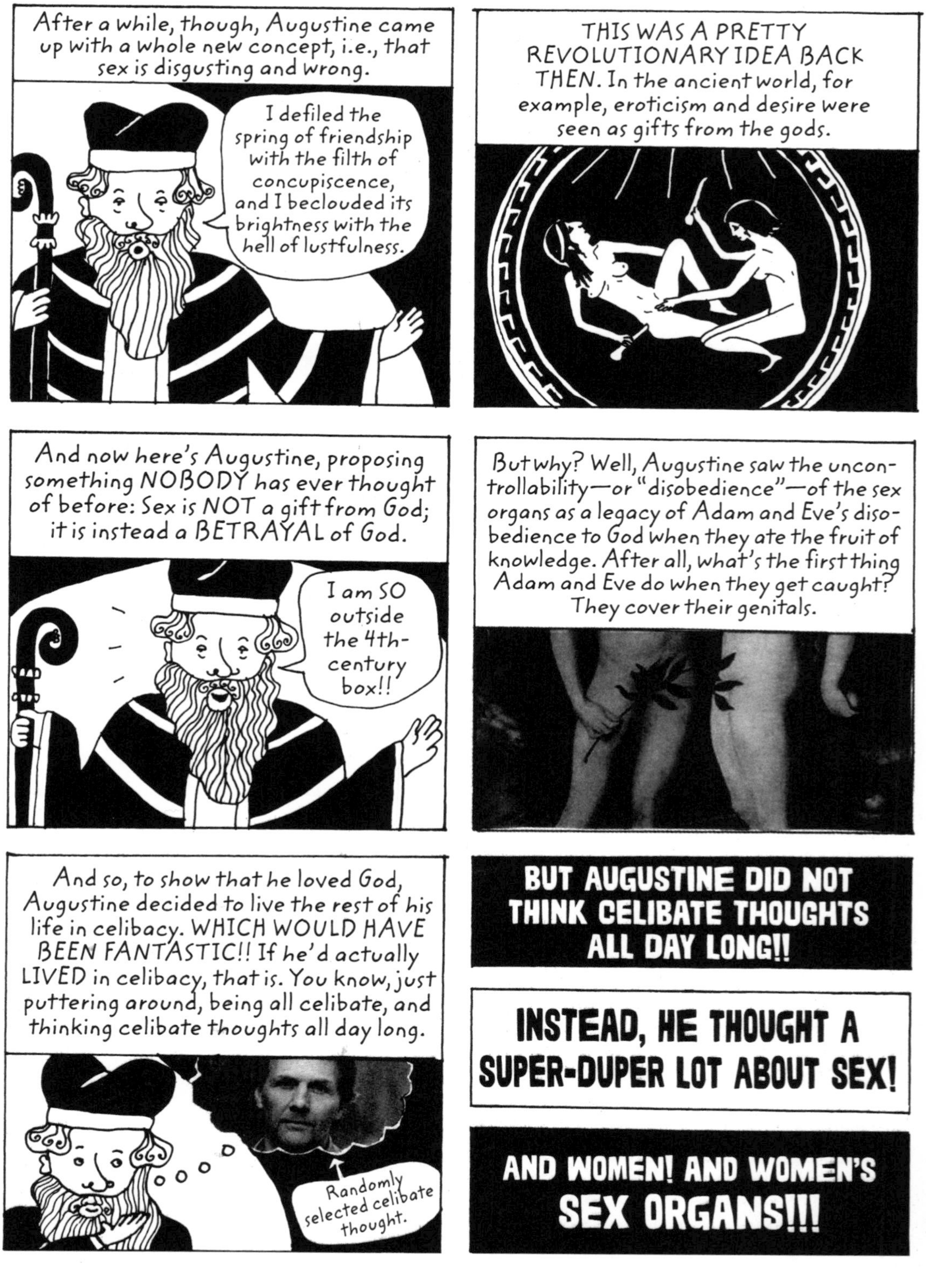
After a while, though, Augustine came up with a whole new concept, i.e., that sex is disgusting and wrong.
I defiled the spring of friendship with the filth of concupiscence, and I beclouded its brightness with the hell of lustfulness.
THIS WAS A PRETTY REVOLUTIONARY IDEA BACK THEN. In the ancient world, for example, eroticism and desire were seen as gifts from the gods.
And now here's Augustine, proposing something NOBODY has ever thought of before: Sex is NOT a gift from God; it is instead a BETRAYAL of God.
I am SO outside the 4th-century box!!
But why? Well, Augustine saw the uncontrollability—or "disobedience"—of the sex organs as a legacy of Adam and Eve's disobedience to God when they ate the fruit of knowledge. After all, what's the first thing Adam and Eve do when they get caught? They cover their genitals.
And so, to show that he loved God, Augustine decided to live the rest of his life in celibacy. WHICH WOULD HAVE BEEN FANTASTIC!! If he'd actually LIVED in celibacy, that is. You know, just puttering around, being all celibate, and thinking celibate thoughts all day long.
Randomly selected celibate thought.
BUT AUGUSTINE DID NOT THINK CELIBATE THOUGHTS ALL DAY LONG!!
INSTEAD, HE THOUGHT A SUPER-DUPER LOT ABOUT SEX!
AND WOMEN! AND WOMEN'S SEX ORGANS!!!

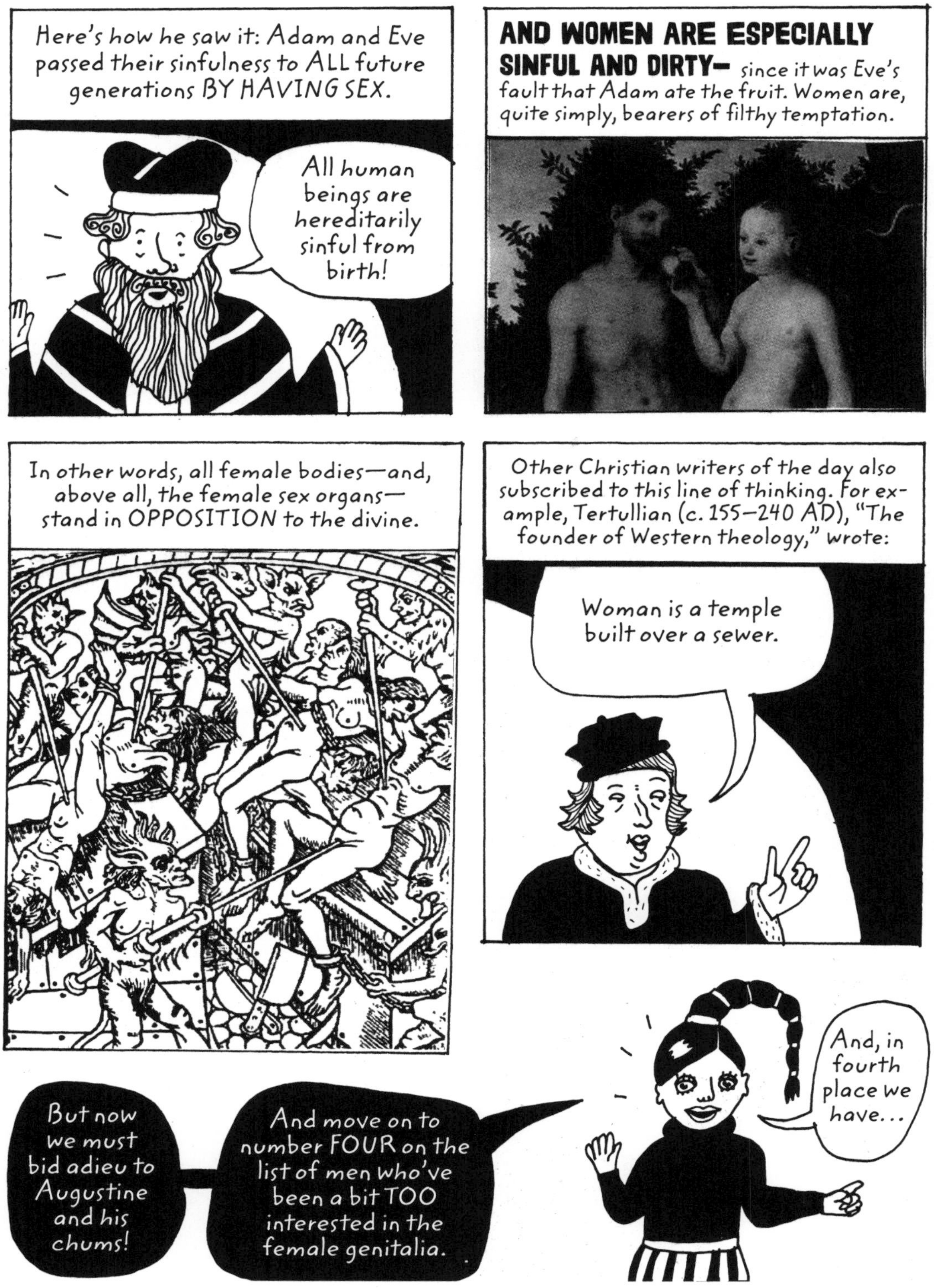
Here's how he saw it: Adam and Eve passed their sinfulness to ALL future generations BY HAVING SEX.
All human beings are hereditarily sinful from birth!
AND WOMEN ARE ESPECIALLY SINFUL AND DIRTY— since it was Eve's fault that Adam ate the fruit. Women are, quite simply, bearers of filthy temptation.
In other words, all female bodies—and, above all, the female sex organs—stand in OPPOSITION to the divine.
Other Christian writers of the day also subscribed to this line of thinking. For example, Tertullian (c. 155–240 AD), "The founder of Western theology," wrote:
Woman is a temple built over a sewer.
But now we must bid adieu to Augustine and his chums!
And move on to number FOUR on the list of men who've been a bit TOO interested in the female genitalia.
And, in fourth place we have...

JOHN MONEY (1921–2006)

John Money was a professor of medical psychology. But he didn't just love medical psychology—he also loved the binary two-gender system!

I'm not just a professor of medical psychology!

I also love the binary two-gender system!

But what is the binary two-gender system? It's the EXTREMELY widespread and revered idea that there are TWO opposing genders in society—male and female—and that these genders are distinguished by the presence of male and female sex organs, respectively.

ONE THING THAT'S PRETTY ANNOYING IN THE BINARY TWO-GENDER SYSTEM IS WHEN BABIES ARE BORN WITH SEX ORGANS THAT DON'T FIT THE TWO-GENDER CULTURAL PARADIGM.

Around 1–2% of all babies are born with sex organs that can't be categorized as "male" or "female."

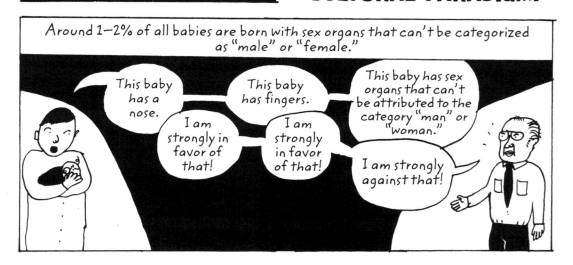

This baby has a nose.

I am strongly in favor of that!

This baby has fingers.

I am strongly in favor of that!

This baby has sex organs that can't be attributed to the category "man" or "woman."

I am strongly against that!

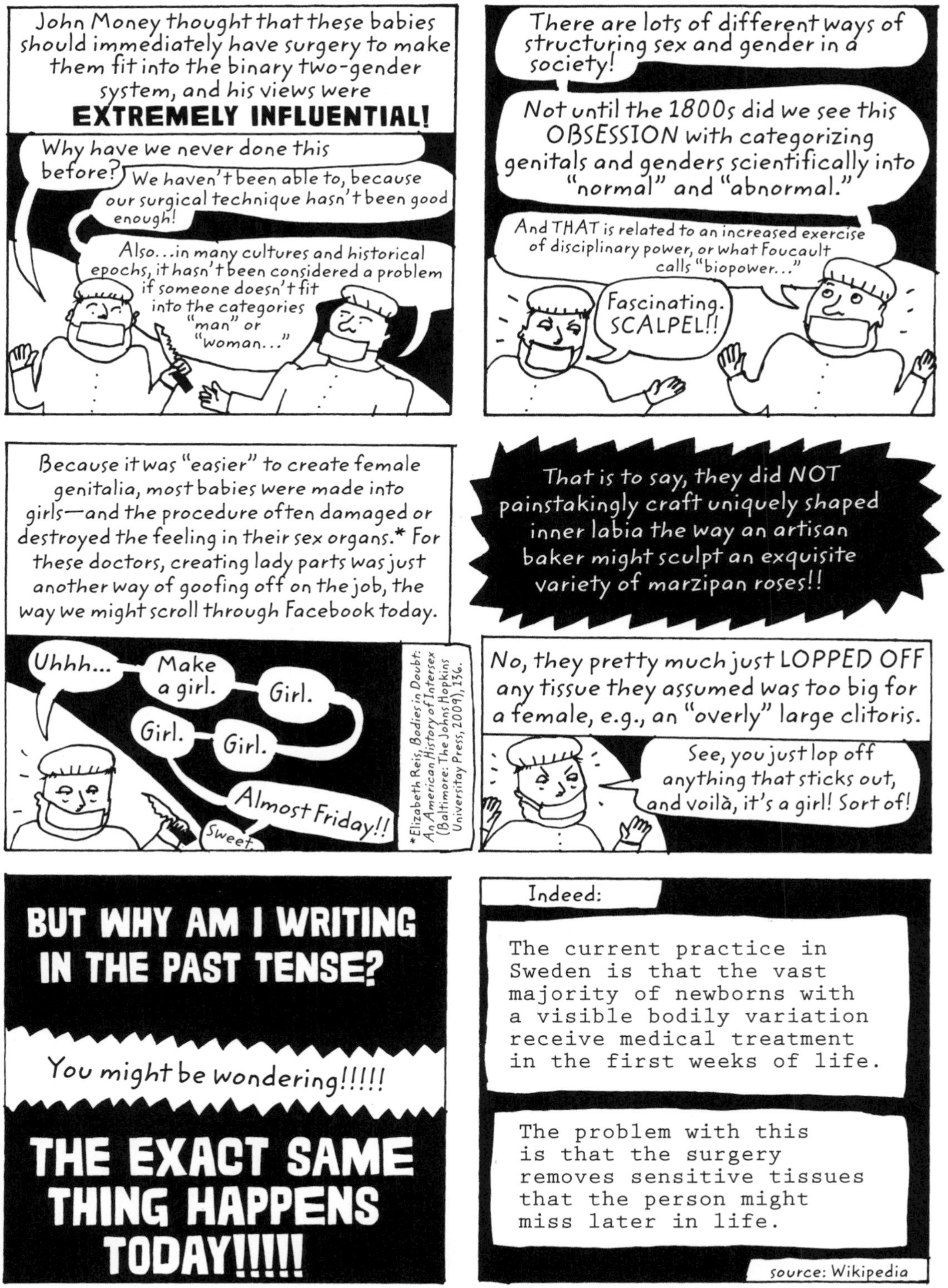
John Money thought that these babies should immediately have surgery to make them fit into the binary two-gender system, and his views were
EXTREMELY INFLUENTIAL!
Why have we never done this before?
We haven't been able to, because our surgical technique hasn't been good enough!
Also... in many cultures and historical epochs, it hasn't been considered a problem if someone doesn't fit into the categories "man" or "woman..."
There are lots of different ways of structuring sex and gender in a society!
Not until the 1800s did we see this OBSESSION with categorizing genitals and genders scientifically into "normal" and "abnormal."
And THAT is related to an increased exercise of disciplinary power, or what Foucault calls "biopower..."
Fascinating. SCALPEL!!
Because it was "easier" to create female genitalia, most babies were made into girls—and the procedure often damaged or destroyed the feeling in their sex organs.* For these doctors, creating lady parts was just another way of goofing off on the job, the way we might scroll through Facebook today.
Uhhh...
Make a girl.
Girl.
Girl.
Girl.
Almost Friday!!
Sweet.
*Elizabeth Reis, Bodies in Doubt: An American History of Intersex (Baltimore: The Johns Hopkins University Press, 2009), 136.
That is to say, they did NOT painstakingly craft uniquely shaped inner labia the way an artisan baker might sculpt an exquisite variety of marzipan roses!!
No, they pretty much just LOPPED OFF any tissue they assumed was too big for a female, e.g., an "overly" large clitoris.
See, you just lop off anything that sticks out, and voilà, it's a girl! Sort of!
BUT WHY AM I WRITING IN THE PAST TENSE?
You might be wondering!!!!!
THE EXACT SAME THING HAPPENS TODAY!!!!!
Indeed:
The current practice in Sweden is that the vast majority of newborns with a visible bodily variation receive medical treatment in the first weeks of life.
The problem with this is that the surgery removes sensitive tissues that the person might miss later in life.
source: Wikipedia

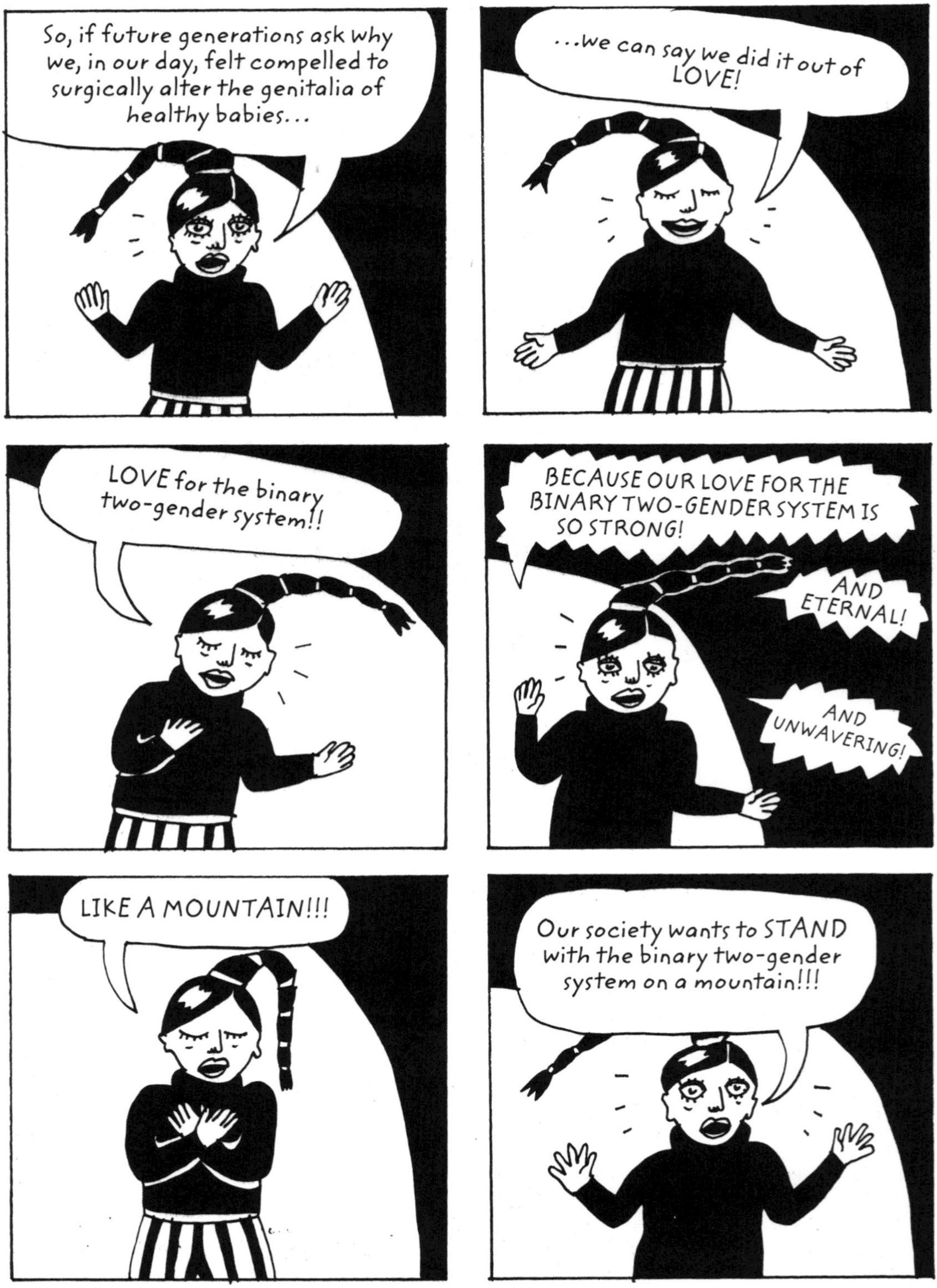
So, if future generations ask why we, in our day, felt compelled to surgically alter the genitalia of healthy babies...
...we can say we did it out of LOVE!
LOVE for the binary two-gender system!!
BECAUSE OUR LOVE FOR THE BINARY TWO-GENDER SYSTEM IS SO STRONG!
AND ETERNAL!
AND UNWAVERING!
LIKE A MOUNTAIN!!!
Our society wants to STAND with the binary two-gender system on a mountain!!!

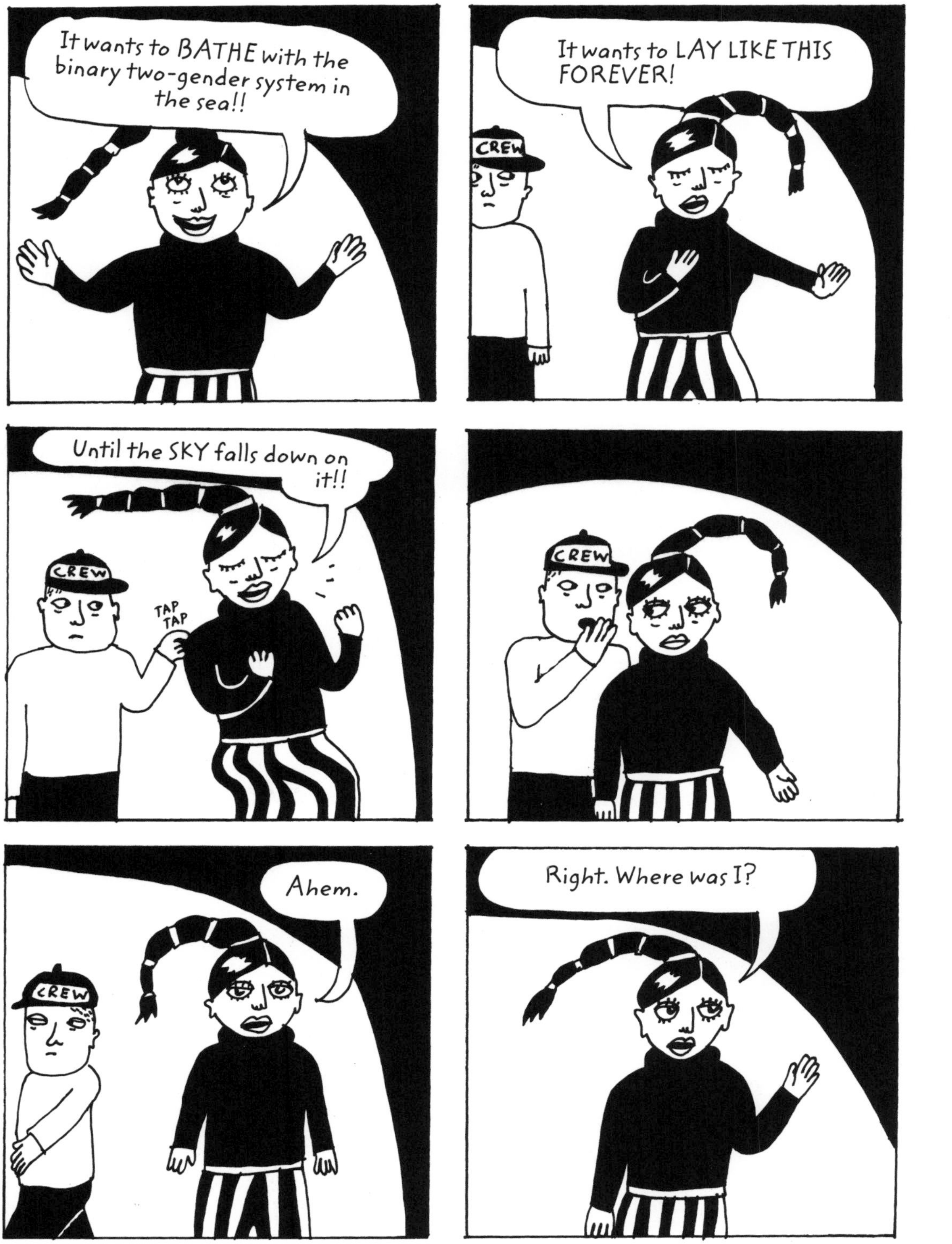
It wants to BATHE with the binary two-gender system in the sea!!
It wants to LAY LIKE THIS FOREVER!
CREW
Until the SKY falls down on it!!
CREW
TAP TAP
CREW
CREW
Ahem.
Right. Where was I?

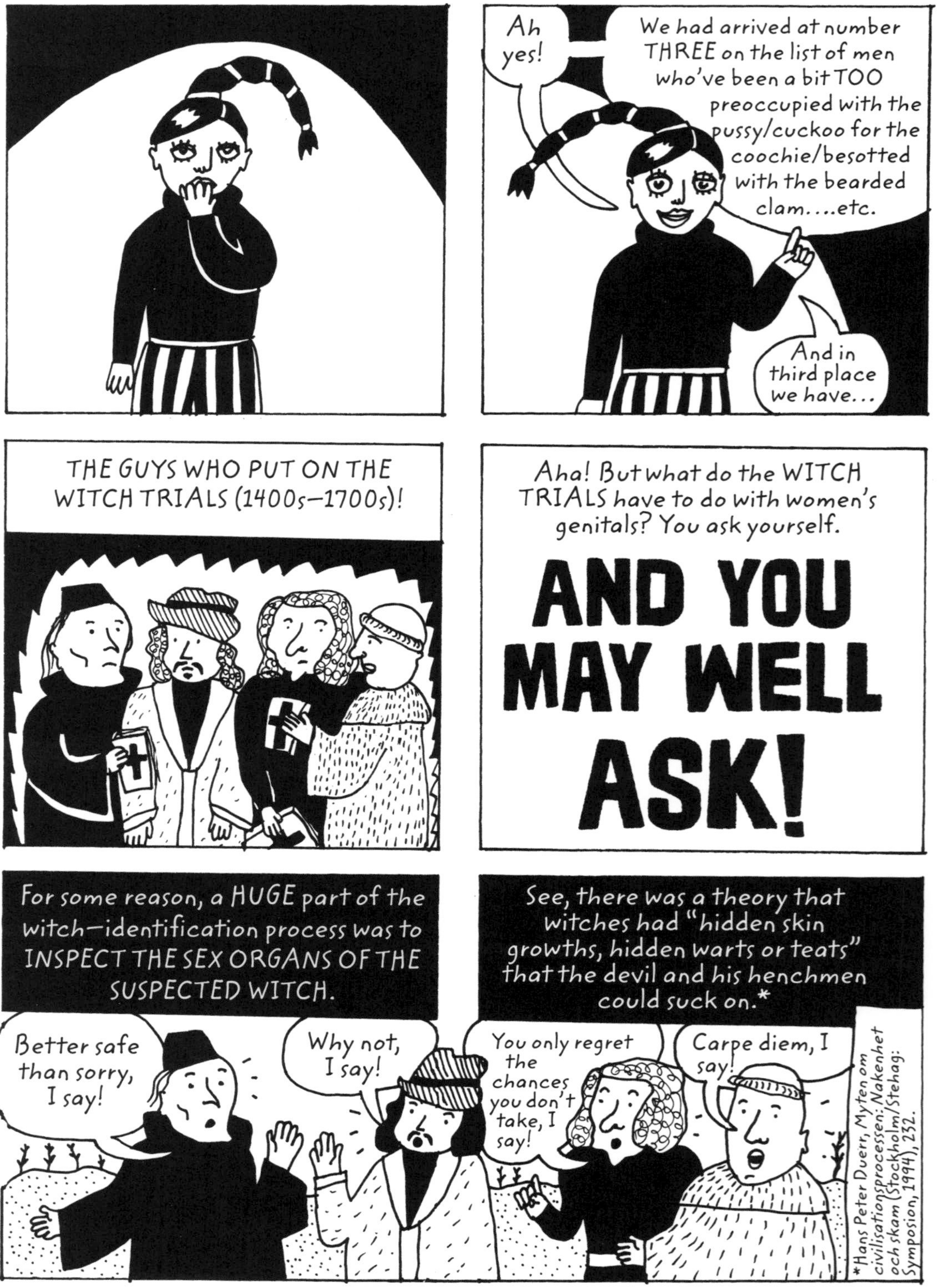

Ah yes!
We had arrived at number THREE on the list of men who've been a bit TOO preoccupied with the pussy/cuckoo for the coochie/besotted with the bearded clam....etc.
And in third place we have...
THE GUYS WHO PUT ON THE WITCH TRIALS (1400s–1700s)!
Aha! But what do the WITCH TRIALS have to do with women's genitals? You ask yourself.
AND YOU MAY WELL ASK!
For some reason, a HUGE part of the witch-identification process was to INSPECT THE SEX ORGANS OF THE SUSPECTED WITCH.
See, there was a theory that witches had "hidden skin growths, hidden warts or teats" that the devil and his henchmen could suck on.*
Better safe than sorry, I say!
Why not, I say!
You only regret the chances you don't take, I say!
Carpe diem, I say!
*Hans Peter Duerr, Myten om civilisationsprocessen: Nakenhet och skam (Stockholm/Stehag: Symposion, 1994), 232.

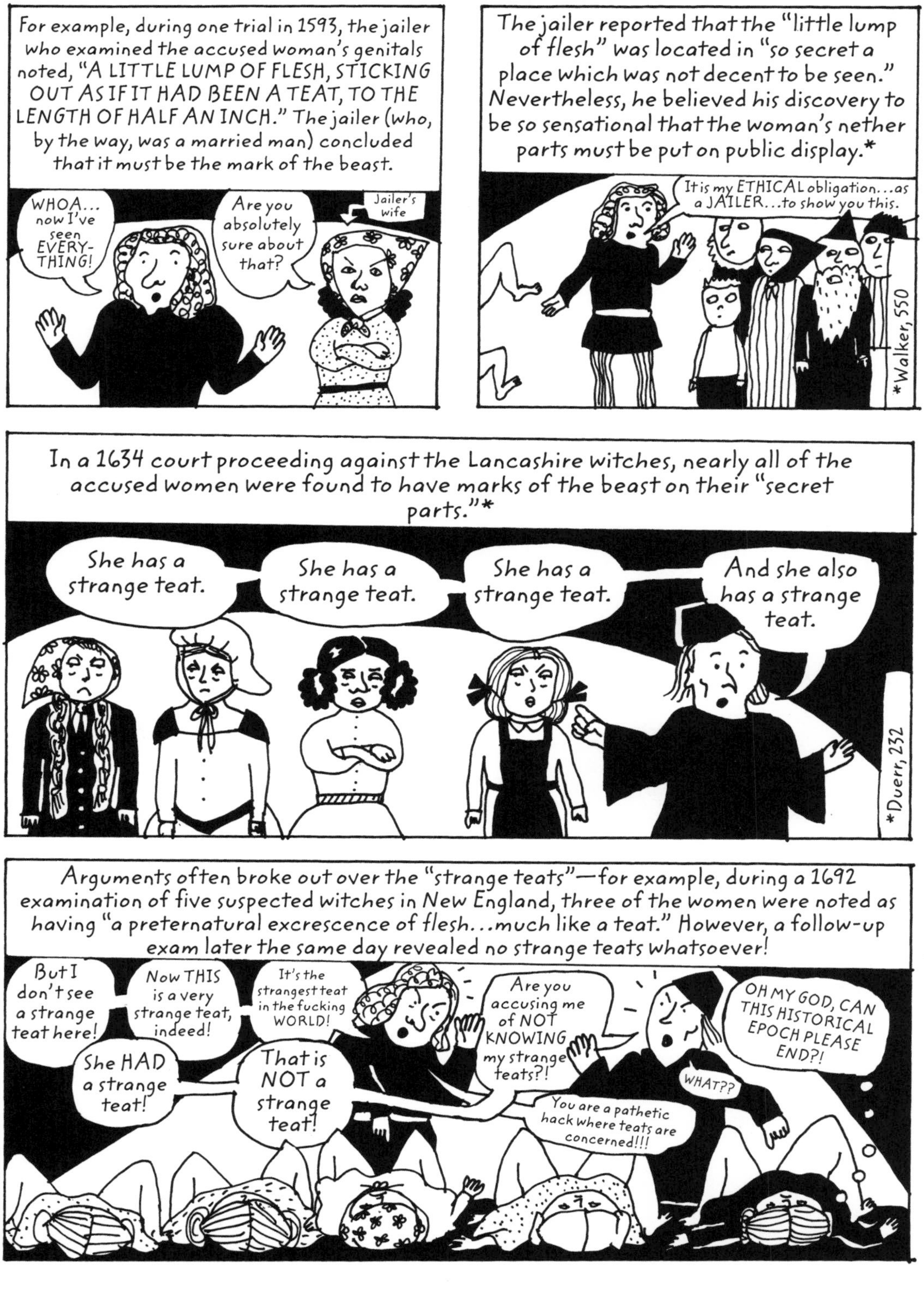
For example, during one trial in 1593, the jailer who examined the accused woman's genitals noted, "A LITTLE LUMP OF FLESH, STICKING OUT AS IF IT HAD BEEN A TEAT, TO THE LENGTH OF HALF AN INCH." The jailer (who, by the way, was a married man) concluded that it must be the mark of the beast.
WHOA... now I've seen EVERYTHING!
Are you absolutely sure about that?
Jailer's wife
The jailer reported that the "little lump of flesh" was located in "so secret a place which was not decent to be seen." Nevertheless, he believed his discovery to be so sensational that the woman's nether parts must be put on public display.*
It is my ETHICAL obligation...as a JAILER...to show you this.
*Walker, 550
In a 1634 court proceeding against the Lancashire witches, nearly all of the accused women were found to have marks of the beast on their "secret parts."*
She has a strange teat.
She has a strange teat.
She has a strange teat.
And she also has a strange teat.
*Duerr, 232
Arguments often broke out over the "strange teats"—for example, during a 1692 examination of five suspected witches in New England, three of the women were noted as having "a preternatural excrescence of flesh...much like a teat." However, a follow-up exam later the same day revealed no strange teats whatsoever!
But I don't see a strange teat here!
Now THIS is a very strange teat, indeed!
It's the strangest teat in the fucking WORLD!
She HAD a strange teat!
That is NOT a strange teat!
Are you accusing me of NOT KNOWING my strange teats?!
You are a pathetic hack where teats are concerned!!!
WHAT??
OH MY GOD, CAN THIS HISTORICAL EPOCH PLEASE END?!

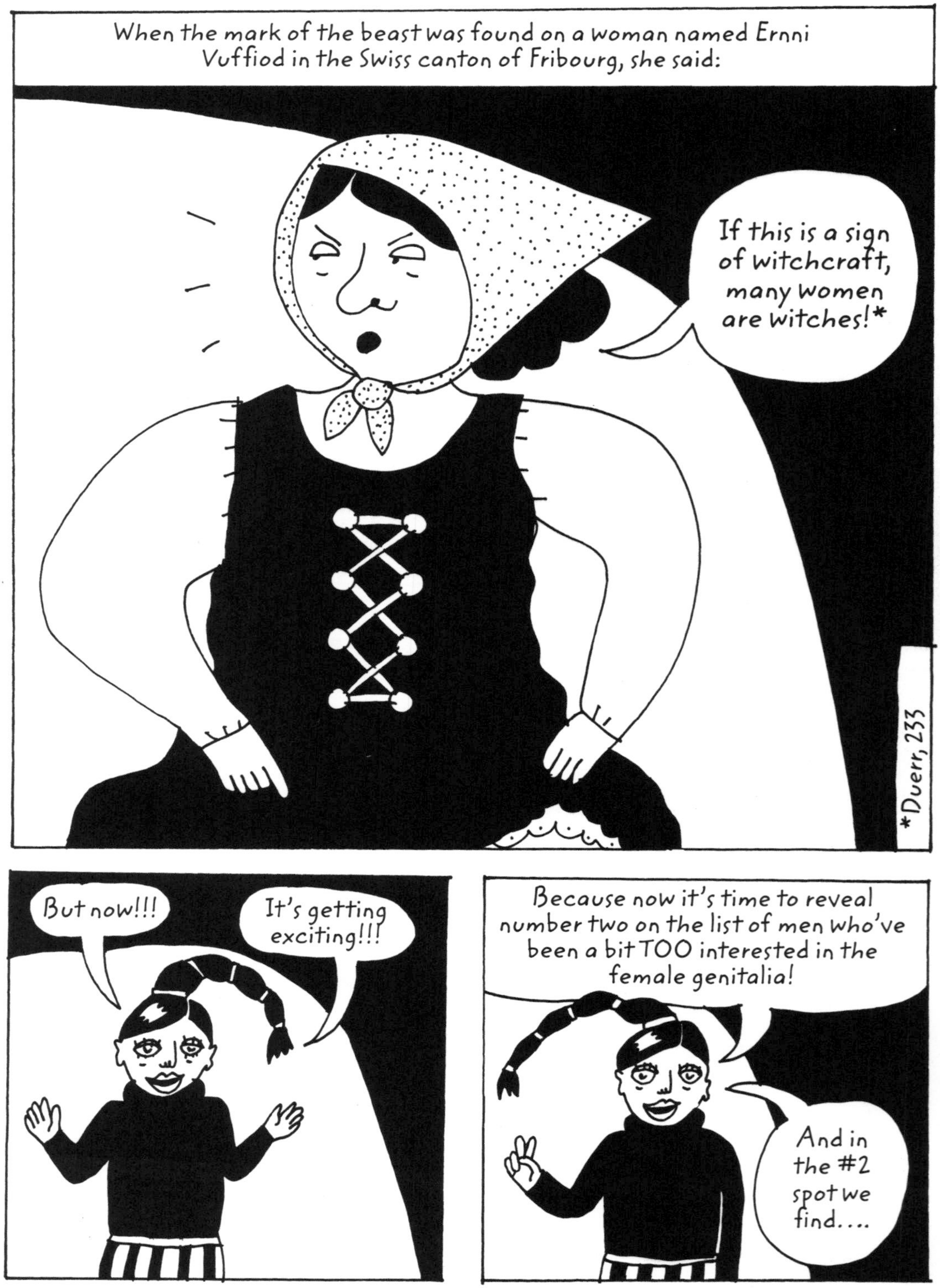
When the mark of the beast was found on a woman named Ernni Vuffiod in the Swiss canton of Fribourg, she said:
If this is a sign of witchcraft, many women are witches!*
*Duerr, 233
But now!!!
It's getting exciting!!!
Because now it's time to reveal number two on the list of men who've been a bit TOO interested in the female genitalia!
And in the #2 spot we find....

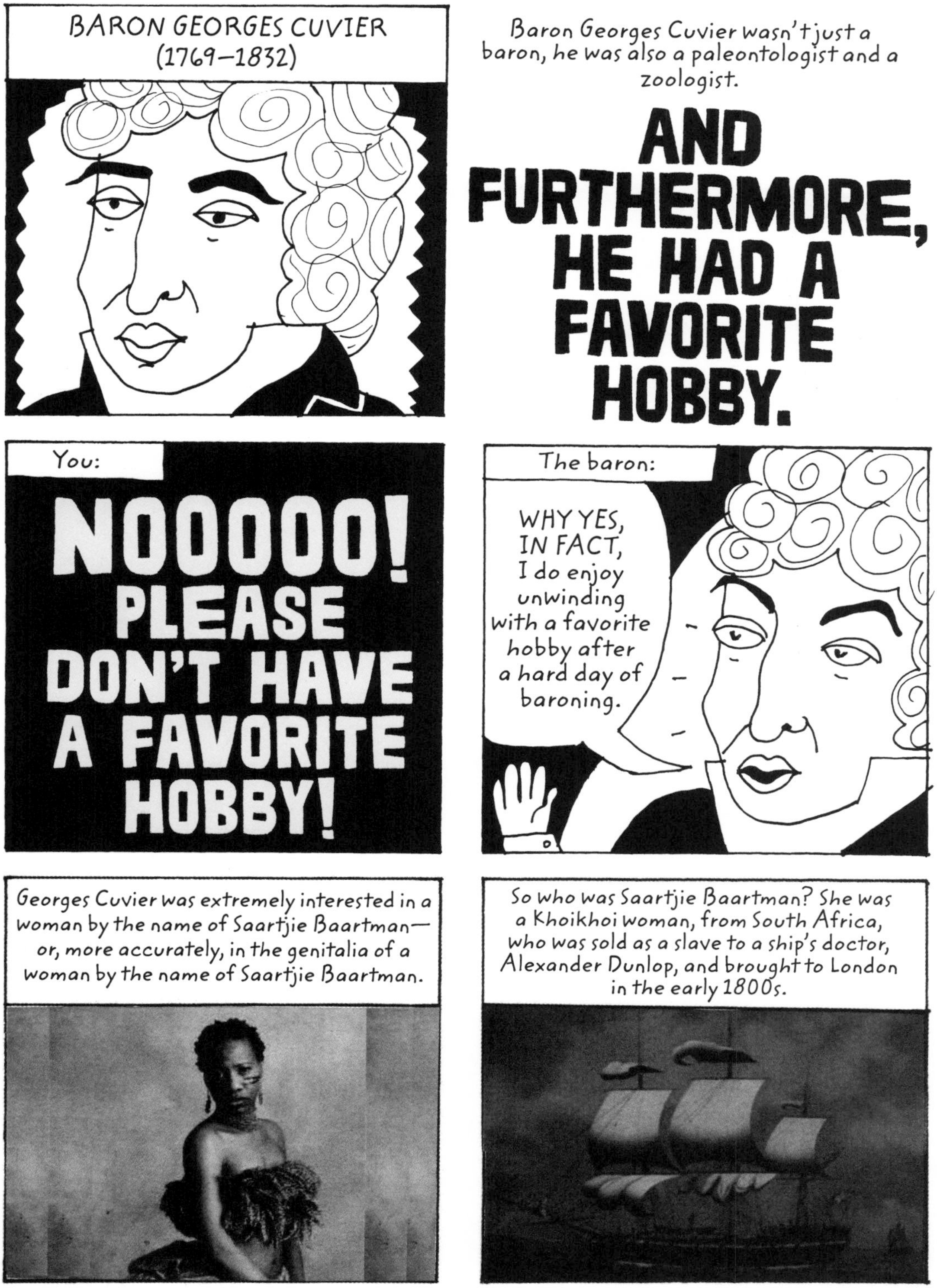
BARON GEORGES CUVIER (1769–1832)
Baron Georges Cuvier wasn't just a baron, he was also a paleontologist and a zoologist.
AND FURTHERMORE, HE HAD A FAVORITE HOBBY.
You:
NOOOOO! PLEASE DON'T HAVE A FAVORITE HOBBY!
The baron:
WHY YES, IN FACT, I do enjoy unwinding with a favorite hobby after a hard day of baroning.
Georges Cuvier was extremely interested in a woman by the name of Saartjie Baartman—or, more accurately, in the genitalia of a woman by the name of Saartjie Baartman.
So who was Saartjie Baartman? She was a Khoikhoi woman, from South Africa, who was sold as a slave to a ship's doctor, Alexander Dunlop, and brought to London in the early 1800s.

In London, Dunlop put Baartman on exhibit and charged admission. Baartman was practically naked, which was a big draw for audiences. She was advertised as the "Hottentot Venus."

The crowds poured in. The main attraction was—you guessed it—Baartman's "enormous buttocks" and "elongated inner labia."

Cartoon of Baartman from that time.

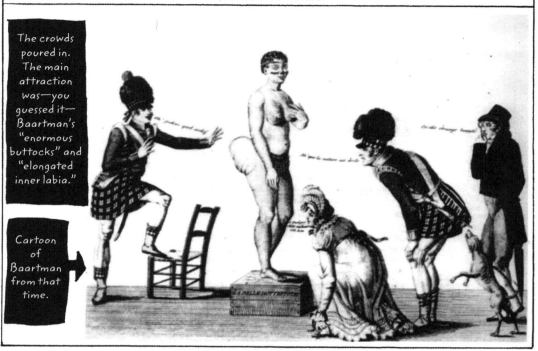

Antislavery protests eventually forced the show to close, and Baartman was sold off to France, where she was again exhibited for money.

LA
VÉNUS
HOTTENTOTE
JARDIN D ACCLIMATATION
Actualité
CRÉÉE PAR
Mlle DERLY

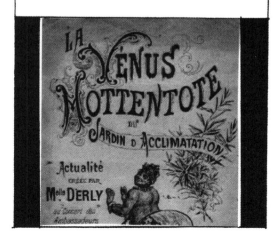

SHORTLY THEREAFTER, BAARTMAN DIED—JUST 26 YEARS OLD—OF AN INFLAMMATORY ILLNESS.

The INSTANT Cuvier got wind of Baartman's death, he RACED to the scene. Within 48 hours he had made a plaster cast of Baartman's body, dissected the parts he found particularly interesting, and PRESERVED Baartman's vulva and brain in alcohol!!!

His sixteen-page autopsy report contains no fewer than

NINE PAGES

about Baartman's vulva

—and exactly

ONE SENTENCE

about her brain.

But why was Georges Cuvier so DAMNED interested in Baartman's vulva? Well, because Cuvier had another major interest: scientific racism.

Cuvier wanted to use Baartman's vulva to demonstrate the supposed inferiority of black people. He believed elongated inner labia were a sign of "animal sexuality."

See for yourselves!

He argued that the inner labia of civilized women (i.e., white women) had shrunk as a result of evolution. Therefore, elongated labia—according to Cuvier—indicated racial inferiority and all-around moral corruption.

So basically:

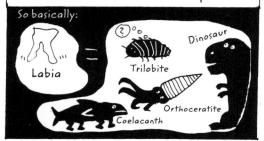

Labia = Trilobite, Dinosaur, Orthoceratite, Coelacanth

CUVIER'S RACE THEORIES ARE WIDESPREAD, AND THEY'VE HAD A MAJOR INFLUENCE ON SCIENTIFIC RACISM!

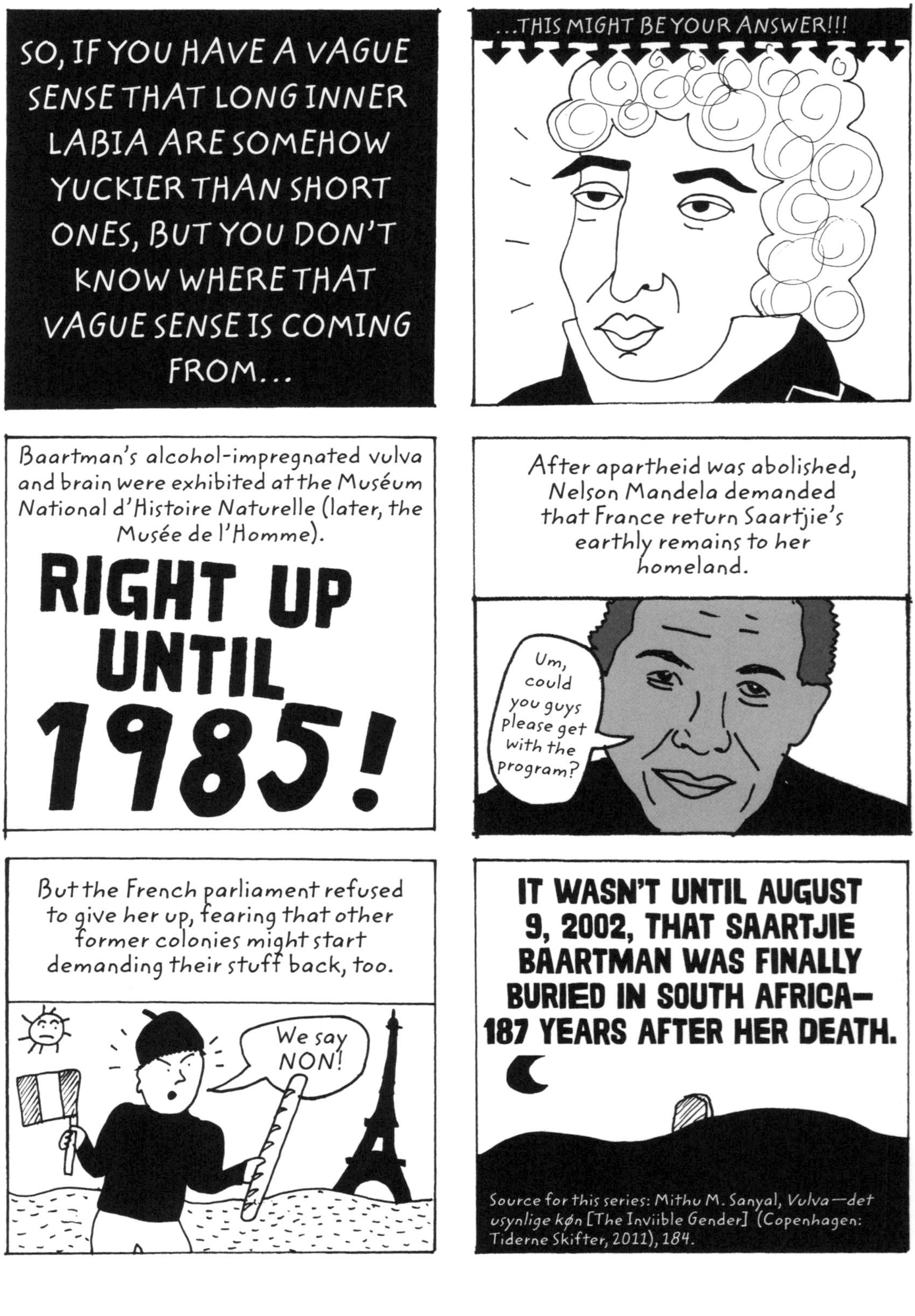
SO, IF YOU HAVE A VAGUE SENSE THAT LONG INNER LABIA ARE SOMEHOW YUCKIER THAN SHORT ONES, BUT YOU DON'T KNOW WHERE THAT VAGUE SENSE IS COMING FROM...
...THIS MIGHT BE YOUR ANSWER!!!
Baartman's alcohol-impregnated vulva and brain were exhibited at the Muséum National d'Histoire Naturelle (later, the Musée de l'Homme).
RIGHT UP UNTIL 1985!
After apartheid was abolished, Nelson Mandela demanded that France return Saartjie's earthly remains to her homeland.
Um, could you guys please get with the program?
But the French parliament refused to give her up, fearing that other former colonies might start demanding their stuff back, too.
We say NON!
IT WASN'T UNTIL AUGUST 9, 2002, THAT SAARTJIE BAARTMAN WAS FINALLY BURIED IN SOUTH AFRICA— 187 YEARS AFTER HER DEATH.
Source for this series: Mithu M. Sanyal, Vulva—det usynlige køn [The Inviible Gender] (Copenhagen: Tiderne Skifter, 2011), 184.

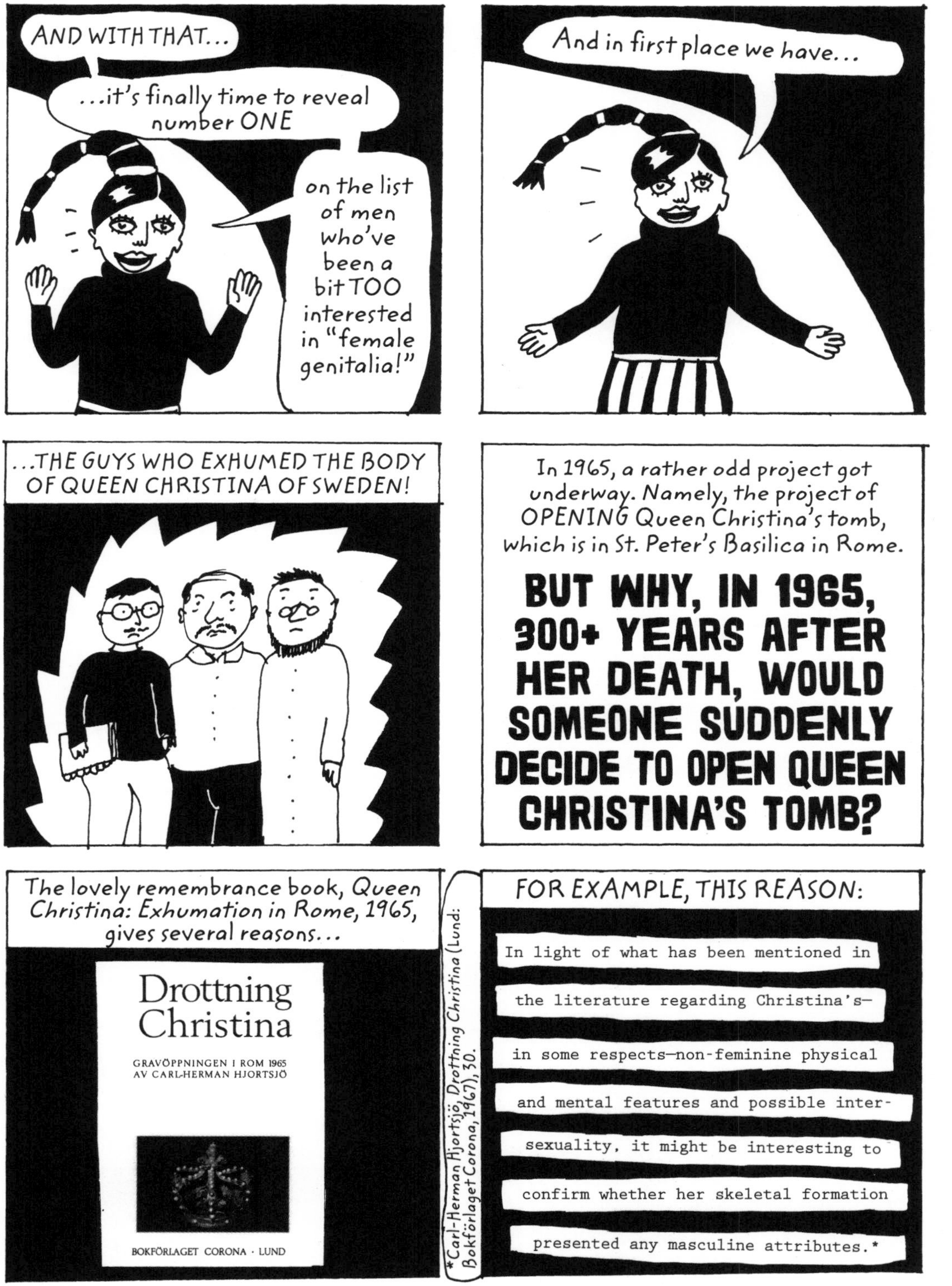
AND WITH THAT...
...it's finally time to reveal number ONE
on the list of men who've been a bit TOO interested in "female genitalia!"
And in first place we have...
...THE GUYS WHO EXHUMED THE BODY OF QUEEN CHRISTINA OF SWEDEN!
In 1965, a rather odd project got underway. Namely, the project of OPENING Queen Christina's tomb, which is in St. Peter's Basilica in Rome.
BUT WHY, IN 1965, 300+ YEARS AFTER HER DEATH, WOULD SOMEONE SUDDENLY DECIDE TO OPEN QUEEN CHRISTINA'S TOMB?
The lovely remembrance book, *Queen Christina: Exhumation in Rome, 1965*, gives several reasons...
Drottning Christina
GRAVÖPPNINGEN I ROM 1965
AV CARL-HERMAN HJORTSJÖ
BOKFÖRLAGET CORONA · LUND
FOR EXAMPLE, THIS REASON:
In light of what has been mentioned in the literature regarding Christina's—in some respects—non-feminine physical and mental features and possible intersexuality, it might be interesting to confirm whether her skeletal formation presented any masculine attributes.*
*Carl-Herman Hjortsjö, *Drottning Christina* (Lund: Bokförlaget Corona, 1967), 30.

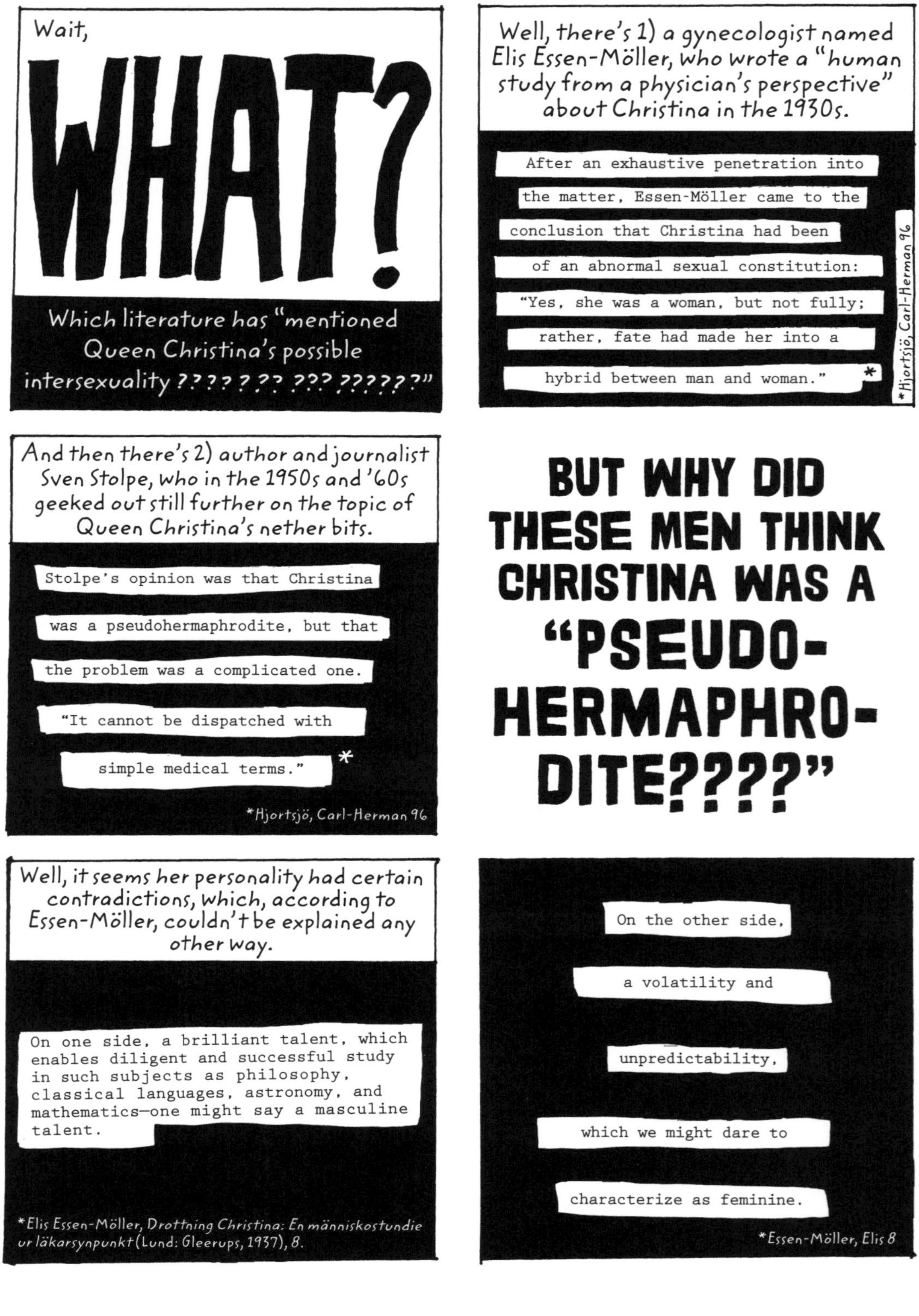

Wait, **WHAT?**

Which literature has "mentioned Queen Christina's possible intersexuality ??? ?? ?? ??? ?????"

Well, there's 1) a gynecologist named Elis Essen-Möller, who wrote a "human study from a physician's perspective" about Christina in the 1930s.

After an exhaustive penetration into the matter, Essen-Möller came to the conclusion that Christina had been of an abnormal sexual constitution: "Yes, she was a woman, but not fully; rather, fate had made her into a hybrid between man and woman." *

*Hjortsjö, Carl-Herman 96

And then there's 2) author and journalist Sven Stolpe, who in the 1950s and '60s geeked out still further on the topic of Queen Christina's nether bits.

Stolpe's opinion was that Christina was a pseudohermaphrodite, but that the problem was a complicated one. "It cannot be dispatched with simple medical terms." *

*Hjortsjö, Carl-Herman 96

BUT WHY DID THESE MEN THINK CHRISTINA WAS A "PSEUDO-HERMAPHRO-DITE????"

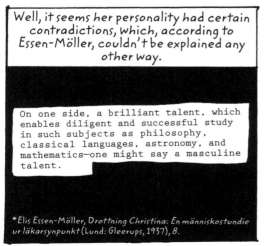

Well, it seems her personality had certain contradictions, which, according to Essen-Möller, couldn't be explained any other way.

On one side, a brilliant talent, which enables diligent and successful study in such subjects as philosophy, classical languages, astronomy, and mathematics—one might say a masculine talent.

*Elis Essen-Möller, Drottning Christina: En människostundie ur läkarsynpunkt (Lund: Gleerups, 1937), 8.

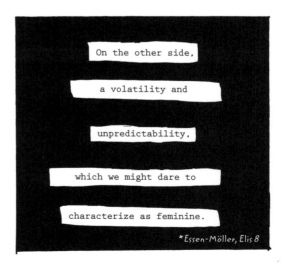

On the other side, a volatility and unpredictability, which we might dare to characterize as feminine.

*Essen-Möller, Elis 8

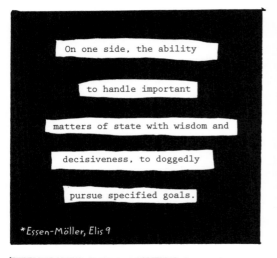

On one side, the ability

to handle important

matters of state with wisdom and

decisiveness, to doggedly

pursue specified goals.

*Essen-Möller, Elis 9

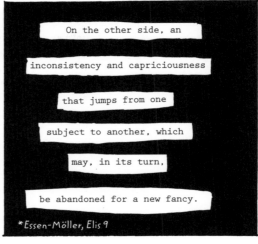

On the other side, an

inconsistency and capriciousness

that jumps from one

subject to another, which

may, in its turn,

be abandoned for a new fancy.

*Essen-Möller, Elis 9

Essen-Möller also notes:

From this perspective, her minimal interest in her clothing, which might seem otherwise unimportant, also takes on a certain significance.

A contemporary observer says: "Never have I seen gold or silver in her hair ornaments, nor on her clothes or around her neck. The only gold she wears is a ring.

She does not care at all for her appearance. Her hair is combed only once a week. Sometimes she can go fourteen days without having it combed."

*Essen-Möller, Elis 46

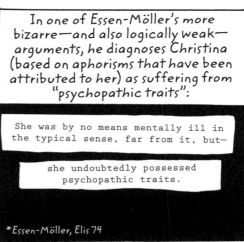

In one of Essen-Möller's more bizarre—and also logically weak—arguments, he diagnoses Christina (based on aphorisms that have been attributed to her) as suffering from "psychopathic traits":

She was by no means mentally ill in the typical sense, far from it, but—

she undoubtedly possessed psychopathic traits.

*Essen-Möller, Elis 74

Essen-Möller continues:

Here it must be pointed out that intersexual individuals also frequently display psychological peculiarities of a psychopathic nature.

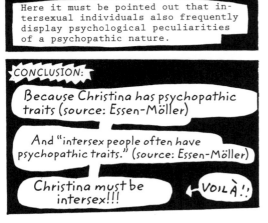

CONCLUSION:

Because Christina has psychopathic traits (source: Essen-Möller)

And "intersex people often have psychopathic traits." (source: Essen-Möller)

Christina must be intersex!!!

← VOILÀ!!

As for Sven Stolpe, he fixated primarily on Christina's refusal to marry—which he saw as incontrovertible proof of his thesis.

A young woman who doesn't want to get married?

Inconceivable!

Only possible explanation? She's a HERMA-PHRODITE.

ANY-WAY!!

Maybe what's weird here is NOT that a loony, sterilization-promoting professor wrote about this stuff in the 1930s, or even that some writer/crackpot popularized his theories a few decades later!!

MAYBE WHAT'S WEIRD IS THAT IN 1965 A MERRY BAND OF GRANDPAS GOT SO FIRED UP ABOUT IT THAT THEY PETITIONED FOR, AND WERE GRANTED, AN EXHUMATION!

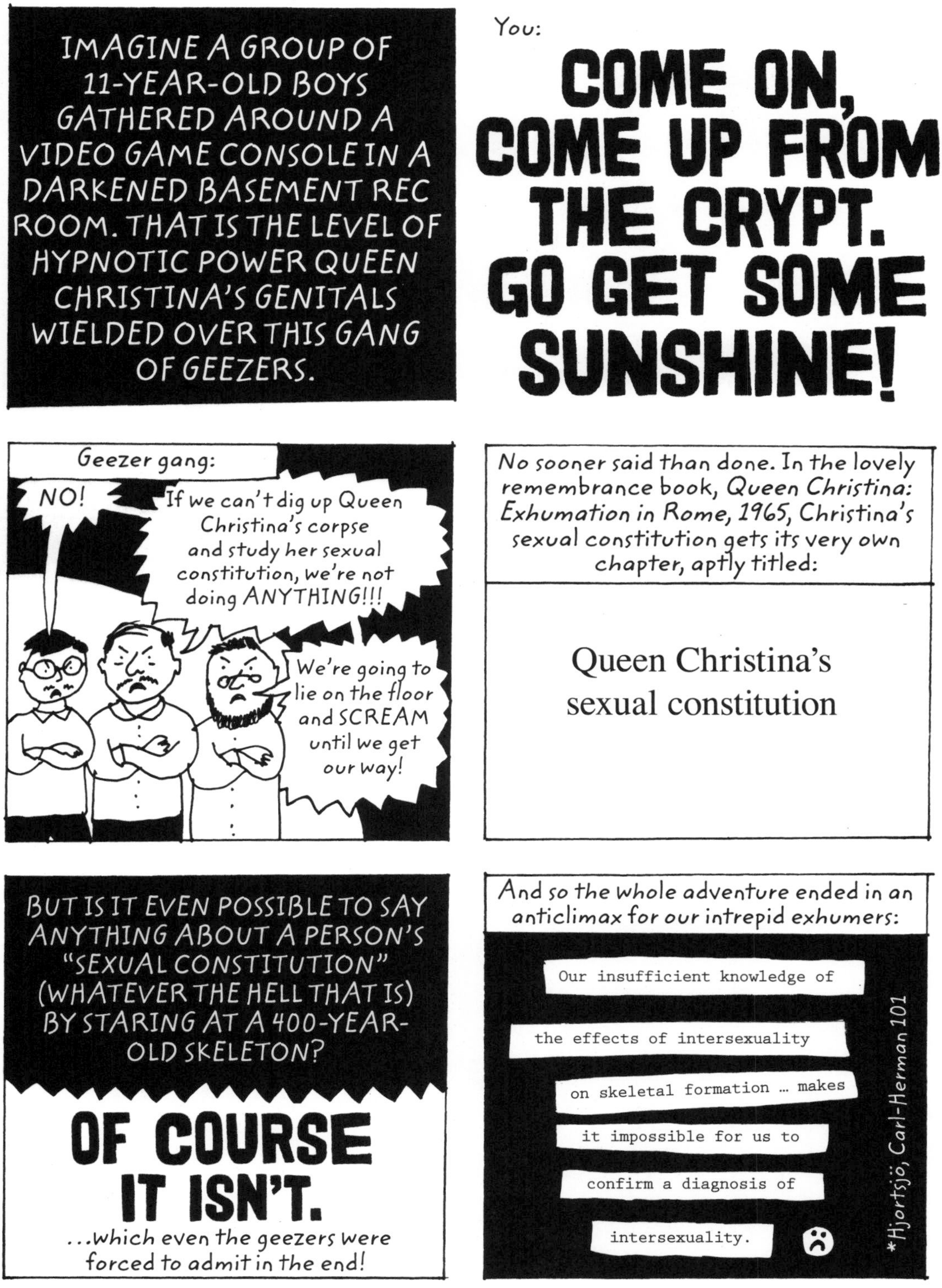
IMAGINE A GROUP OF 11-YEAR-OLD BOYS GATHERED AROUND A VIDEO GAME CONSOLE IN A DARKENED BASEMENT REC ROOM. THAT IS THE LEVEL OF HYPNOTIC POWER QUEEN CHRISTINA'S GENITALS WIELDED OVER THIS GANG OF GEEZERS.
You:
COME ON, COME UP FROM THE CRYPT. GO GET SOME SUNSHINE!
Geezer gang:
NO!
If we can't dig up Queen Christina's corpse and study her sexual constitution, we're not doing ANYTHING!!!
We're going to lie on the floor and SCREAM until we get our way!
No sooner said than done. In the lovely remembrance book, *Queen Christina: Exhumation in Rome, 1965*, Christina's sexual constitution gets its very own chapter, aptly titled:
Queen Christina's sexual constitution
BUT IS IT EVEN POSSIBLE TO SAY ANYTHING ABOUT A PERSON'S "SEXUAL CONSTITUTION" (WHATEVER THE HELL THAT IS) BY STARING AT A 400-YEAR-OLD SKELETON?
OF COURSE IT ISN'T.
...which even the geezers were forced to admit in the end!
And so the whole adventure ended in an anticlimax for our intrepid exhumers:
Our insufficient knowledge of
the effects of intersexuality
on skeletal formation ... makes
it impossible for us to
confirm a diagnosis of
intersexuality.
*Hjortsjö, Carl-Herman 101

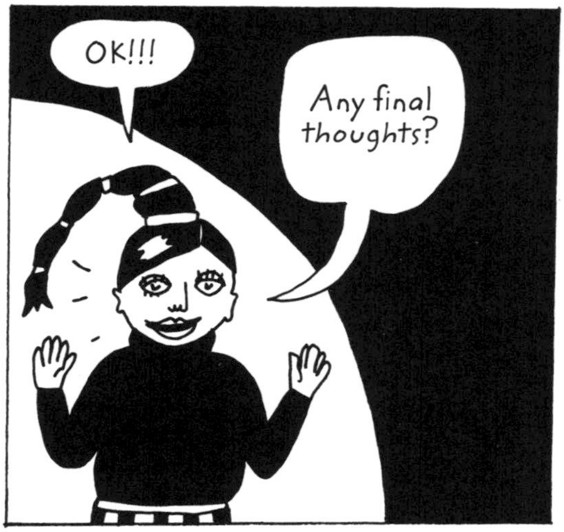
OK!!!
Any final thoughts?

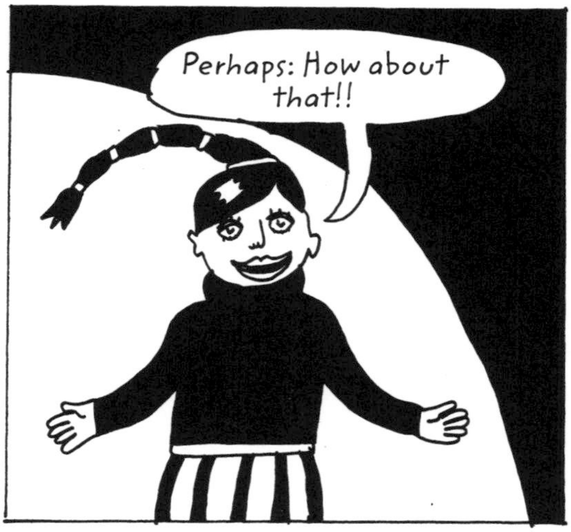
Perhaps: How about that!!

Or even:

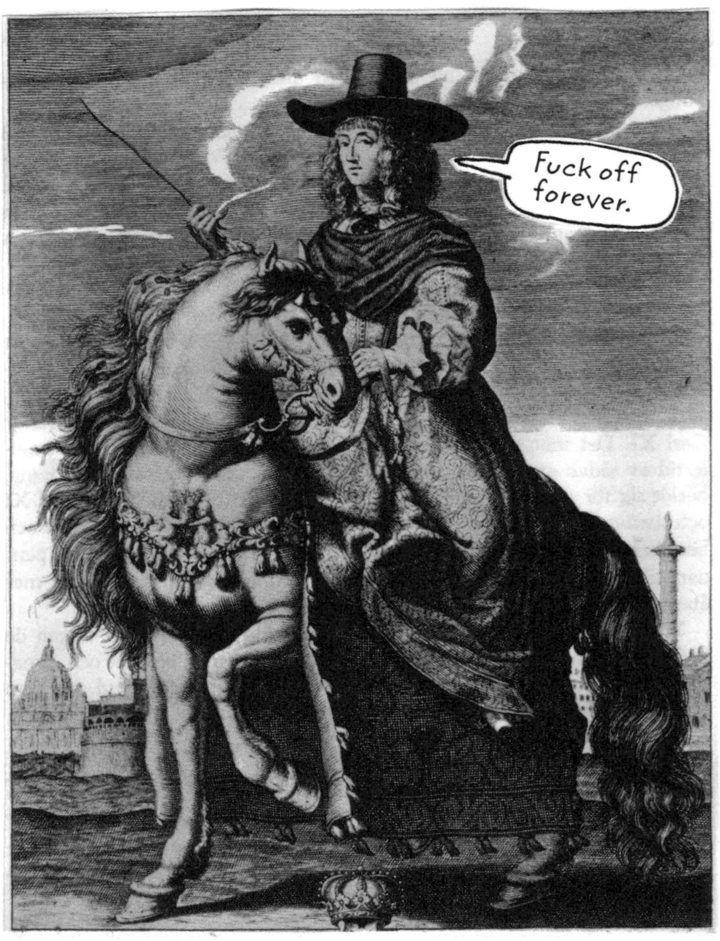
Fuck off forever.

The End

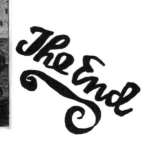

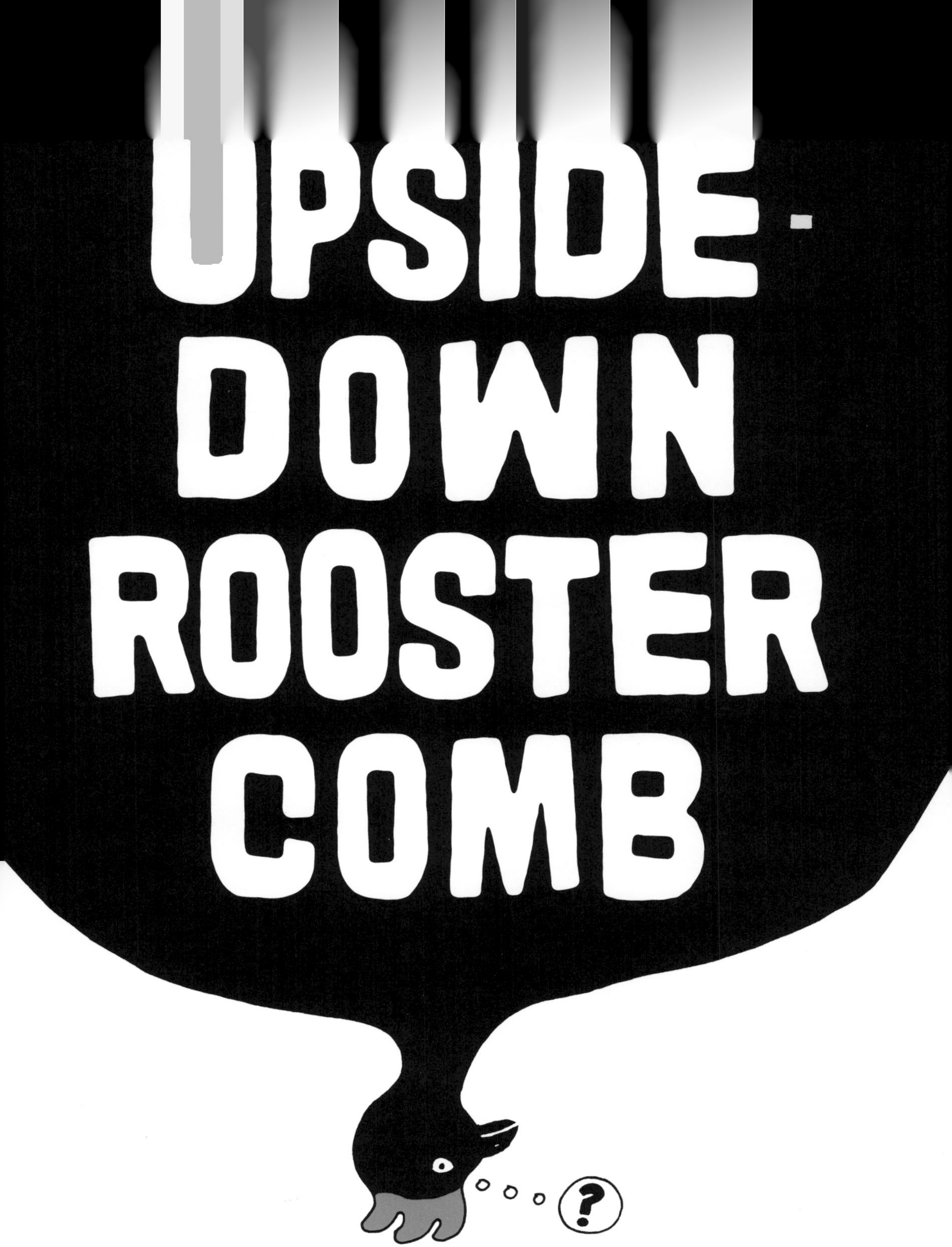
UPSIDE-
DOWN
ROOSTER
COMB
?

Aftonbladet featured an article about a type of plastic surgery that has become increasingly popular:

More and more women choose labia enlargement.

Intimate cosmetic surgical procedures have

doubled in the past ten years, according to an

estimate by Jan Jernbeck, plastic surgeon

at Akademikliniken.

For example, women think that

their labia, often the inner labia,

are too small.

They're unhappy with their appearance

and don't like being naked in front of other

people. For example, when they're with their

partner or in the showers at the pool.

So, they want to "tidy things up."

Jernbeck, who also appears on the program *Plastikkirurgerna* [The Plastic Surgeons] on TV4+, says that women from all walks of life come to the clinic for this type of surgery.

"We talk more openly about these things now than we used to, and patients can see what's possible."

Sexologist Malena Ivarsson says women

today are more concerned about their

sex lives.

"Many of them think their labia

are too small."

In Ivarsson's opinion, some women overestimate how much men actually care about these things. She advises women to think things through and weigh the pros and cons before electing to have surgery.

"Often it's a matter of self–esteem.

Go and talk with a therapist. It's

important to understand why you want

to enlarge your labia."

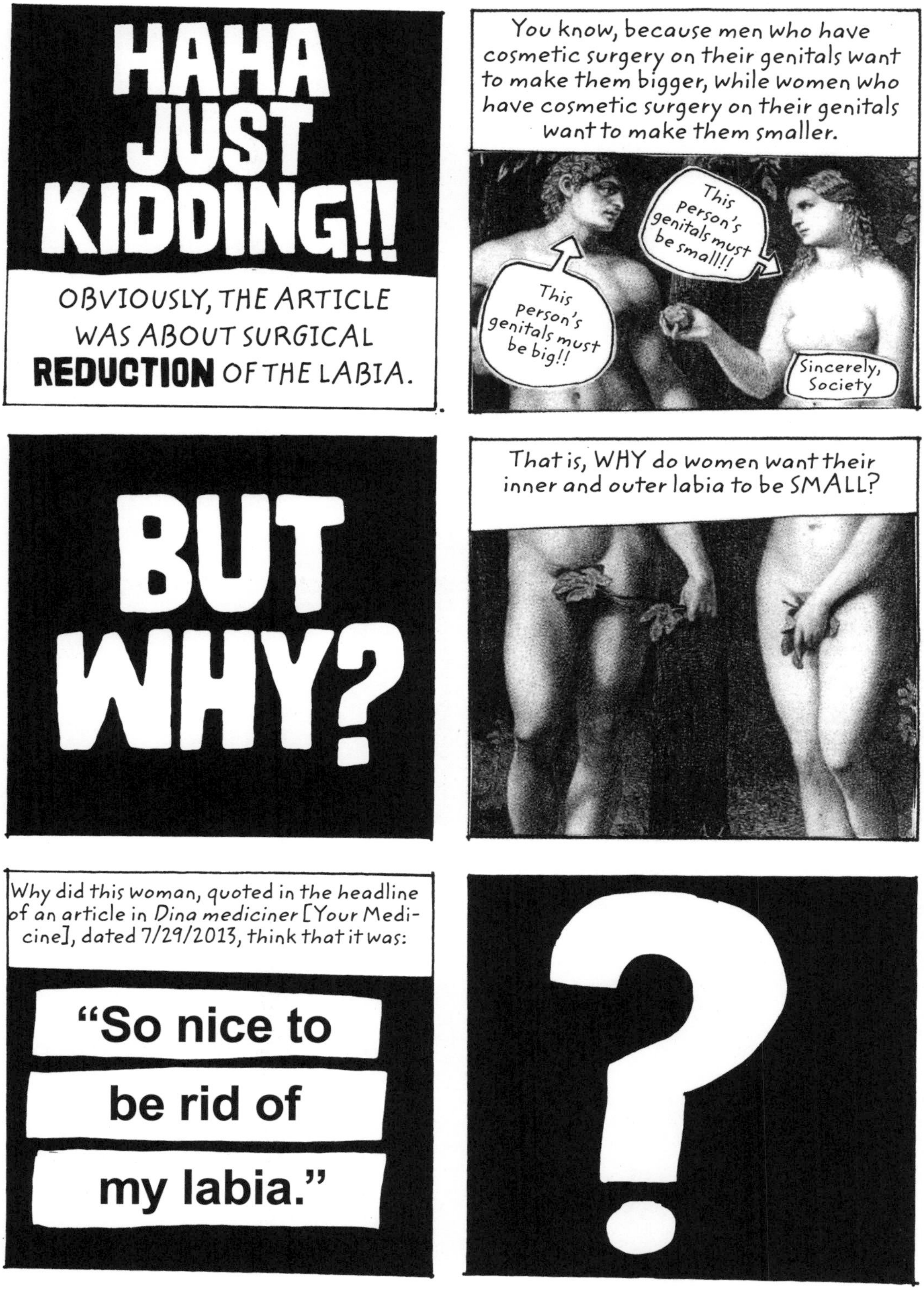
HAHA JUST KIDDING!!
OBVIOUSLY, THE ARTICLE WAS ABOUT SURGICAL **REDUCTION** OF THE LABIA.
You know, because men who have cosmetic surgery on their genitals want to make them bigger, while women who have cosmetic surgery on their genitals want to make them smaller.
This person's genitals must be small!!!
This person's genitals must be big!!
Sincerely, Society
BUT WHY?
That is, WHY do women want their inner and outer labia to be SMALL?
Why did this woman, quoted in the headline of an article in *Dina mediciner* [Your Medicine], dated 7/29/2013, think that it was:
"So nice to be rid of my labia."
?

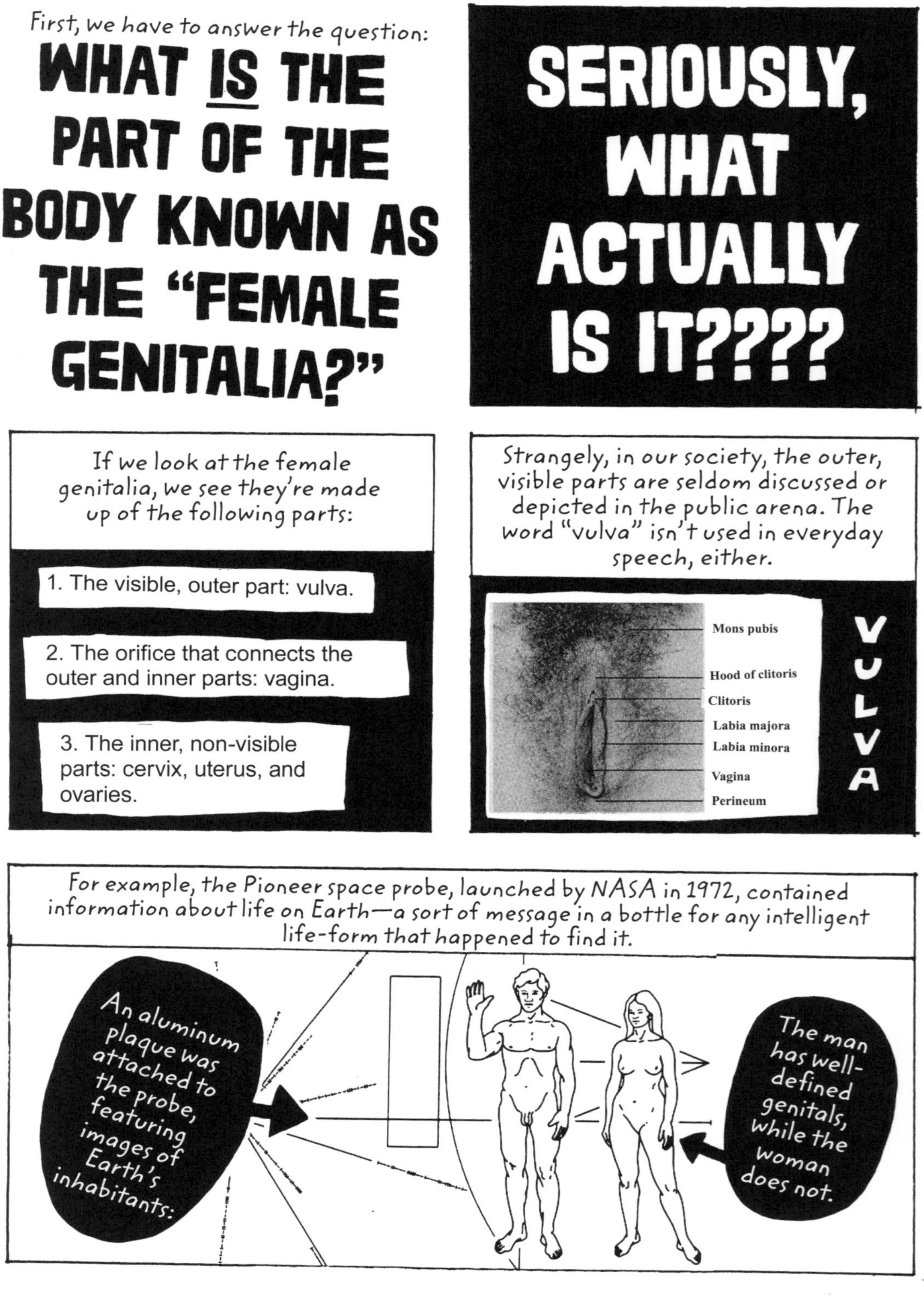

First, we have to answer the question:

WHAT IS THE PART OF THE BODY KNOWN AS THE "FEMALE GENITALIA?"

SERIOUSLY, WHAT ACTUALLY IS IT????

If we look at the female genitalia, we see they're made up of the following parts:

1. The visible, outer part: vulva.

2. The orifice that connects the outer and inner parts: vagina.

3. The inner, non-visible parts: cervix, uterus, and ovaries.

Strangely, in our society, the outer, visible parts are seldom discussed or depicted in the public arena. The word "vulva" isn't used in everyday speech, either.

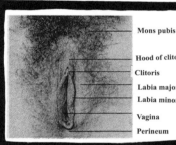

Mons pubis

Hood of clitoris

Clitoris

Labia majora

Labia minora

Vagina

Perineum

VULVA

For example, the Pioneer space probe, launched by NASA in 1972, contained information about life on Earth—a sort of message in a bottle for any intelligent life-form that happened to find it.

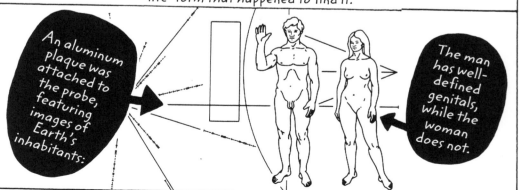

An aluminum plaque was attached to the probe, featuring images of Earth's inhabitants:

The man has well-defined genitals, while the woman does not.

In fact, the original sketch for the plaque DID have a "short line indicating the woman's vulva."*

*Mark Wolverton, The Depths of Space: The Story of the Pioneer Planetary Probes (Washington, D.C.: Joseph Henry Press, 2004), 79.

Hmm, something about this feels wrong!! I can't quite put my finger on it!!

But the line was erased, because the plaque's creators were afraid NASA leadership wouldn't approve an accurate depiction of a vulva.

Ah!!! Yes!!! There!! Much better!!

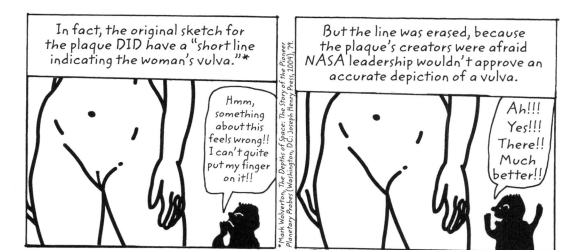

In other words, the general understanding at NASA was that EVEN ALIENS ON OTHER PLANETS would be uncomfortable if confronted with an illustrated vulva— that if they DID include the "short line," it might lead to something like this:

EWWW!! We are NOT replying to this!

ABSO-LUTELY NOT!

If they ask, we'll just tell them we never received it!!

Good idea!

Cultural historian Mithu M. Sanyal says that women's genitals are often described as an empty space, a kind of deprivation or deficiency, or the absence of a penis.* This is evident in many ways, e.g., how we talk:

Boys are the ones with a penis and girls are the ones without a penis!

HOW WE USUALLY SAY IT.

Girls are the ones with a vulva and boys are the ones without a vulva!

HOW WE RARELY SAY IT.**

**Even MORE uncommon is talking about sexual parts WITHOUT linking them to a particular gender, e.g., "Girls are the ones with a penis or a vulva."

*Mithu M. Sanyal, Vulva—det usynlige køn (Copenhagen: Tiderne Skrifter, 2011).

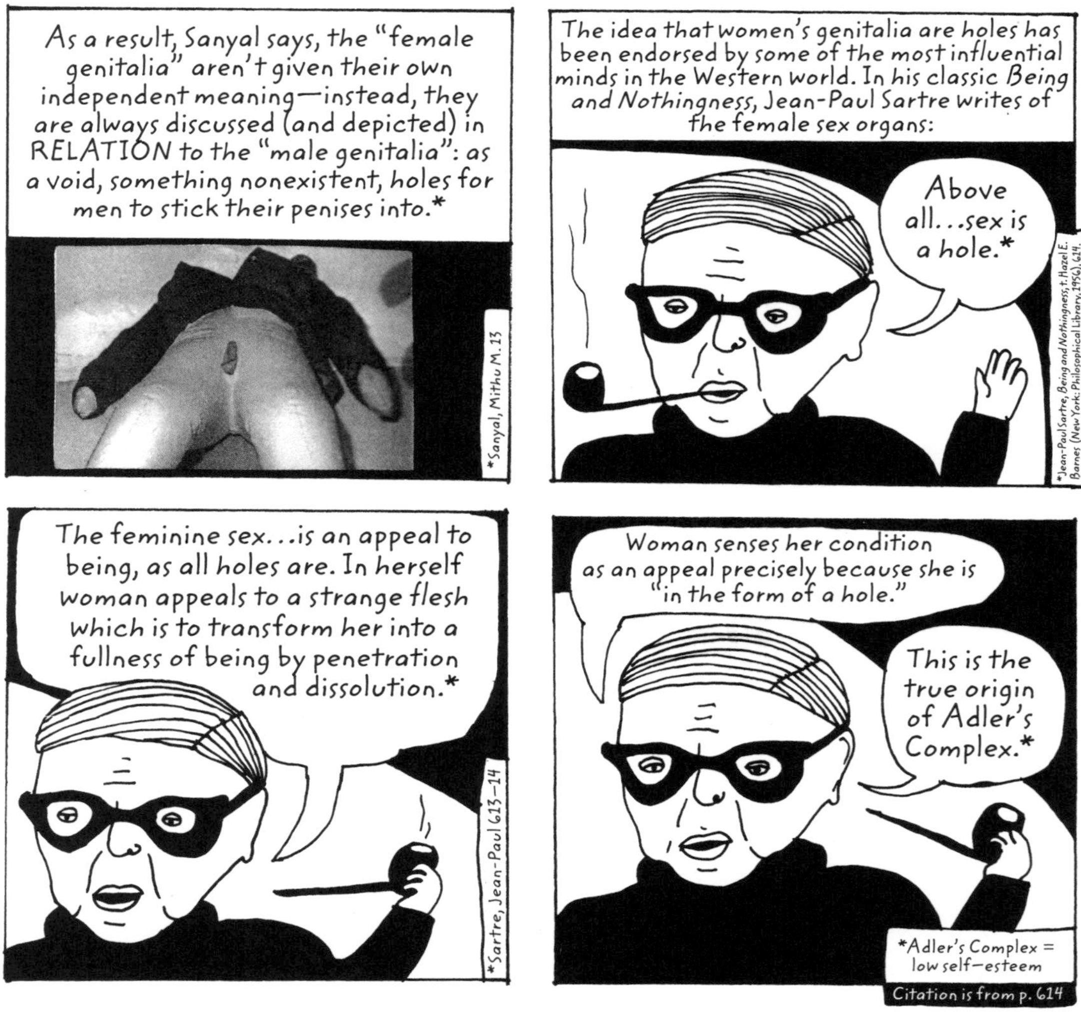

As a result, Sanyal says, the "female genitalia" aren't given their own independent meaning—instead, they are always discussed (and depicted) in RELATION to the "male genitalia": as a void, something nonexistent, holes for men to stick their penises into.*
*Sanyal, Mithu M. 13
The idea that women's genitalia are holes has been endorsed by some of the most influential minds in the Western world. In his classic *Being and Nothingness*, Jean-Paul Sartre writes of the female sex organs:
Above all...sex is a hole.*
*Jean-Paul Sartre, *Being and Nothingness*, t. Hazel E. Barnes (New York: Philosophical Library, 1956), 614.
The feminine sex...is an appeal to being, as all holes are. In herself woman appeals to a strange flesh which is to transform her into a fullness of being by penetration and dissolution.*
*Sartre, Jean-Paul 613–14
Woman senses her condition as an appeal precisely because she is "in the form of a hole."
This is the true origin of Adler's Complex.*
*Adler's Complex = low self–esteem
Citation is from p. 614

IN OTHER WORDS, THE WOMAN HAS LOW SELF-ESTEEM BECAUSE SHE <u>HAS</u> NO SEX; SHE IS HOLLOW, AND MUST PLEAD FOR A PENIS TO FILL HER INADEQUACY (THE EMPTY PLACE WHERE A SEX ORGAN SHOULD BE).

No doubt deeply influenced by Sartre, the author of the children's book *Kärlekboken* [The Love Book] describes the sex organs this way:

The man has a penis that sticks out.
The woman has a tuft of hair with a hole that goes in.

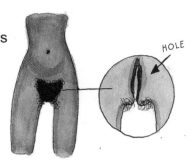

HOLE

*Pernilla Stalfelt, Kärlekboken (Stockholm: Rabën & Sjögren, 2011).

The penis fits into the hole.

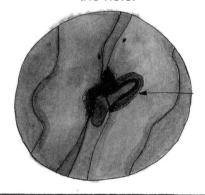

Women's external sex organs are essentially erased in many areas of our culture. Euphemisms and metaphors for the "female genitalia" often look something like this, from "Det e dej jag vill ha" [That's What I Want] by The Latin Kings:

In and out, in and out...

You with your gash and me with my spear.

But there are lots of other metaphors they could have chosen for the woman's parts— an upside-down rooster comb, for example. Why not something like this:

Me with my garden gnome and you with your rooster comb.

JUST A SUGGESTION, WORDSMITHS/ BALLADEERS. FEEL FREE TO RUN WITH IT! CONSIDER IT MY GIFT TO YOU!!

As I mentioned earlier, the collective term for the outer sexual parts, "VULVA," is hardly ever used in everyday speech.

INSTEAD, PEOPLE USE THE INCORRECT TERM "VAGINA," WHEN WHAT THEY'RE REALLY TALKING ABOUT IS THE VULVA.

FOR EXAMPLE: This "vagina necklace," as described in the Swedish magazine QX in January 2012...

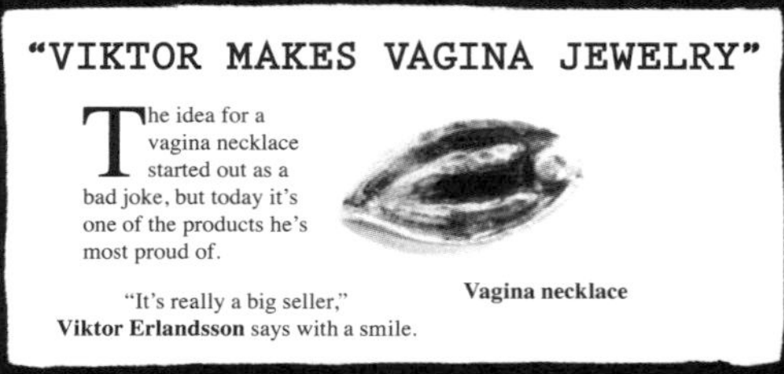

"VIKTOR MAKES VAGINA JEWELRY"

The idea for a vagina necklace started out as a bad joke, but today it's one of the products he's most proud of.

"It's really a big seller," **Viktor Erlandsson** says with a smile.

Vagina necklace

...actually depicts a vulva and should be called a "vulva necklace."

The entrepreneur behind this product, "Vagina whiten cream," which aims to give the genitals a more Aryan hue...

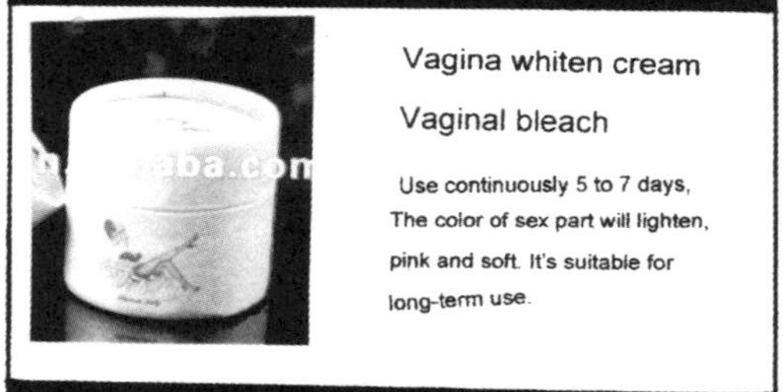
Vagina whiten cream
Vaginal bleach
Use continuously 5 to 7 days,
The color of sex part will lighten,
pink and soft. It's suitable for
long-term use.

...should—to be correct—have called it "Vulva whiten cream" instead.

On the Flashback message boards, user "Humbug" had this to say about pop singer Jasmine Kara...

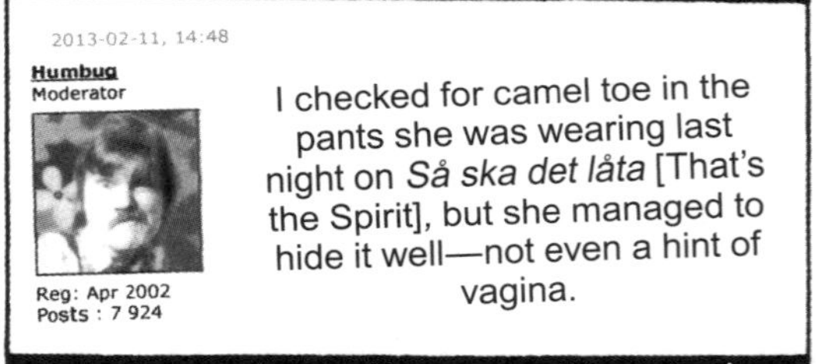
2013-02-11, 14:48
Humbug
Moderator
Reg: Apr 2002
Posts : 7 924
I checked for camel toe in the pants she was wearing last night on *Så ska det låta* [That's the Spirit], but she managed to hide it well—not even a hint of vagina.

...however, to use the correct terminology, Humbug should have said she or he didn't see a hint of Jasmine Kara's VULVA.

When author Stig Larsson,* appearing on the talk show *Malou efter tio* [Malou After Ten] (11/18/2012), was asked about a section in his book where he writes that younger women's pussies taste sweeter...

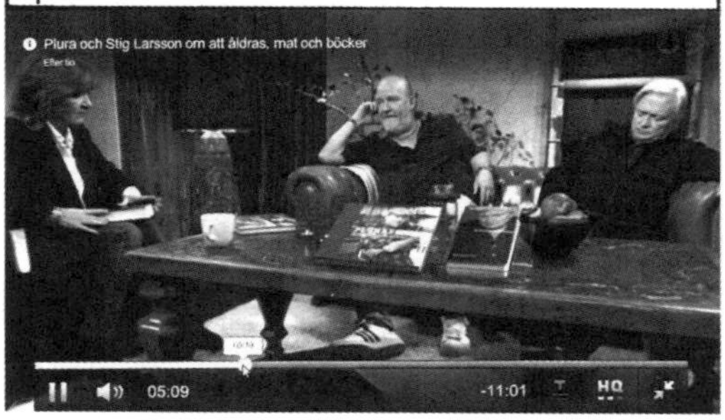
Plura och Stig Larsson om att åldras, mat och böcker
05:09
-11:01
HQ

*Not the Dragon Tattoo guy—that's Stieg!

...here's how he answered:

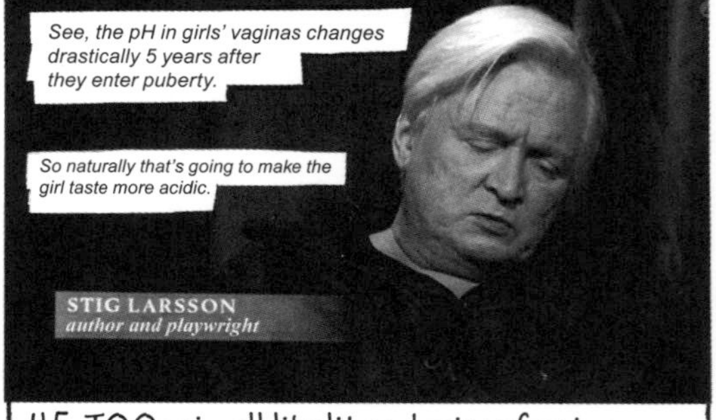
See, the pH in girls' vaginas changes drastically 5 years after they enter puberty.
So naturally that's going to make the girl taste more acidic.
STIG LARSSON
author and playwright

HE, TOO—in all likelihood—is referring primarily to the EXTERNAL genitalia and should therefore have used the word VULVA.

OK, SO THERE'S THIS COLLECTIVE CONFUSION OVER WHAT TO CALL THE VARIOUS SEXUAL PARTS. BUT DOES IT REALLY MATTER?
Psychologist Harriet Lerner has been writing since the 1970s about the consequences of mislabeling the vulva as the vagina. She likens this misuse of language to "psychic genital mutilation."*
What is not named does not exist!
*Sanyal, Mithu M. 22
To illustrate her point, she cites a popular sex-education book from the 1980s:
A girl has two ovaries, a uterus, and a vagina, which are her sex organs. A boy's sex organs are a penis and testicles.
One of the first changes (at puberty) will be the growth of hair around the vaginal opening of the girl.
Sanyal, Mithu M. 22
Lerner writes:
Such partial and inaccurate labeling of female genitalia might inspire any young girl to sit on the bathroom floor with a mirror and conclude that she is a freak.*
*Sanyal, Mithu M. 22
The editors of this 2002 biology textbook saw no reason to include an image of the external genitalia, either. They were content just to publish these two figures, under the heading "The female sex organs."
uterus
bladder
pubic bone
urethra
clitoris
labia majora
labia minora
oviduct
ovary
cervix
rectum
vagina
Female sex organs, side view.
Anders Henriksson, Biologi (Malmö: Gleerups, 2002), 288.
Uterus, oviducts and ovaries, seen from the front.
oviduct
ovary with follicles
uterus
endometrium
vagina

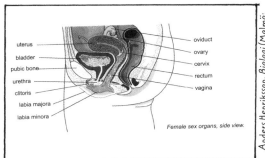

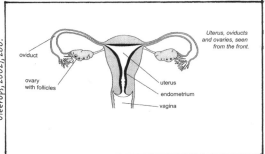

On the other hand, it does seem extremely important to inform readers that the vagina's preordained purpose is to be filled with a penis in the heat of heterosexual passion:

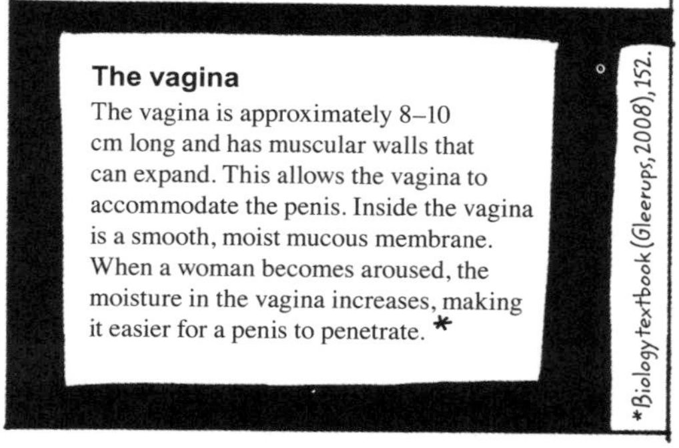

The vagina

The vagina is approximately 8–10 cm long and has muscular walls that can expand. This allows the vagina to accommodate the penis. Inside the vagina is a smooth, moist mucous membrane. When a woman becomes aroused, the moisture in the vagina increases, making it easier for a penis to penetrate. *

*Biology textbook (Gleerups, 2008), 152.

It doesn't take Einstein to figure out my point here: Our CULTURAL unwillingness to name and visually depict the vulva has is likely a major factor for women who want to surgically reduce their labia.

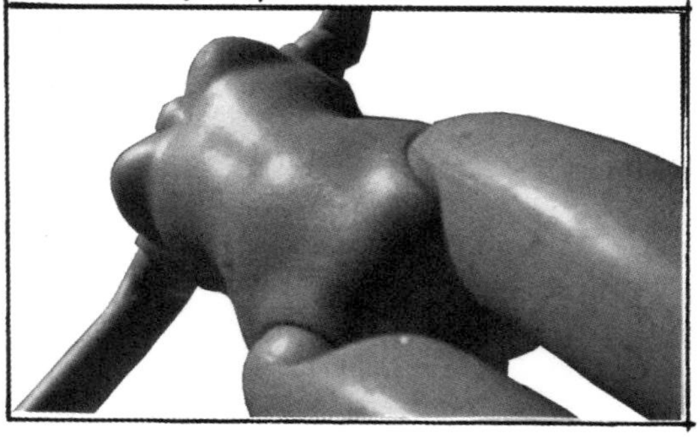

Our culture simply WANTS things a CERTAIN WAY: 1) There are two genders; 2) They are each other's opposite; and 3) They physically complement each other like a "sword and sheath," as manifested in heterosexual intercourse. Based on these cultural ideals, women's genitals are construed as a "hole" waiting to be filled with a cock—not as organs that exist in their own right.

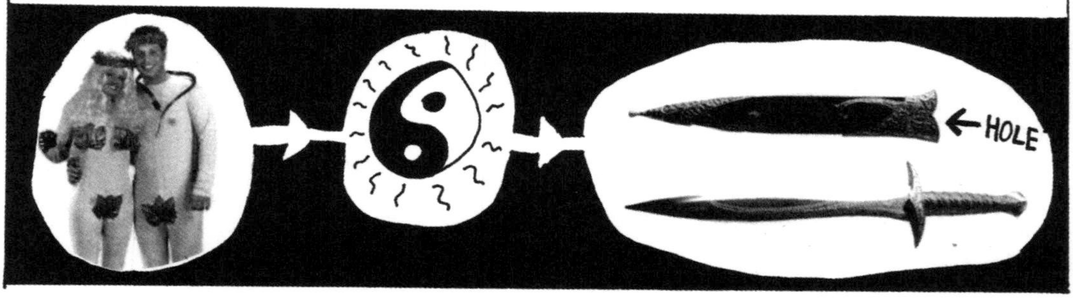
←HOLE

SO IT'S OBVIOUSLY A HUGE DISAPPOINTMENT WHEN REALITY DOESN'T LIVE UP TO EXPECTATIONS!

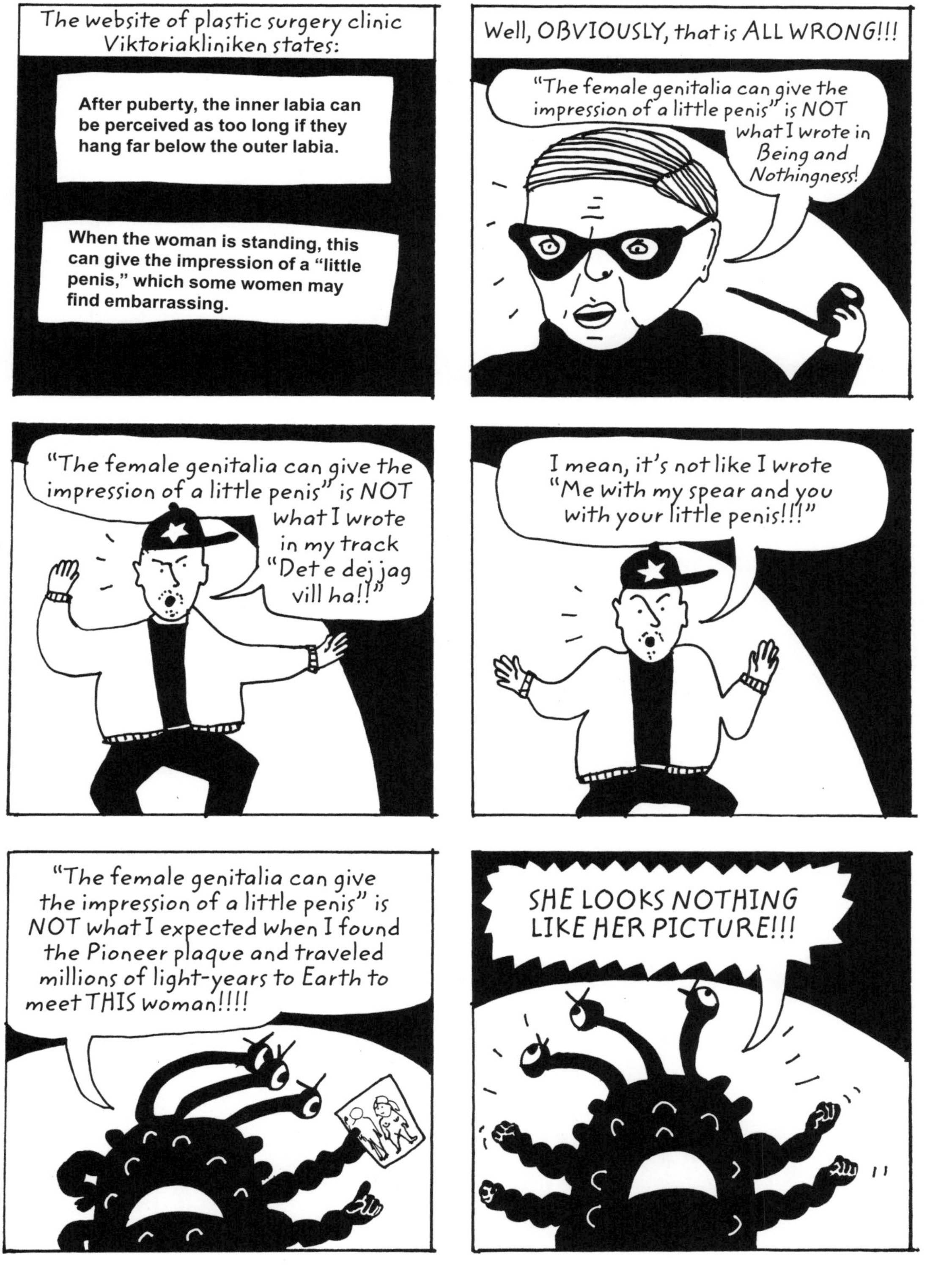
The website of plastic surgery clinic Viktoriakliniken states:
After puberty, the inner labia can be perceived as too long if they hang far below the outer labia.
When the woman is standing, this can give the impression of a "little penis," which some women may find embarrassing.
Well, OBVIOUSLY, that is ALL WRONG!!!
"The female genitalia can give the impression of a little penis" is NOT what I wrote in Being and Nothingness!
"The female genitalia can give the impression of a little penis" is NOT what I wrote in my track "Det e dej jag vill ha!!"
I mean, it's not like I wrote "Me with my spear and you with your little penis!!!"
"The female genitalia can give the impression of a little penis" is NOT what I expected when I found the Pioneer plaque and traveled millions of light-years to Earth to meet THIS woman!!!!
SHE LOOKS NOTHING LIKE HER PICTURE!!!

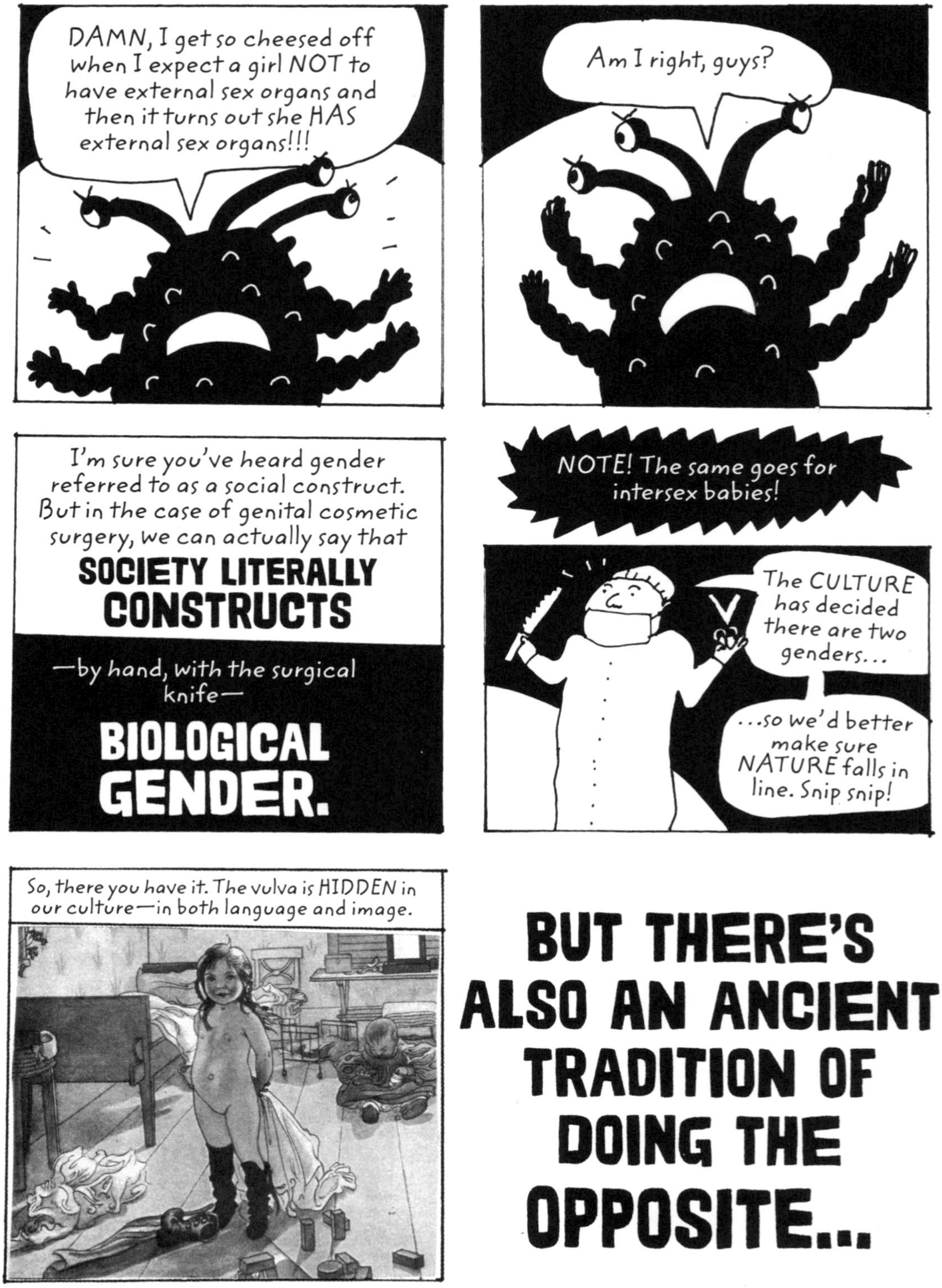
DAMN, I get so cheesed off when I expect a girl NOT to have external sex organs and then it turns out she HAS external sex organs!!!
Am I right, guys?
I'm sure you've heard gender referred to as a social construct. But in the case of genital cosmetic surgery, we can actually say that
SOCIETY LITERALLY CONSTRUCTS
—by hand, with the surgical knife—
BIOLOGICAL GENDER.
NOTE! The same goes for intersex babies!
The CULTURE has decided there are two genders...
...so we'd better make sure NATURE falls in line. Snip snip!
So, there you have it. The vulva is HIDDEN in our culture—in both language and image.
BUT THERE'S ALSO AN ANCIENT TRADITION OF DOING THE OPPOSITE...

...THAT IS, PUTTING THE **VULVA** ON DISPLAY.

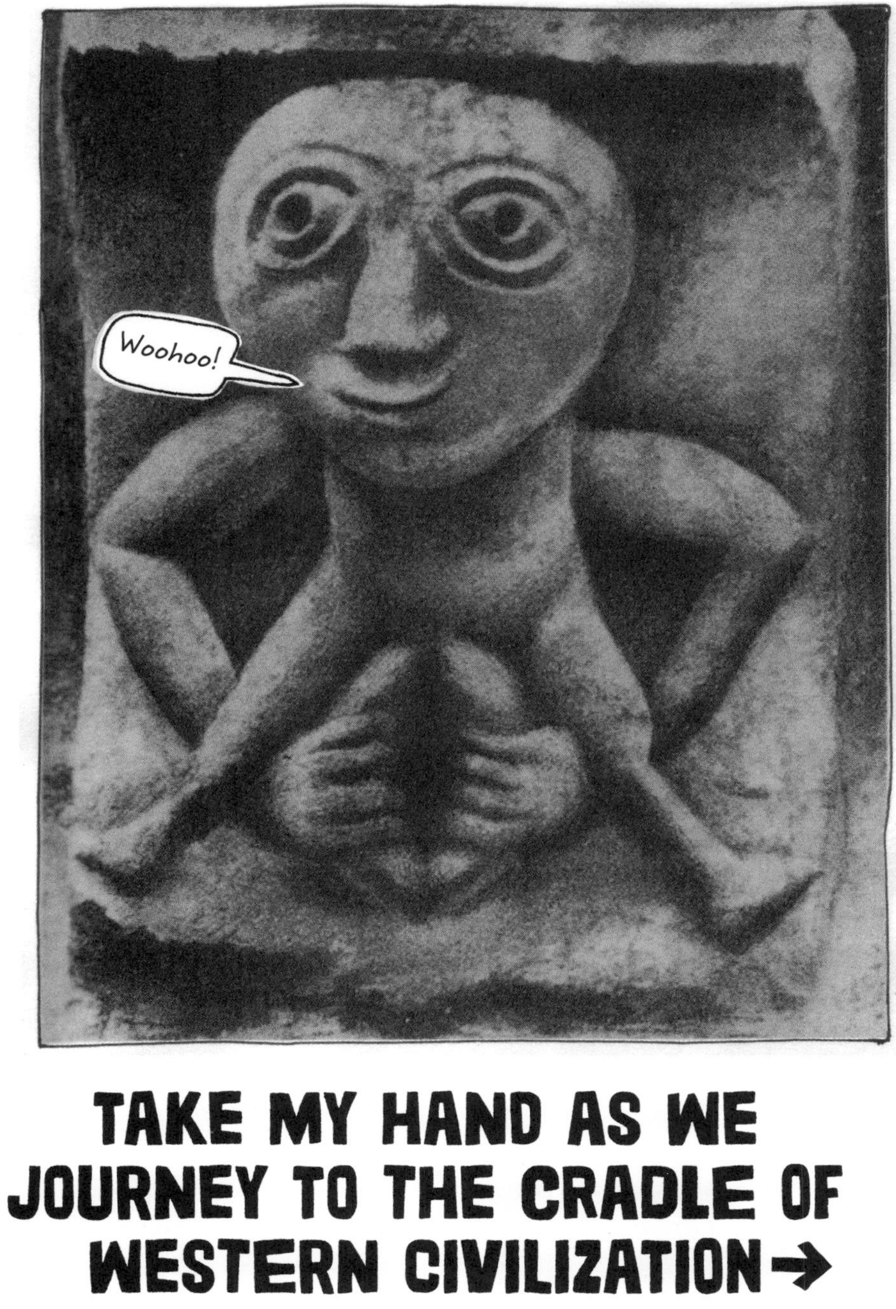
Woohoo!

TAKE MY HAND AS WE JOURNEY TO THE CRADLE OF WESTERN CIVILIZATION →

In one of the *Homeric Hymns* (33 anonymous poems from ca. 600–500 BC) there is a myth called "To Demeter," which goes like this:

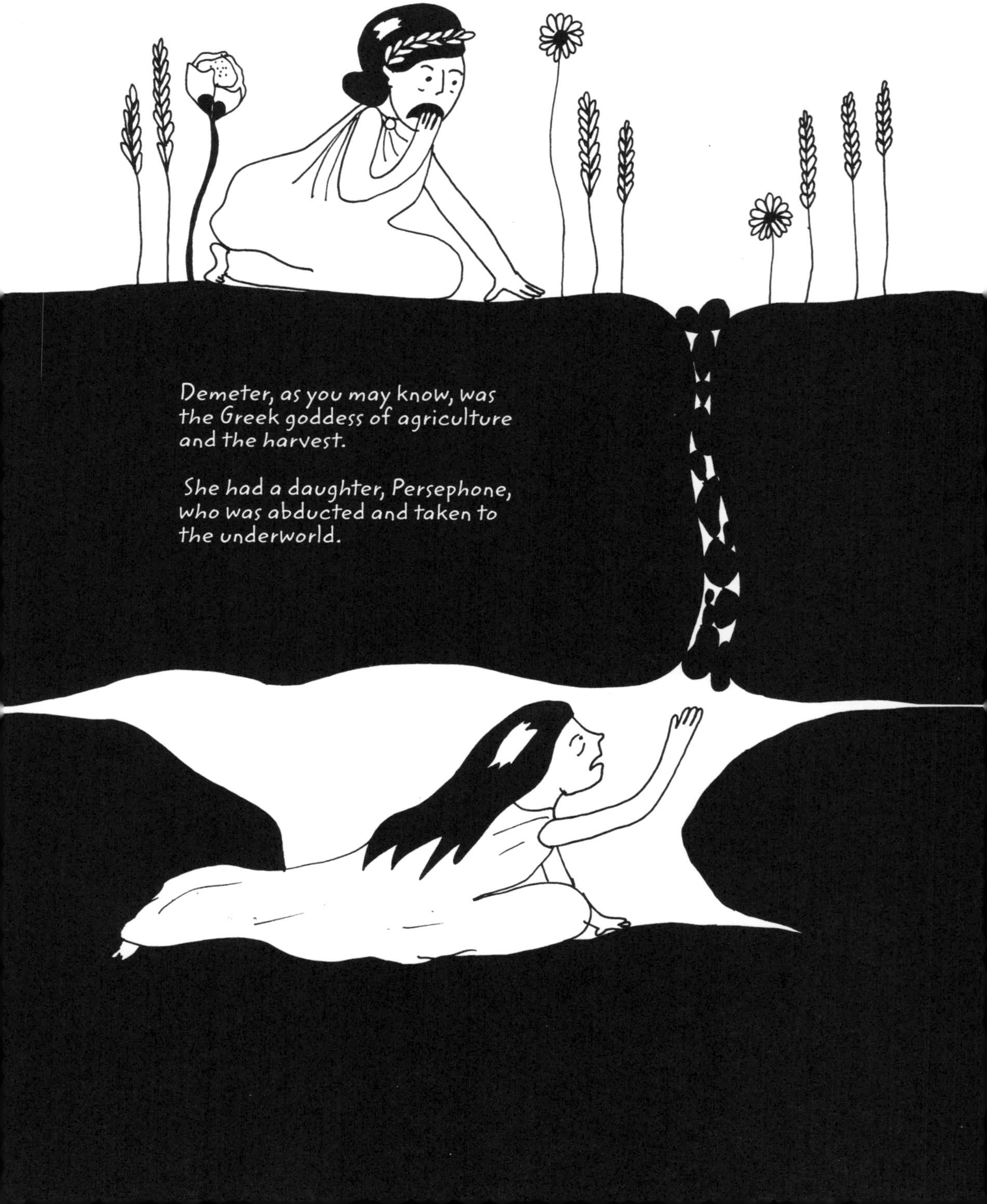
Demeter, as you may know, was the Greek goddess of agriculture and the harvest.
She had a daughter, Persephone, who was abducted and taken to the underworld.

Beside herself with despair over her daughter's disappearance, Demeter wanders the countryside, lacking the will to eat or drink.

As her body grows more and more emaciated, all the plants and crops around her stop growing and eventually die. On the brink of starvation, the people beg the gods for help.

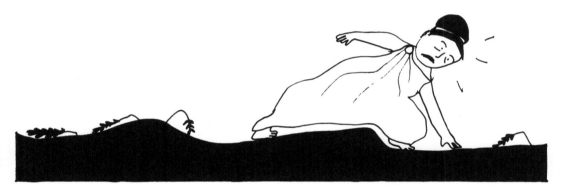

But the gods cannot lift Demeter's sprits. She remains inconsolable and wracked with grief.

AND THEN A VERY INTERESTING CHARACTER SHOWS UP IN THE STORY: IAMBE.

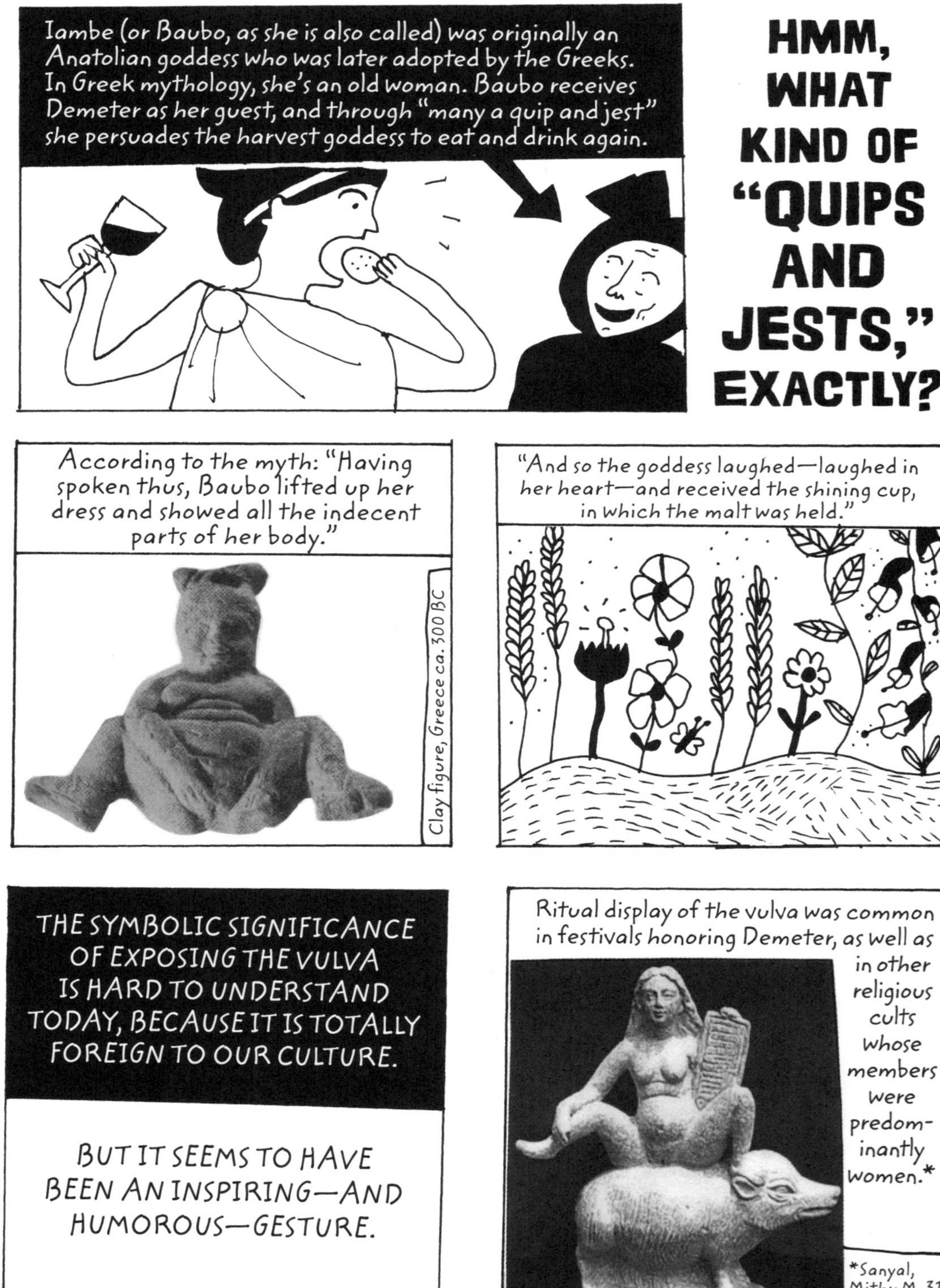
Iambe (or Baubo, as she is also called) was originally an Anatolian goddess who was later adopted by the Greeks. In Greek mythology, she's an old woman. Baubo receives Demeter as her guest, and through "many a quip and jest" she persuades the harvest goddess to eat and drink again.
HMM, WHAT KIND OF "QUIPS AND JESTS," EXACTLY?
According to the myth: "Having spoken thus, Baubo lifted up her dress and showed all the indecent parts of her body."
Clay figure, Greece ca. 300 BC
"And so the goddess laughed—laughed in her heart—and received the shining cup, in which the malt was held."
THE SYMBOLIC SIGNIFICANCE OF EXPOSING THE VULVA IS HARD TO UNDERSTAND TODAY, BECAUSE IT IS TOTALLY FOREIGN TO OUR CULTURE.
BUT IT SEEMS TO HAVE BEEN AN INSPIRING—AND HUMOROUS—GESTURE.
Ritual display of the vulva was common in festivals honoring Demeter, as well as in other religious cults whose members were predominantly women.*
*Sanyal, Mithu M. 31

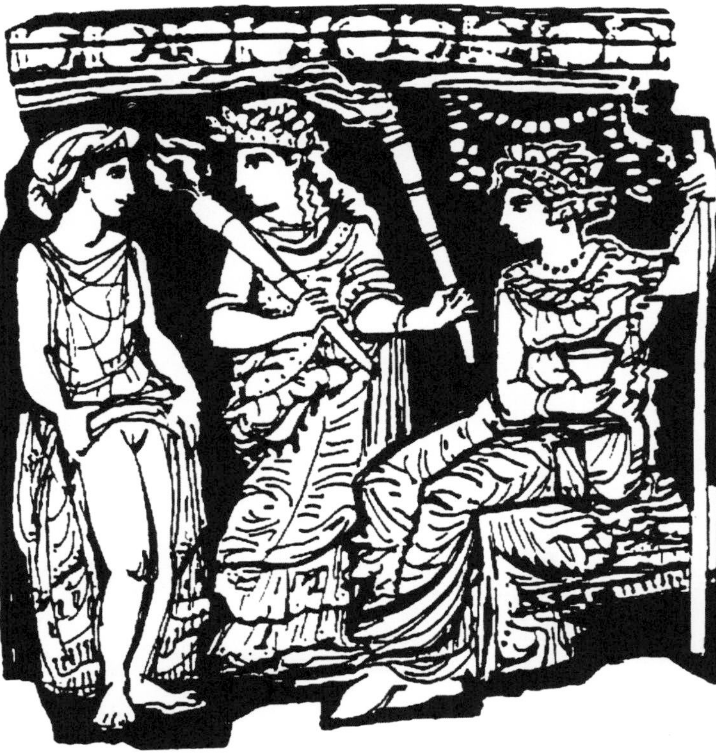

Aristophanes writes about women in the Greek city of Eleusis who gathered at the temple of Demeter, exposed their genitals to one another, sang, and ate sesame-honey cakes in the shape of vulvas.*

*Sanyal, Mithu M. 31

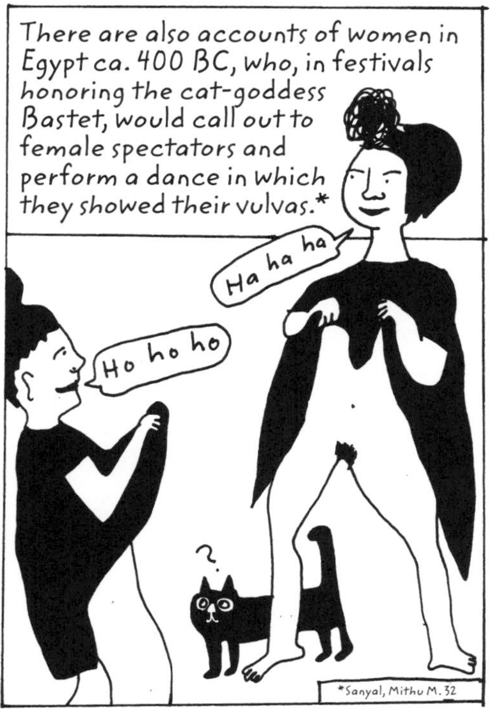

There are also accounts of women in Egypt ca. 400 BC, who, in festivals honoring the cat-goddess Bastet, would call out to female spectators and perform a dance in which they showed their vulvas.*
Ha ha ha
Ho ho ho
?
*Sanyal, Mithu M. 32

As recently as the 1800s, European fables featured women defeating the devil by exposing their genitals to him (*Vulva*, p. 9).

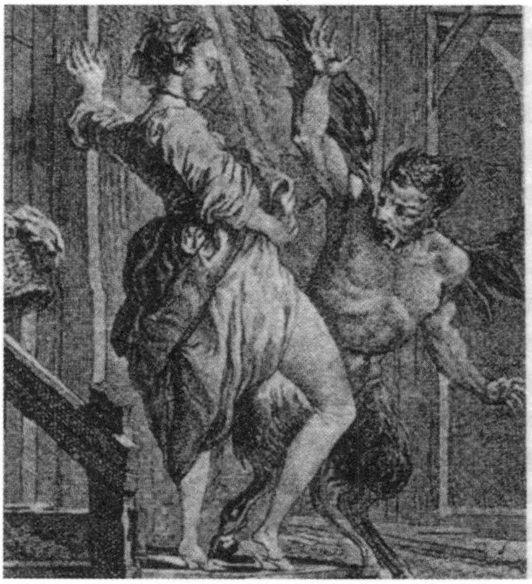

Copperplate engraving by Charles Eisen for a fable by Jean de La Fontaine.

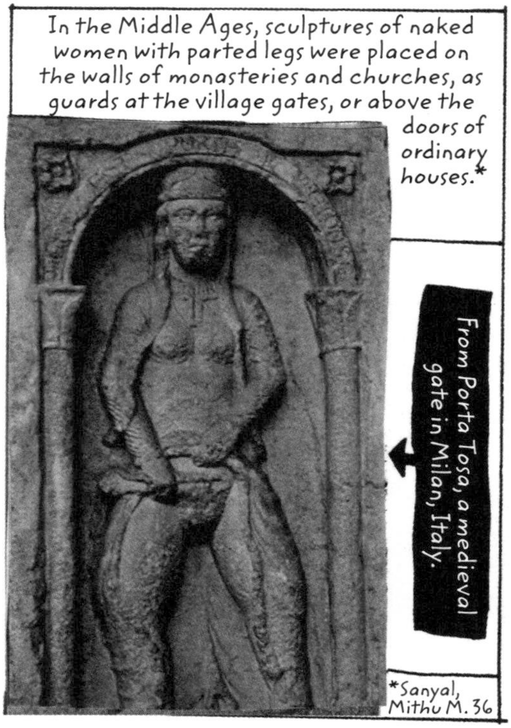
In the Middle Ages, sculptures of naked women with parted legs were placed on the walls of monasteries and churches, as guards at the village gates, or above the doors of ordinary houses.*
From Porta Tosa, a medieval gate in Milan, Italy.
*Sanyal, Mithu M. 36

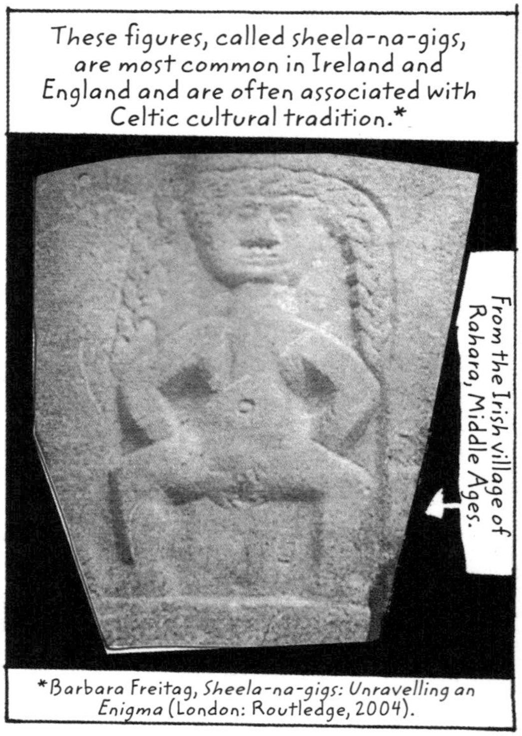
These figures, called sheela-na-gigs, are most common in Ireland and England and are often associated with Celtic cultural tradition.*
From the Irish village of Rahara, Middle Ages.
*Barbara Freitag, Sheela-na-gigs: Unravelling an Enigma (London: Routledge, 2004).

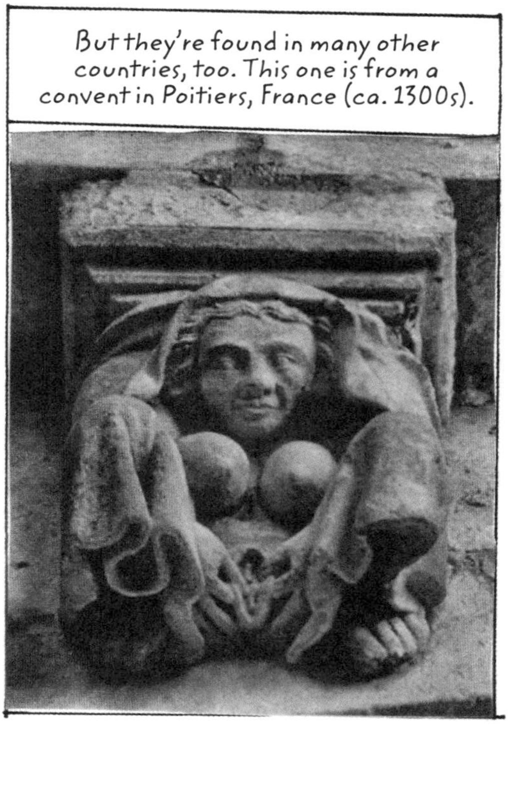
But they're found in many other countries, too. This one is from a convent in Poitiers, France (ca. 1300s).

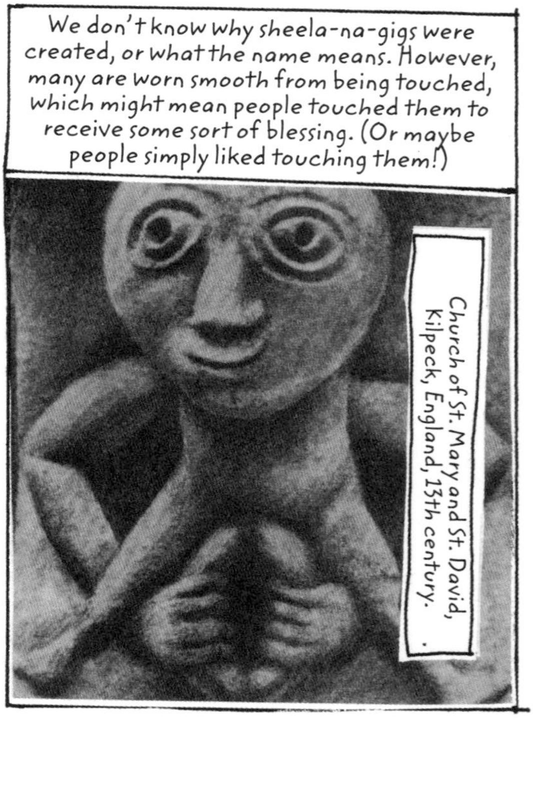
We don't know why sheela-na-gigs were created, or what the name means. However, many are worn smooth from being touched, which might mean people touched them to receive some sort of blessing. (Or maybe people simply liked touching them!)
Church of St. Mary and St. David, Kilpeck, England, 13th century.

One theory is that sheela-na-gigs represent an Irish/Celtic mythological figure called the Morrigan. She was a goddess of war who could transform into a raven as one of her powers. One recorded myth describes her as "a huge big-mouthed woman, whose labia reached to her knee."*

These days, Morrigan is a popular fantasy character who, regrettably, is usually drawn like this:

When she should be drawn like this:

Patrick K. Ford, "Celtic Women: The Opposing Sex," Viator 19 (1988): 417.

Figures with exposed vulvas are found all over the world. Another example is the Dilukai of Micronesia: wood sculptures with legs spread wide and hands on their thighs, exposing a large, triangular vulva. Dilukai were placed above the entrances to houses, where they were thought to ward off evil spirits.

Christian missionaries weren't exactly thrilled about the Dilukai (what? no way!), so they insisted the carvings were meant to shame women who behaved immorally.

This one is from the Caroline Islands, Palau, ca. 1800s–early 1900s.

Another example is yoni worship, which is widely practiced in India. The yoni (vulva) is celebrated as a sacred place, a channel for subtle powers, the gateway to cosmic mysteries (*Vulva*, p. 82).

Sculptures depict the goddess either lying on her back with her legs apart, or standing in a straddle position while her worshippers stand beneath her.*

Stone sculpture inside temple, Bhedaghat, India, 13th century.

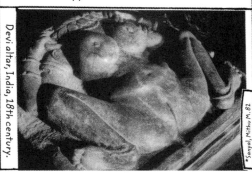

Devi altar, India, 18th century.

*Sanyal, Mithu M. 82

Displays of the vulva go REALLY far back in our culture. The world's oldest known carvings and sculptures are a veritable cornucopia of vulvas.

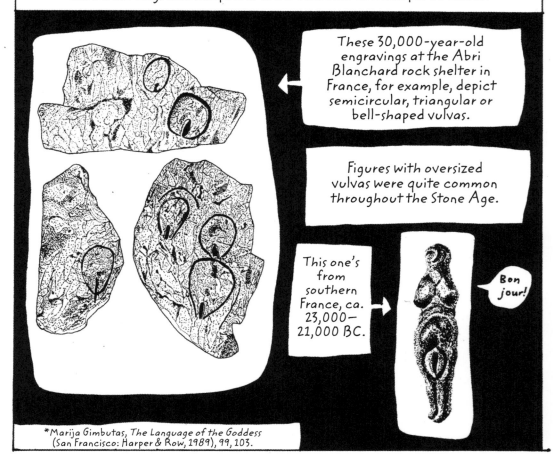

These 30,000-year-old engravings at the Abri Blanchard rock shelter in France, for example, depict semicircular, triangular or bell-shaped vulvas.

Figures with oversized vulvas were quite common throughout the Stone Age.

This one's from southern France, ca. 23,000 – 21,000 BC.

Bon jour!

*Marija Gimbutas, *The Language of the Goddess* (San Francisco: Harper & Row, 1989), 99, 103.

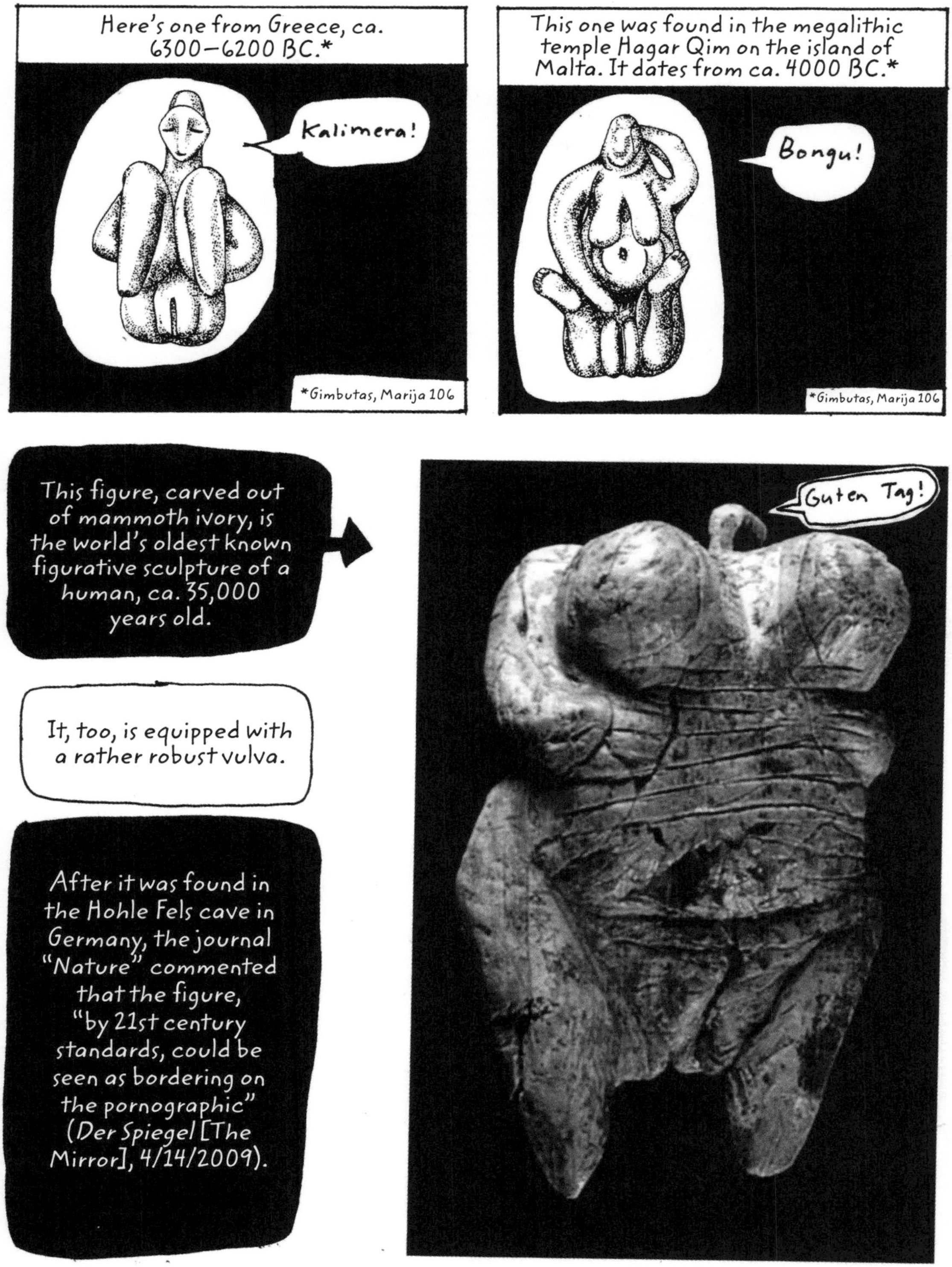
Here's one from Greece, ca. 6300–6200 BC.*
Kalimera!
*Gimbutas, Marija 106
This one was found in the megalithic temple Hagar Qim on the island of Malta. It dates from ca. 4000 BC.*
Bongu!
*Gimbutas, Marija 106
This figure, carved out of mammoth ivory, is the world's oldest known figurative sculpture of a human, ca. 35,000 years old.
It, too, is equipped with a rather robust vulva.
After it was found in the Hohle Fels cave in Germany, the journal "Nature" commented that the figure, "by 21st century standards, could be seen as bordering on the pornographic" (Der Spiegel [The Mirror], 4/14/2009).
Guten Tag!

This relief from Laussel, France, has one hand on its belly and the other holding a horn. The horn has thirteen notches—the number of lunar months/menstrual cycles in a year (25,000–20,000 BC).

Archaeologists have the annoying habit of christening these figures "Venus," as in the goddess of love.

For example, some dude named this one the "Venus of Laussel," which it automatically associates it with love and sex.

BUT A LOT OF EVIDENCE SUGGESTS THAT THE SYMBOL OF A VULVA HAD A MUCH BROADER EXISTENTIAL SIGNIFICANCE.

Vulva-bearing figures like these have been found in graves all over eastern Europe. These two were found in Bulgaria. Others have been found, for example, in the graves of 9–10-year-old girls in Moldova (5000–3000 BC).

Здравей !

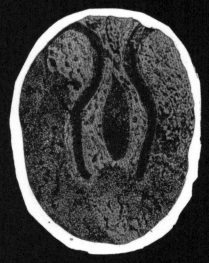

This egg-shaped stone figure from ca. 6000 BC, with a vulva engraved on one side, was found at the head of a stone altar in the former Yugoslavia (Gimbutas, p. 101).

Of course, it's **EXTREMELY** difficult to know why people in the Stone Age, etc., kept drawing/sculpting vulvas like this. **NOBODY KNOWS!!!**

So naturally there are lots of theories. But two things are UNDENIABLE:

1. During this era, the vulva (as evidenced by its depiction in graves and temples) was **PART OF** the sacred/spiritual/existential, and not—as it would later be viewed—**CONTRARY TO** the sacred/spiritual/existential.

2. People didn't feel the same sort of panic about connection with the vulva that has developed in recent history.

In other words, if the **STONE AGE** had sent a picture of humans into space, it would **NOT** have looked like this:

But instead more like this:

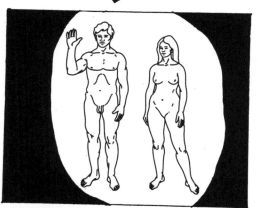

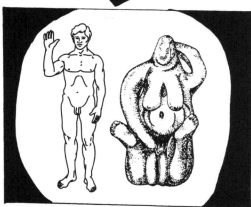

OK!!!!! END OF CHAPTER !!!!!!

MEANWHILE, IN SPACE:

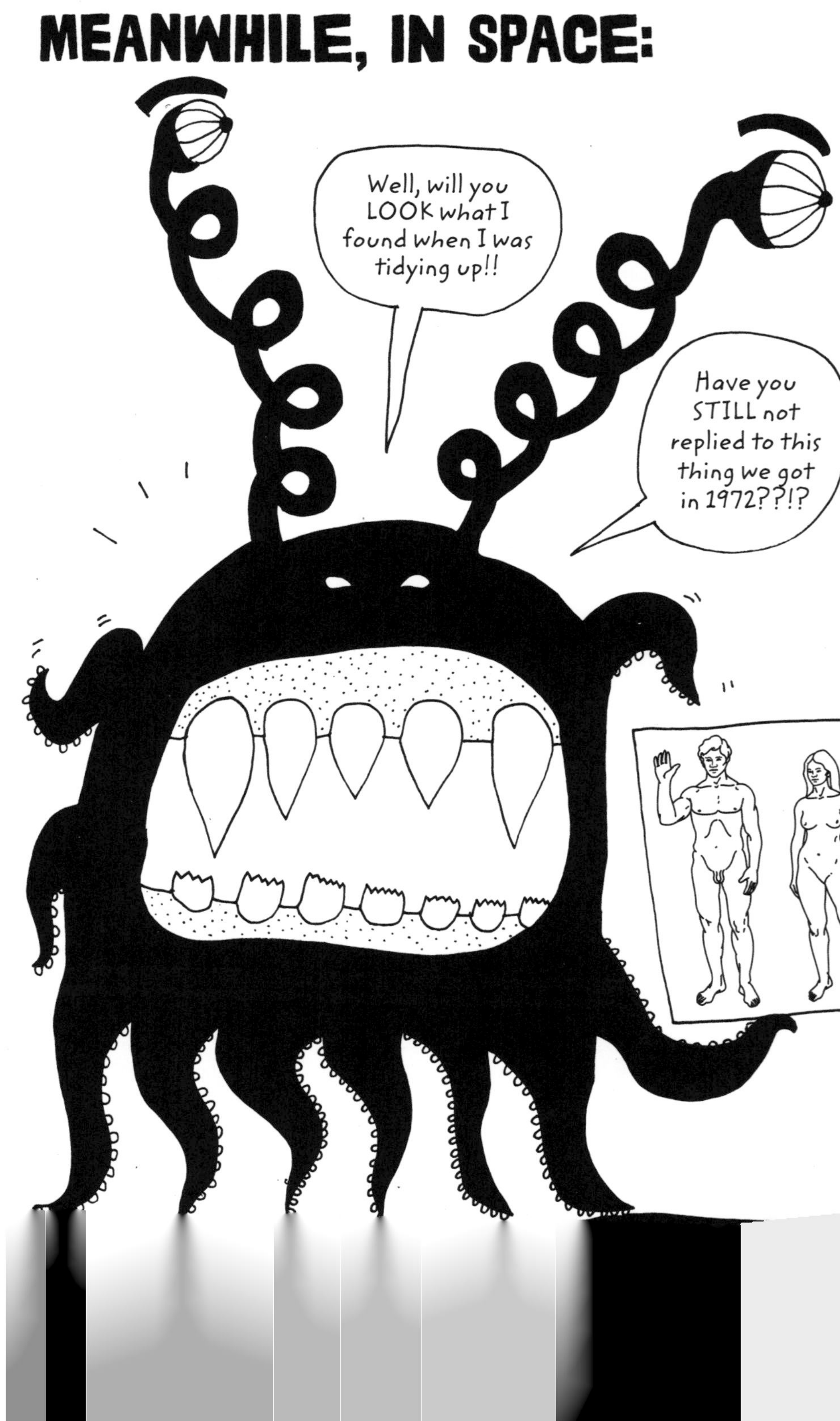
Well, will you LOOK what I found when I was tidying up!!
Have you STILL not replied to this thing we got in 1972??!?

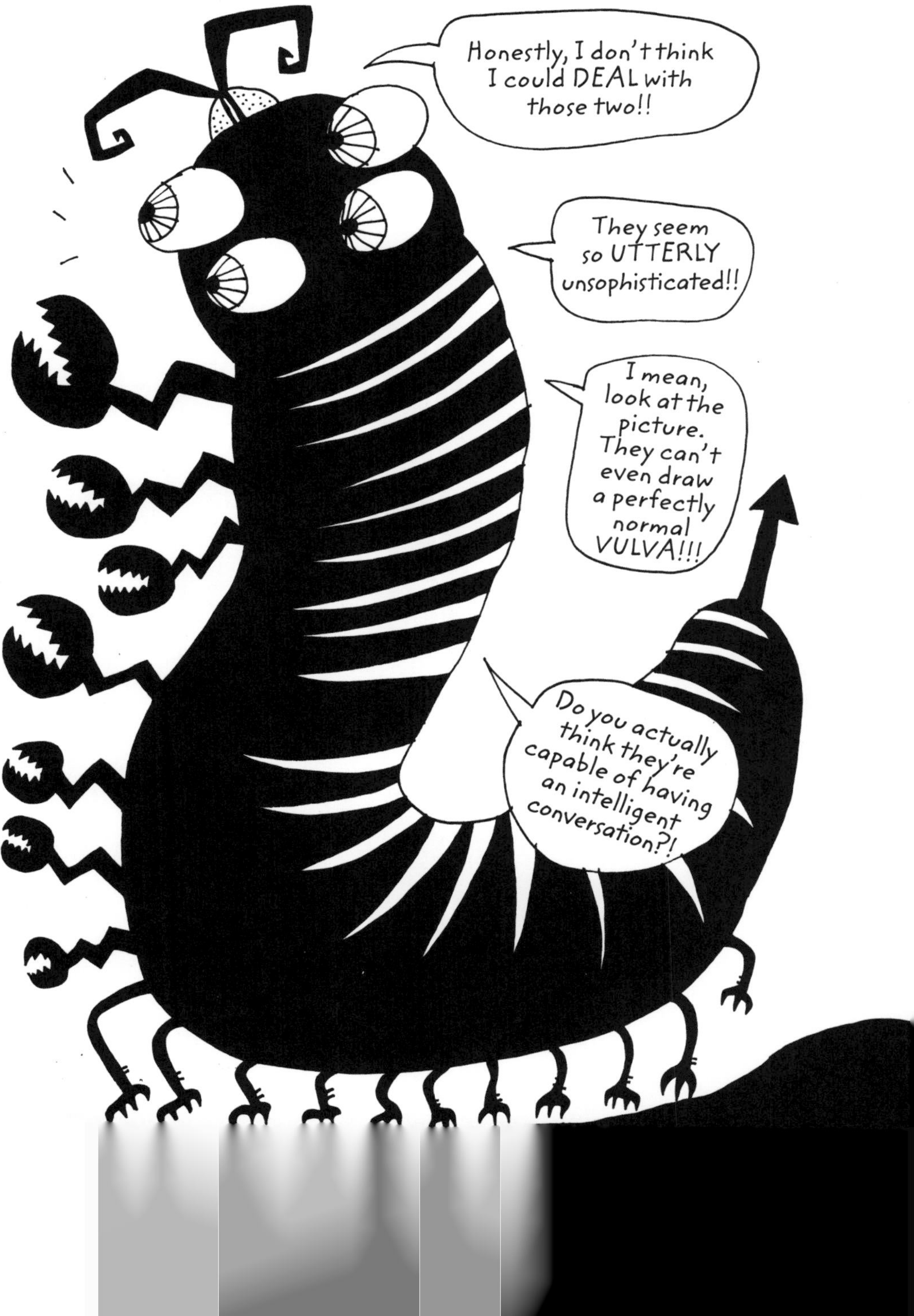
Honestly, I don't think I could DEAL with those two!!
They seem so UTTERLY unsophisticated!!
I mean, look at the picture. They can't even draw a perfectly normal VULVA!!!
Do you actually think they're capable of having an intelligent conversation?!

OK!!! Here comes a
chapter about orgasms

AAH

HAA

AS YOU MAY HAVE NOTICED, GOVERNMENT AGENCIES, ORGANIZATIONS, NEWSPAPERS, MEDICAL EXPERTS, AND OTHERS IN SOCIETY PRODUCE INFORMATIONAL MATERIALS ABOUT SEX.

ON THE SUBJECT OF ORGASMS, THIS INFORMATION—THAT IS, THE CULTURAL NARRATIVE—HAS SOME COMMON THEMES. FOR EXAMPLE:

Getting a woman to enjoy sex is *not* the same thing as getting her to have an orgasm, since women can enjoy other things about sex more than the orgasm.

Web4Health, "Female Orgasm: How to give a Woman an Orgasm"

Some women are incapable of having an orgasm, no matter what tools or tricks they try.

Even the world's best lover can't give a woman an orgasm if she won't allow herself to relax and let go.

iform.se, "Orgasmens Hemligheter"

A woman doesn't necessarily want to have an orgasm every time she has sex.

Sometimes she's satisfied just to feel the man inside her, to feel intimacy and tenderness.

iform.se, "Orgasmens Hemligheter"

Coitus interruptus

Coitus interruptus is when the man withdraws his penis from the vagina before ejaculating.

Biology textbook (Gleerups, 2008).

IF WE SWAP THE GENDERS IN THESE TEXTS, WE SEE THAT THE CULTURAL NARRATIVES AROUND MEN'S AND WOMEN'S ORGASMS ARE VERY DIFFERENT.

It's hard to imagine informational materials on sex that look like this:

Getting a man to enjoy sex is *not* the same thing as getting him to have an orgasm, since men can enjoy other things about sex more than the orgasm.

Some men are incapable of having an orgasm, no matter what tools or tricks they try.

Even the world's best lover can't give a man an orgasm if he won't allow himself to relax and let go.

A man doesn't necessarily want to have an orgasm every time he has sex.

Sometimes he's satisfied just to feel close to the woman, to feel intimacy and tenderness.

Coitus interruptus

Coitus interruptus is when the sex act terminates before the woman has had an orgasm.

WHY IS THIS?

THAT IS, WHY DOES THE CULTURAL NARRATIVE TELL US THAT FEMALE AND MALE ORGASMS ARE TWO DIFFERENT THINGS: THAT THE FEMALE ORGASM IS COMPLICATED, HARD TO ACHIEVE, AND NOT NECESSARILY IMPORTANT TO THE WOMAN,

WHILE THE MALE ORGASM IS (TOO) EASY TO ACHIEVE, INDISPUTEDLY DESIRED BY THE MAN, AND TAKEN FOR GRANTED AS PART OF "HAVING SEX?"

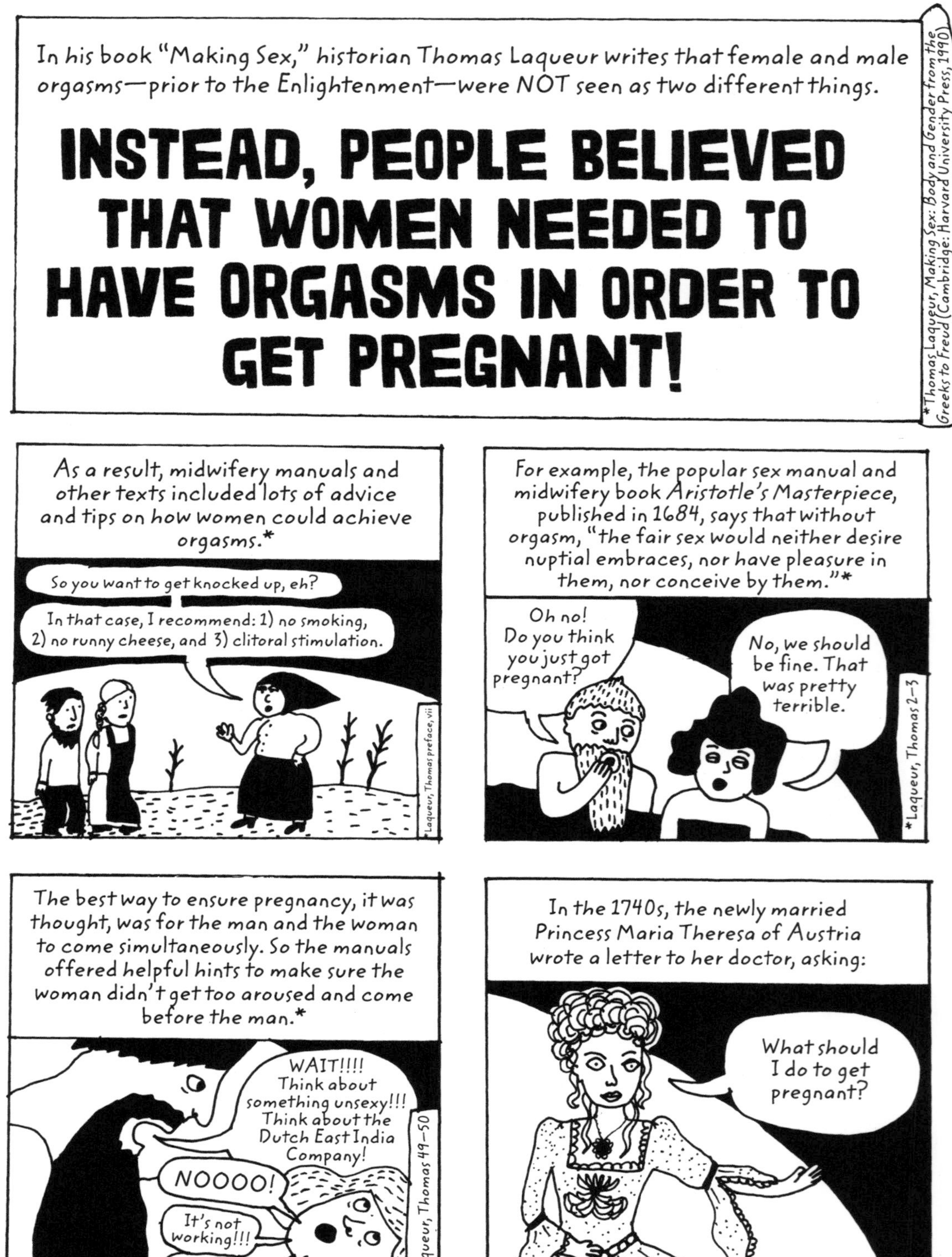
In his book "Making Sex," historian Thomas Laqueur writes that female and male orgasms—prior to the Enlightenment—were NOT seen as two different things.
INSTEAD, PEOPLE BELIEVED THAT WOMEN NEEDED TO HAVE ORGASMS IN ORDER TO GET PREGNANT!
*Thomas Laqueur, Making Sex: Body and Gender from the Greeks to Freud (Cambridge: Harvard University Press, 1990)
As a result, midwifery manuals and other texts included lots of advice and tips on how women could achieve orgasms.*
So you want to get knocked up, eh?
In that case, I recommend: 1) no smoking, 2) no runny cheese, and 3) clitoral stimulation.
*Laqueur, Thomas preface, vii
For example, the popular sex manual and midwifery book Aristotle's Masterpiece, published in 1684, says that without orgasm, "the fair sex would neither desire nuptial embraces, nor have pleasure in them, nor conceive by them."*
Oh no! Do you think you just got pregnant?
No, we should be fine. That was pretty terrible.
*Laqueur, Thomas 2–3
The best way to ensure pregnancy, it was thought, was for the man and the woman to come simultaneously. So the manuals offered helpful hints to make sure the woman didn't get too aroused and come before the man.*
WAIT!!!! Think about something unsexy!!! Think about the Dutch East India Company!
NOOOO!
It's not working!!!
Sorry.
*Laqueur, Thomas 49–50
In the 1740s, the newly married Princess Maria Theresa of Austria wrote a letter to her doctor, asking:
What should I do to get pregnant?

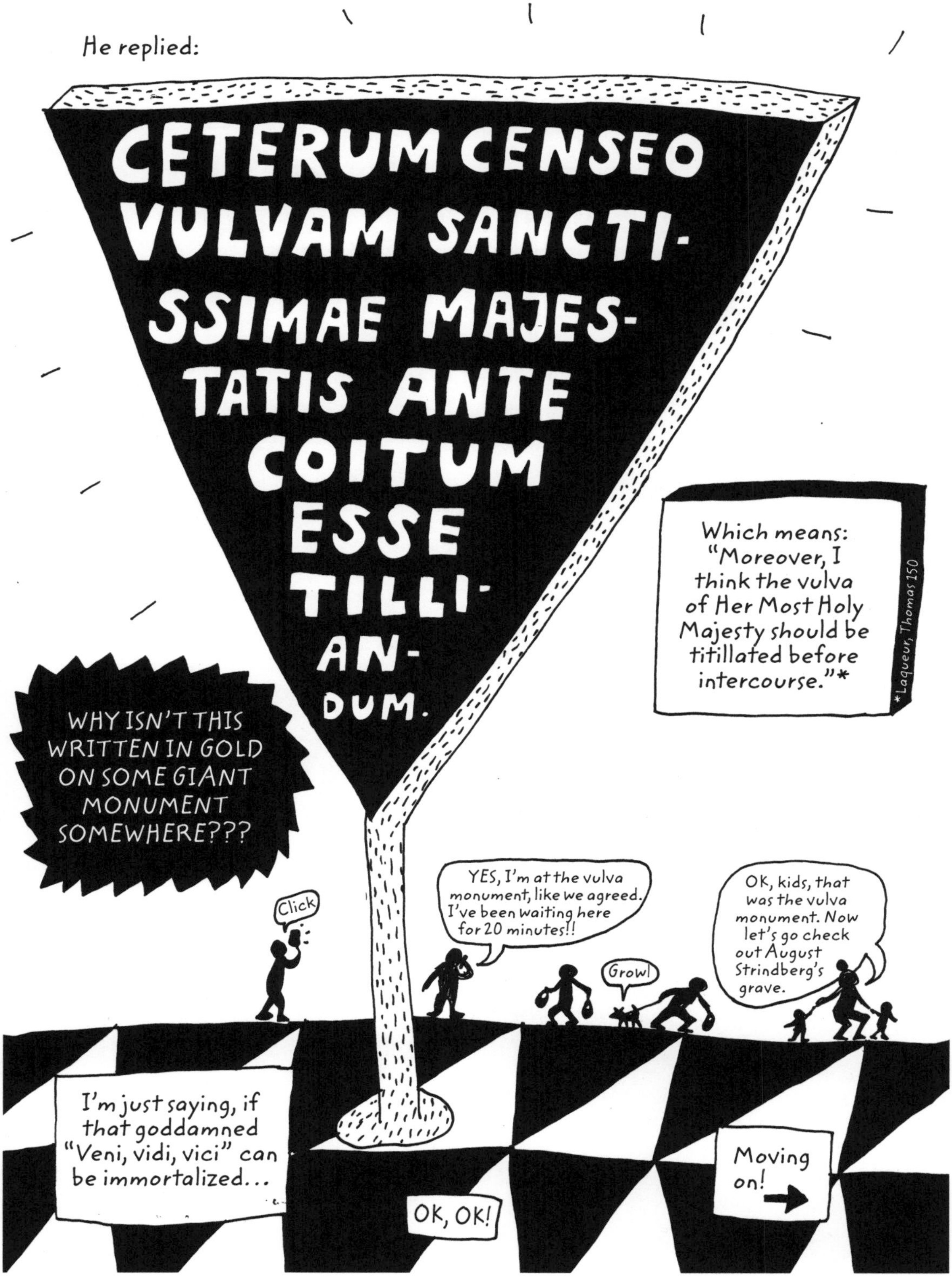
He replied:
CETERUM CENSEO VULVAM SANCTI-SSIMAE MAJES-TATIS ANTE COITUM ESSE TILLI-AN-DUM.
Which means: "Moreover, I think the vulva of Her Most Holy Majesty should be titillated before intercourse."*
*Laqueur, Thomas 150
WHY ISN'T THIS WRITTEN IN GOLD ON SOME GIANT MONUMENT SOMEWHERE???
Click
YES, I'm at the vulva monument, like we agreed. I've been waiting here for 20 minutes!!
Growl
OK, kids, that was the vulva monument. Now let's go check out August Strindberg's grave.
I'm just saying, if that goddamned "Veni, vidi, vici" can be immortalized...
OK, OK!
Moving on!

TOWARD THE END OF THE ENLIGHTENMENT, HOWEVER, MEDICAL SCIENCE (AND THOSE WHO BELIEVED IN IT) STOPPED REGARDING THE FEMALE ORGASM AS PART OF THE REPRODUCTIVE PROCESS.

New theory!

Women do not, I repeat, DO NOT, need an orgasm to get pregnant!!!

Rewrite all the medical books!!!

This was NOT the result of scientific progress in the field of human reproduction.

PEOPLE IN THE 1800s WERE STILL COMPLETELY CLUELESS ABOUT REPRODUCTIVE BIOLOGY!!!

1. For example, in reproduction manuals at that time, the standard advice for women who wanted to <u>avoid</u> getting pregnant was to have sex about a week after the end of their period (i.e., what we now know to be the MOST fertile time).

When is the safest time?

It's...the SAME TIME as ovulation!

OK, but what's ovulation?

It's the same thing as... BREAD!

Whatever! The main thing is that YOU don't need to have an orgasm!!!

No, removal of the female orgasm from the reproductive process was part of a much larger cultural shift—IN THE WAY WOMEN'S AND MEN'S BODIES WERE PERCEIVED.

BEFORE THE ENLIGHTENMENT, women's and men's bodies had been viewed—for thousands of years—as IDENTICAL. Their genitals, too, were seen as the same thing, just turned in different directions.

The vagina was simply an inside-out penis, the labia were the foreskin, the uterus was the scrotum, and the ovaries were testicles.

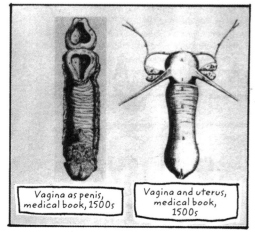

Vagina as penis, medical book, 1500s

Vagina and uterus, medical book, 1500s

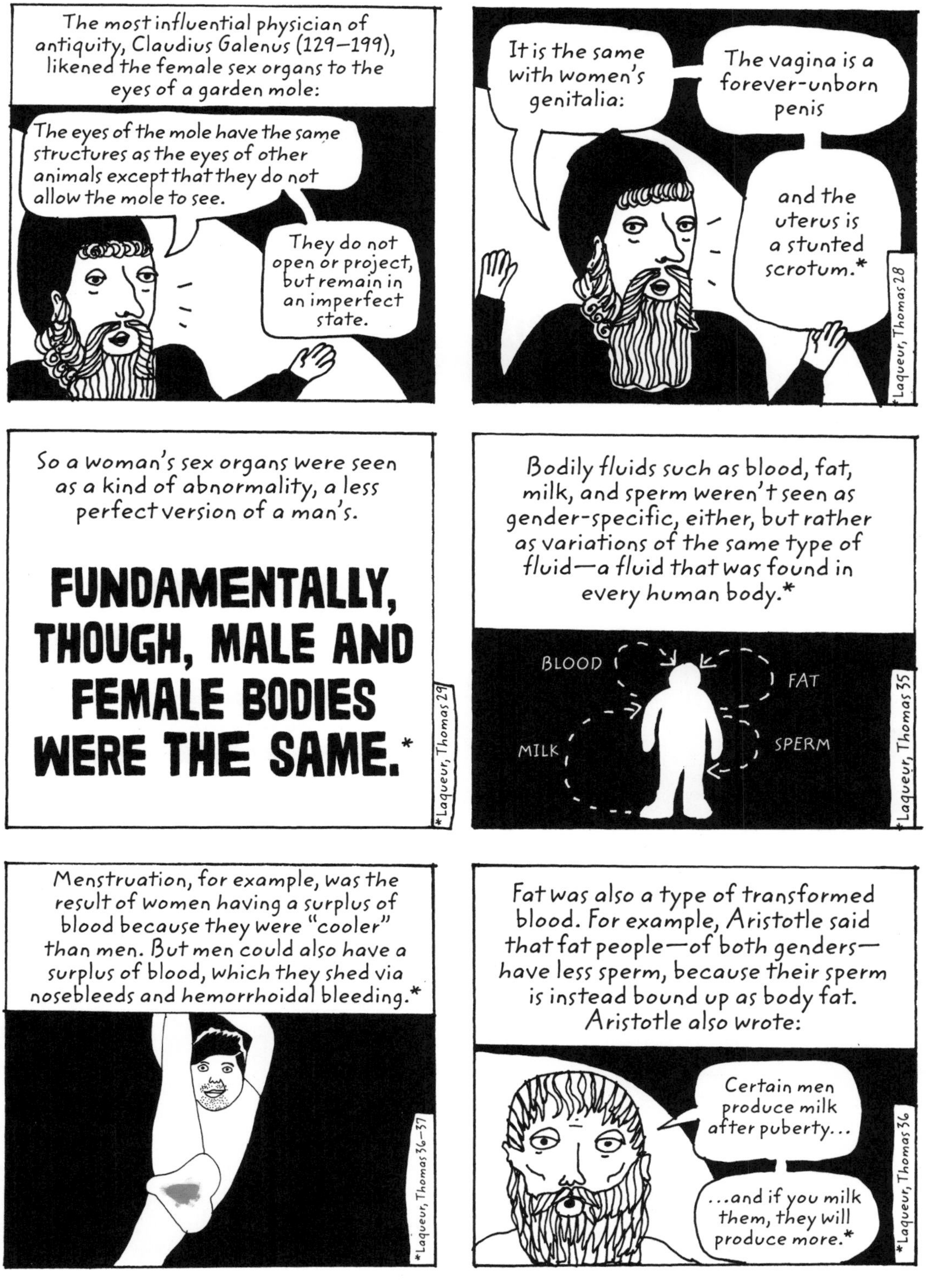

The most influential physician of antiquity, Claudius Galenus (129–199), likened the female sex organs to the eyes of a garden mole:

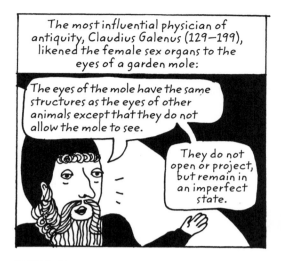

The eyes of the mole have the same structures as the eyes of other animals except that they do not allow the mole to see.

They do not open or project, but remain in an imperfect state.

It is the same with women's genitalia:

The vagina is a forever-unborn penis

and the uterus is a stunted scrotum.*

*Laqueur, Thomas 28

So a woman's sex organs were seen as a kind of abnormality, a less perfect version of a man's.

FUNDAMENTALLY, THOUGH, MALE AND FEMALE BODIES WERE THE SAME.*

*Laqueur, Thomas 29

Bodily fluids such as blood, fat, milk, and sperm weren't seen as gender-specific, either, but rather as variations of the same type of fluid—a fluid that was found in every human body.*

BLOOD

FAT

MILK

SPERM

*Laqueur, Thomas 35

Menstruation, for example, was the result of women having a surplus of blood because they were "cooler" than men. But men could also have a surplus of blood, which they shed via nosebleeds and hemorrhoidal bleeding.*

*Laqueur, Thomas 36–37

Fat was also a type of transformed blood. For example, Aristotle said that fat people—of both genders—have less sperm, because their sperm is instead bound up as body fat. Aristotle also wrote:

Certain men produce milk after puberty...

...and if you milk them, they will produce more.*

*Laqueur, Thomas 36

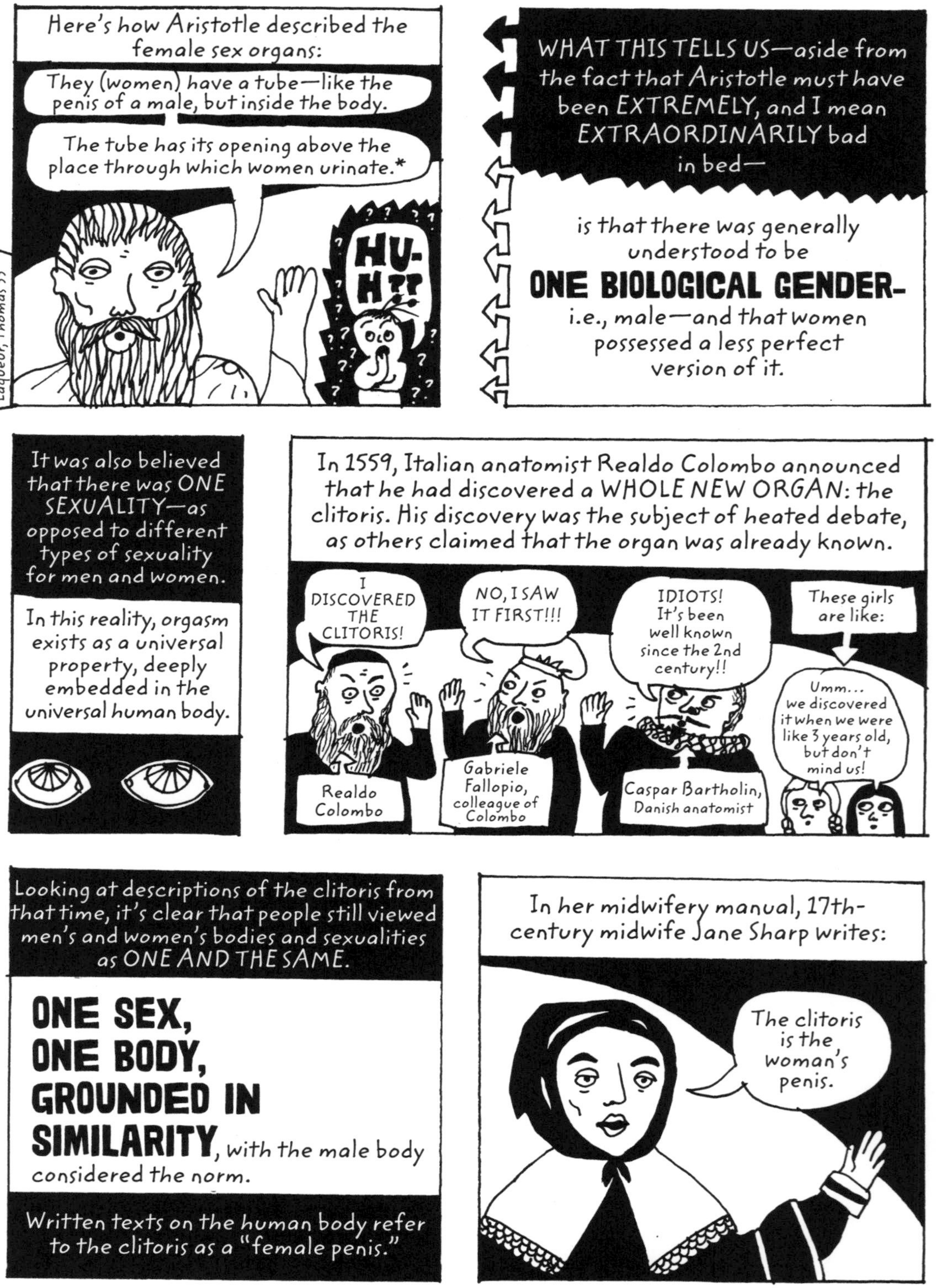

Here's how Aristotle described the female sex organs:
They (women) have a tube—like the penis of a male, but inside the body.
The tube has its opening above the place through which women urinate.*
HU-H??
*Laqueur, Thomas 35
WHAT THIS TELLS US—aside from the fact that Aristotle must have been EXTREMELY, and I mean EXTRAORDINARILY bad in bed—
is that there was generally understood to be ONE BIOLOGICAL GENDER—i.e., male—and that women possessed a less perfect version of it.
It was also believed that there was ONE SEXUALITY—as opposed to different types of sexuality for men and women.
In this reality, orgasm exists as a universal property, deeply embedded in the universal human body.
In 1559, Italian anatomist Realdo Colombo announced that he had discovered a WHOLE NEW ORGAN: the clitoris. His discovery was the subject of heated debate, as others claimed that the organ was already known.
I DISCOVERED THE CLITORIS!
NO, I SAW IT FIRST!!!
IDIOTS! It's been well known since the 2nd century!!
These girls are like:
Umm... we discovered it when we were like 3 years old, but don't mind us!
Realdo Colombo
Gabriele Fallopio, colleague of Colombo
Caspar Bartholin, Danish anatomist
Looking at descriptions of the clitoris from that time, it's clear that people still viewed men's and women's bodies and sexualities as ONE AND THE SAME.
ONE SEX, ONE BODY, GROUNDED IN SIMILARITY, with the male body considered the norm.
Written texts on the human body refer to the clitoris as a "female penis."
In her midwifery manual, 17th-century midwife Jane Sharp writes:
The clitoris is the woman's penis.

It will stand and fall as the male member doth, and makes women lustful and take delight in copulation.*

*Laqueur, Thomas 65

In 1612, physician Jacques Duval wrote:

In French it is called the female rod and the scorner of men:

and women who will admit their lewdness call it their "great joy."*

*Laqueur, Thomas 240

Realdo Colombo described the clitoris this way:

If you rub it vigorously with a penis, or touch it even with a little finger,

semen swifter than air flies this way and that on account of the pleasure,

even with them (women) unwilling.*

*Laqueur, Thomas 66

Also in the 17th century, obstetrician François Maurice wrote:

The clitoris is where the Author of Nature has placed the seat of voluptuousness—as He has in the glans penis—

where the most exquisite sensibility is located, and where He placed the origins of lasciviousness in women.

And he concluded:

The clitoris functions just like the penis.*

*Laqueur, Thomas 239

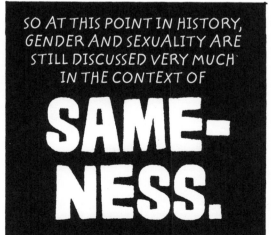

SO AT THIS POINT IN HISTORY, GENDER AND SEXUALITY ARE STILL DISCUSSED VERY MUCH IN THE CONTEXT OF

SAME-NESS.

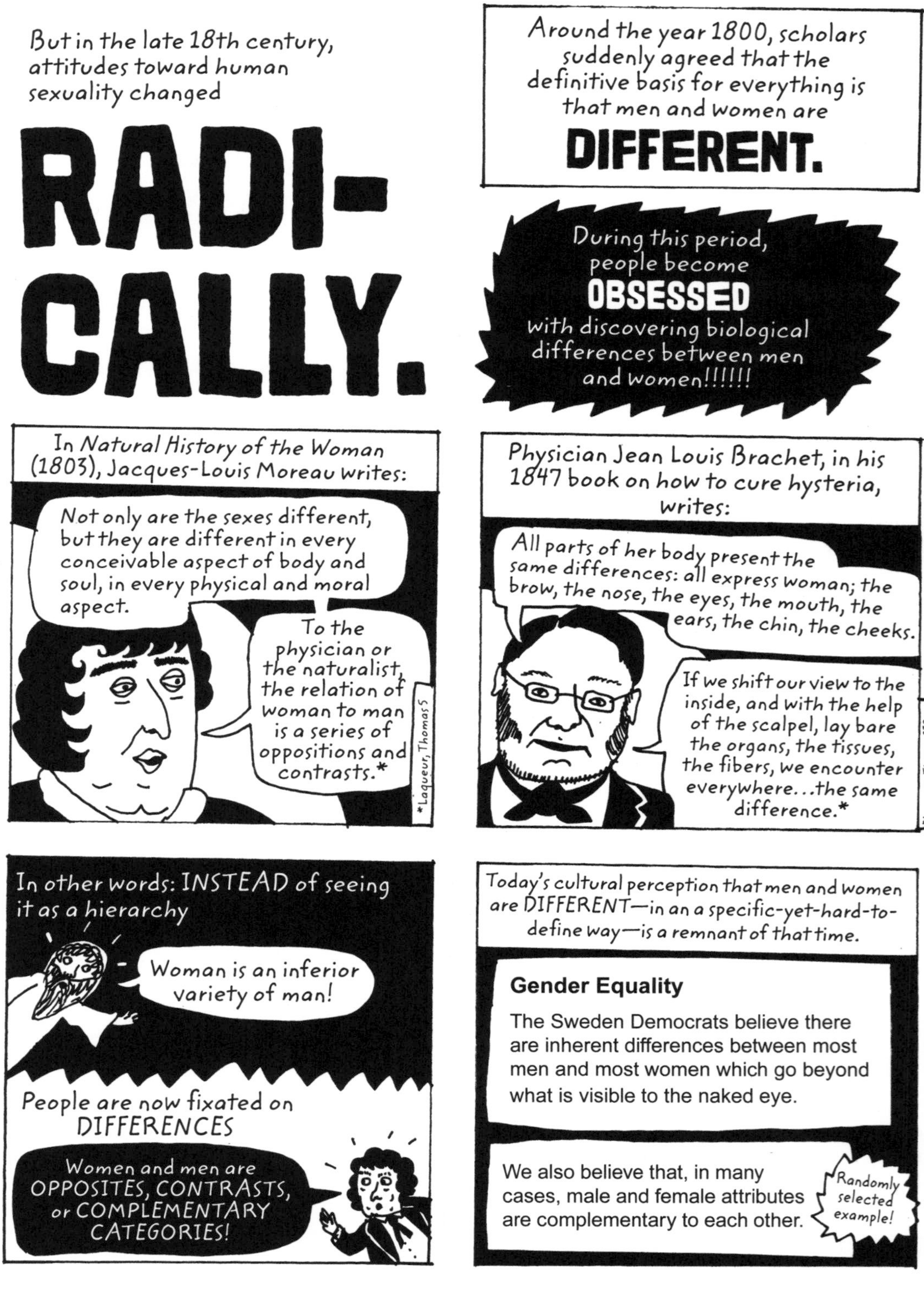

But in the late 18th century, attitudes toward human sexuality changed
RADI-CALLY.
Around the year 1800, scholars suddenly agreed that the definitive basis for everything is that men and women are DIFFERENT.
During this period, people become OBSESSED with discovering biological differences between men and women!!!!!!
In Natural History of the Woman (1803), Jacques-Louis Moreau writes:
Not only are the sexes different, but they are different in every conceivable aspect of body and soul, in every physical and moral aspect.
To the physician or the naturalist, the relation of woman to man is a series of oppositions and contrasts.*
*Laqueur, Thomas 5
Physician Jean Louis Brachet, in his 1847 book on how to cure hysteria, writes:
All parts of her body present the same differences: all express woman; the brow, the nose, the eyes, the mouth, the ears, the chin, the cheeks.
If we shift our view to the inside, and with the help of the scalpel, lay bare the organs, the tissues, the fibers, we encounter everywhere...the same difference.*
*Laqueur, Thomas 239
In other words: INSTEAD of seeing it as a hierarchy
Woman is an inferior variety of man!
People are now fixated on DIFFERENCES
Women and men are OPPOSITES, CONTRASTS, or COMPLEMENTARY CATEGORIES!
Today's cultural perception that men and women are DIFFERENT—in an a specific-yet-hard-to-define way—is a remnant of that time.
Gender Equality
The Sweden Democrats believe there are inherent differences between most men and most women which go beyond what is visible to the naked eye.
We also believe that, in many cases, male and female attributes are complementary to each other.
Randomly selected example!

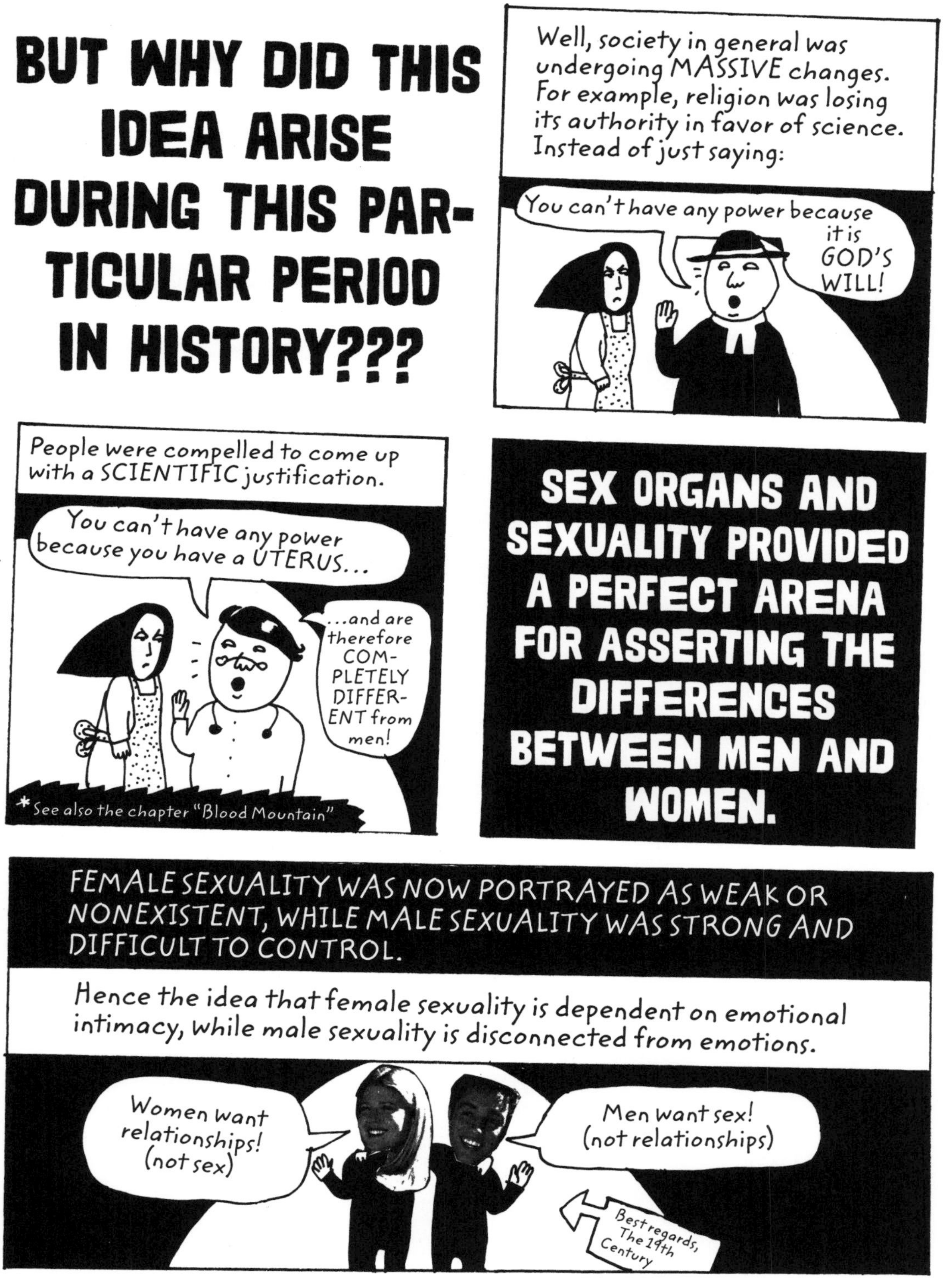
BUT WHY DID THIS IDEA ARISE DURING THIS PARTICULAR PERIOD IN HISTORY???
Well, society in general was undergoing MASSIVE changes. For example, religion was losing its authority in favor of science. Instead of just saying:
You can't have any power because it is GOD'S WILL!
People were compelled to come up with a SCIENTIFIC justification.
You can't have any power because you have a UTERUS...
...and are therefore COMPLETELY DIFFERENT from men!
* See also the chapter "Blood Mountain"
SEX ORGANS AND SEXUALITY PROVIDED A PERFECT ARENA FOR ASSERTING THE DIFFERENCES BETWEEN MEN AND WOMEN.
FEMALE SEXUALITY WAS NOW PORTRAYED AS WEAK OR NONEXISTENT, WHILE MALE SEXUALITY WAS STRONG AND DIFFICULT TO CONTROL.
Hence the idea that female sexuality is dependent on emotional intimacy, while male sexuality is disconnected from emotions.
Women want relationships! (not sex)
Men want sex! (not relationships)
Best regards, The 19th Century

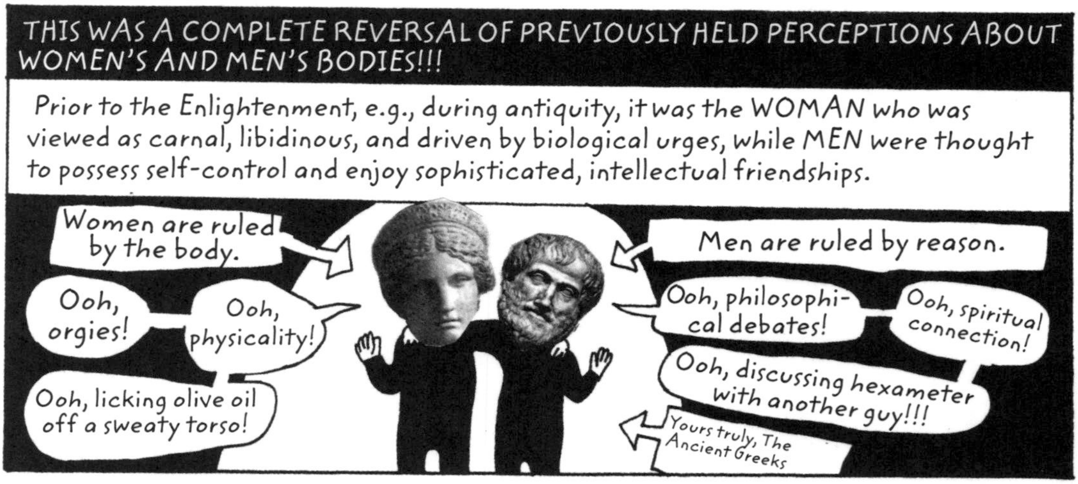
THIS WAS A COMPLETE REVERSAL OF PREVIOUSLY HELD PERCEPTIONS ABOUT WOMEN'S AND MEN'S BODIES!!!
Prior to the Enlightenment, e.g., during antiquity, it was the WOMAN who was viewed as carnal, libidinous, and driven by biological urges, while MEN were thought to possess self-control and enjoy sophisticated, intellectual friendships.
Women are ruled by the body.
Ooh, orgies!
Ooh, physicality!
Ooh, licking olive oil off a sweaty torso!
Men are ruled by reason.
Ooh, philosophical debates!
Ooh, spiritual connection!
Ooh, discussing hexameter with another guy!!!
Yours truly, The Ancient Greeks

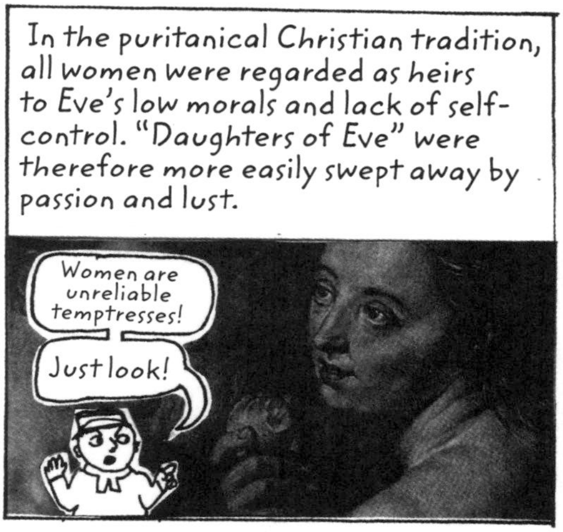
In the puritanical Christian tradition, all women were regarded as heirs to Eve's low morals and lack of self-control. "Daughters of Eve" were therefore more easily swept away by passion and lust.
Women are unreliable temptresses!
Just look!

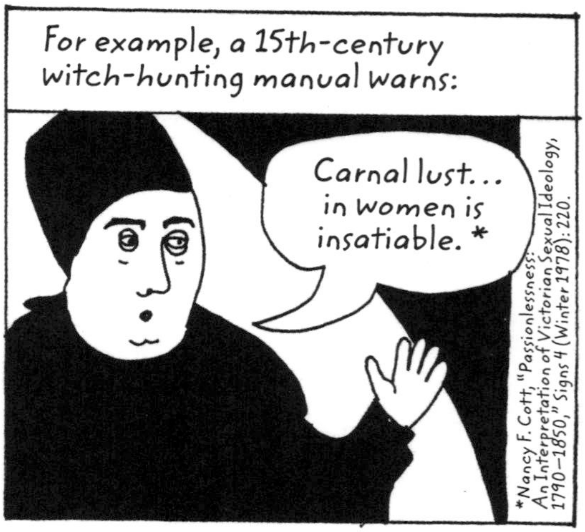
For example, a 15th-century witch-hunting manual warns:
Carnal lust... in women is insatiable. *
*Nancy F. Cott, "Passionlessness: An Interpretation of Victorian Sexual Ideology, 1790–1850," Signs 4 (Winter 1978): 220.

BUT AFTER THE ENLIGHTENMENT, A WHOLE NEW IDEA TOOK HOLD: WOMEN'S EROTIC DESIRES WERE VERY WEAK—OR COMPLETELY LACKING.

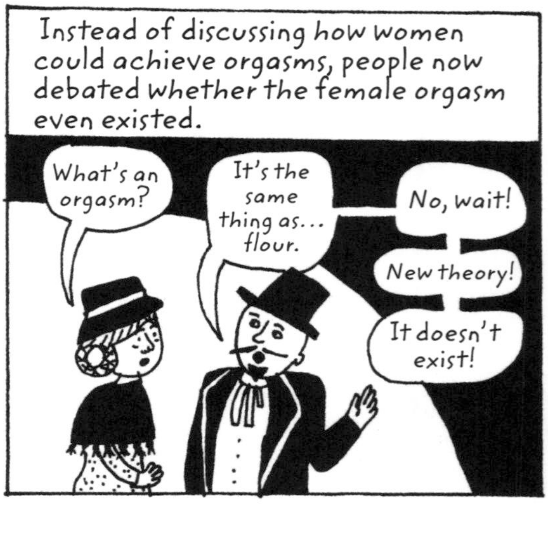
Instead of discussing how women could achieve orgasms, people now debated whether the female orgasm even existed.
What's an orgasm?
It's the same thing as... flour.
No, wait!
New theory!
It doesn't exist!

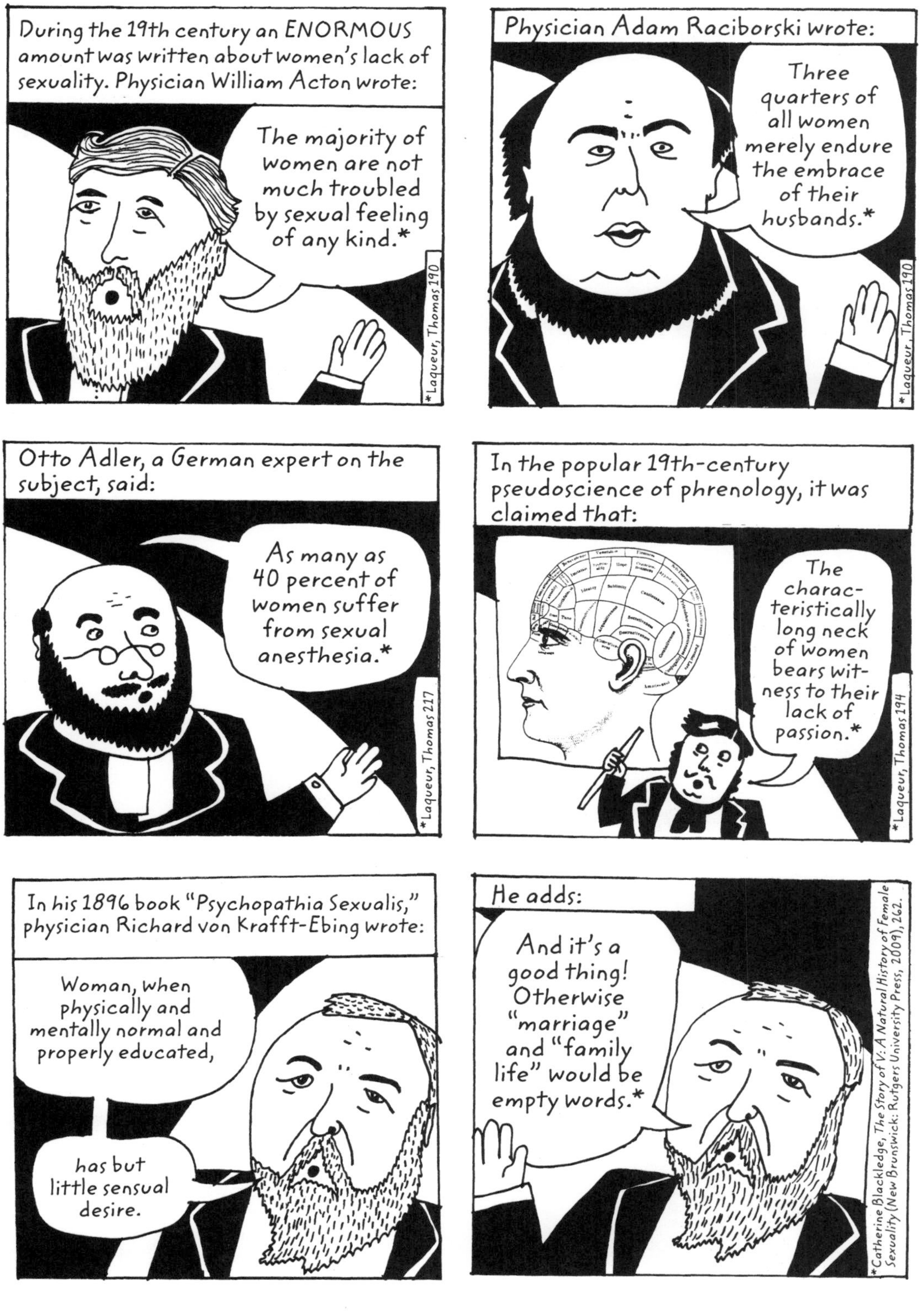
During the 19th century an ENORMOUS amount was written about women's lack of sexuality. Physician William Acton wrote:
The majority of women are not much troubled by sexual feeling of any kind.*
*Laqueur, Thomas 190
Physician Adam Raciborski wrote:
Three quarters of all women merely endure the embrace of their husbands.*
*Laqueur, Thomas 190
Otto Adler, a German expert on the subject, said:
As many as 40 percent of women suffer from sexual anesthesia.*
*Laqueur, Thomas 217
In the popular 19th-century pseudoscience of phrenology, it was claimed that:
The charac-teristically long neck of women bears wit-ness to their lack of passion.*
*Laqueur, Thomas 194
In his 1896 book "Psychopathia Sexualis," physician Richard von Krafft-Ebing wrote:
Woman, when physically and mentally normal and properly educated,
has but little sensual desire.
He adds:
And it's a good thing! Otherwise "marriage" and "family life" would be empty words.*
*Catherine Blackledge, The Story of V: A Natural History of Female Sexuality (New Brunswick: Rutgers University Press, 2009), 262.

WOMEN'S LACK OF PASSION WAS ESSENTIALLY TREATED LIKE A BIOLOGICAL MARKER DIFFERENTIATING THEM FROM MEN.

But there were other reasons the "asexual woman" theory became so popular! For women, it represented liberation from the Christian image of the woman as unpredictable and sexually deceitful. Many welcomed the idea that women were devoid of sexual desire.

We are not wanton temptresses!!

Quite the contrary! We NEVER EVER want to have sex. EVER!!!

The construct of the passionless woman meant that women were perceived as more moral and civilized than men, which gave them a sort of pseudo-power.* Socialist feminist Anna Wheeler (1780–1848) wrote:

Moral aptitude for legislation is more probable in women than men.

*Cott, Nancy F. 228

Liberal feminist Mary Wollstonecraft (1759–1797), author of one of the first feminist texts, *A Vindication of the Rights of Woman*, wrote:

Men are certainly more under the influence of their appetites than women!

But I must warn of the nasty and immodest habits girls learn at boarding school!*

Code for masturbation

*Laqueur, Thomas 232

BUT THE PRICE OF THIS MODEST PROMOTION IN SOCIAL STATUS WAS THE TOTAL ERADICATION OF THEIR OWN SEXUALITY.

NOTE! THE "WANTON TEMPTRESS" IDEA WASN'T DEAD, OF COURSE. IT LIVED ON IN PARALLEL, AS A CONSTANT LOOMING THREAT!

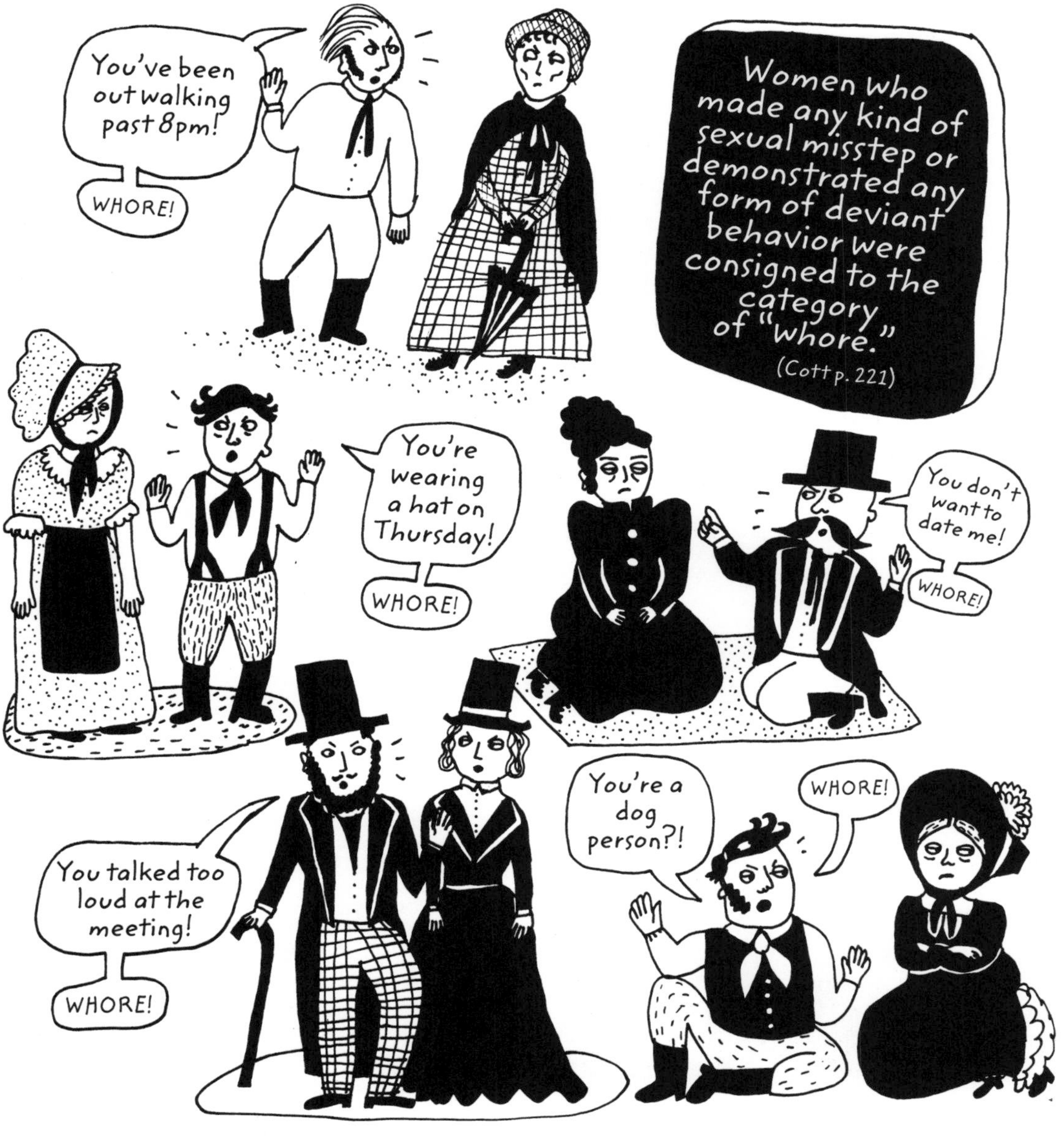

You've been out walking past 8pm!
WHORE!
Women who made any kind of sexual misstep or demonstrated any form of deviant behavior were consigned to the category of "whore."
(Cott p. 221)
You're wearing a hat on Thursday!
WHORE!
You don't want to date me!
WHORE!
You talked too loud at the meeting!
WHORE!
You're a dog person?!
WHORE!

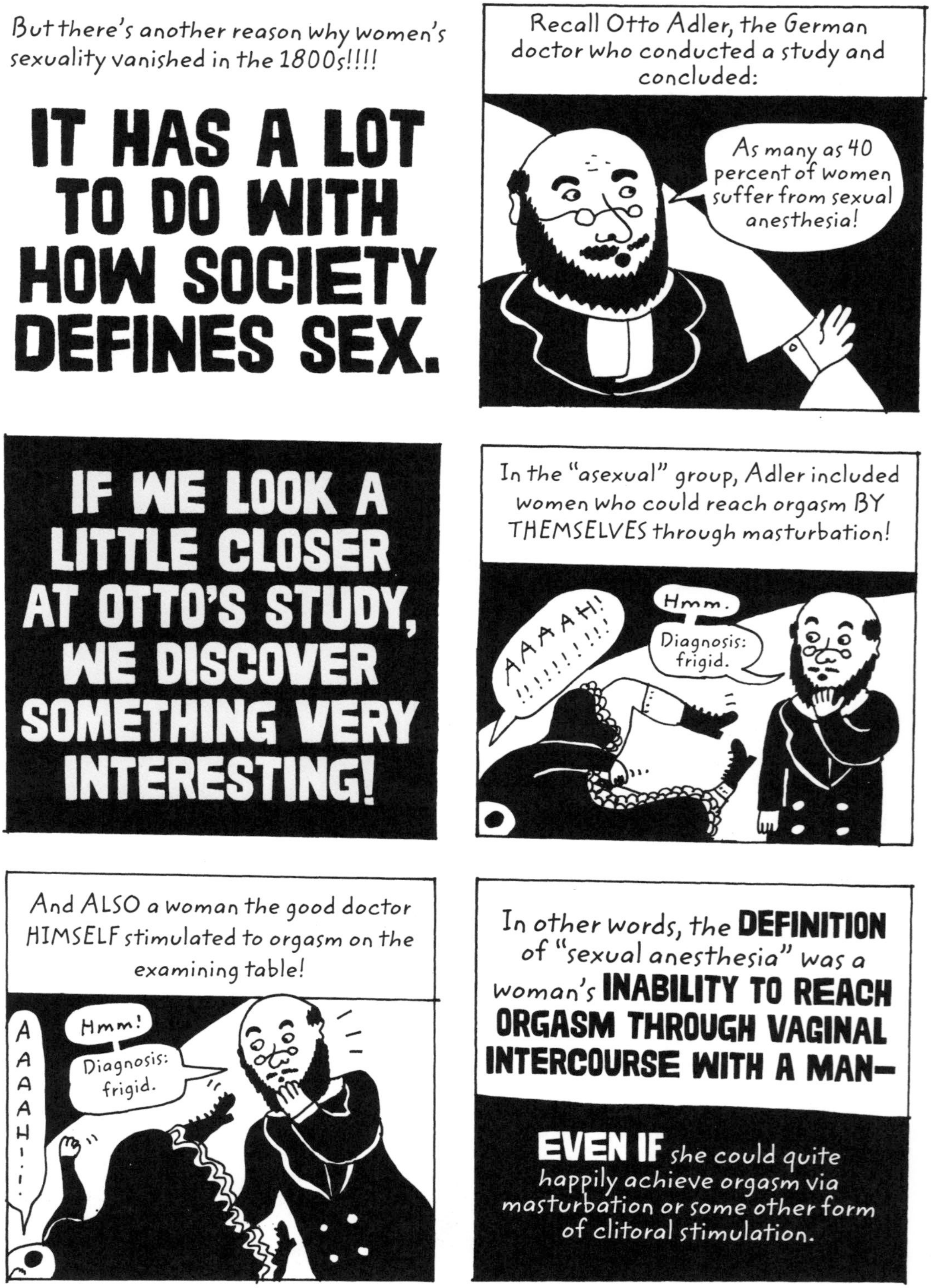
But there's another reason why women's sexuality vanished in the 1800s!!!!
IT HAS A LOT TO DO WITH HOW SOCIETY DEFINES SEX.
Recall Otto Adler, the German doctor who conducted a study and concluded:
As many as 40 percent of women suffer from sexual anesthesia!
IF WE LOOK A LITTLE CLOSER AT OTTO'S STUDY, WE DISCOVER SOMETHING VERY INTERESTING!
In the "asexual" group, Adler included women who could reach orgasm BY THEMSELVES through masturbation!
AAAAH!!!!!!!!!!
Hmm.
Diagnosis: frigid.
And ALSO a woman the good doctor HIMSELF stimulated to orgasm on the examining table!
AAAAH!..!
Hmm!
Diagnosis: frigid.
In other words, the DEFINITION of "sexual anesthesia" was a woman's INABILITY TO REACH ORGASM THROUGH VAGINAL INTERCOURSE WITH A MAN—
EVEN IF she could quite happily achieve orgasm via masturbation or some other form of clitoral stimulation.

THIS IS THE SAME CULTURAL VIEW OF SEXUALITY EXPRESSED BY FREUD SEVERAL YEARS LATER IN HIS FAMOUS PRONOUNCEMENT ON CLITORAL VS. VAGINAL ORGASMS.

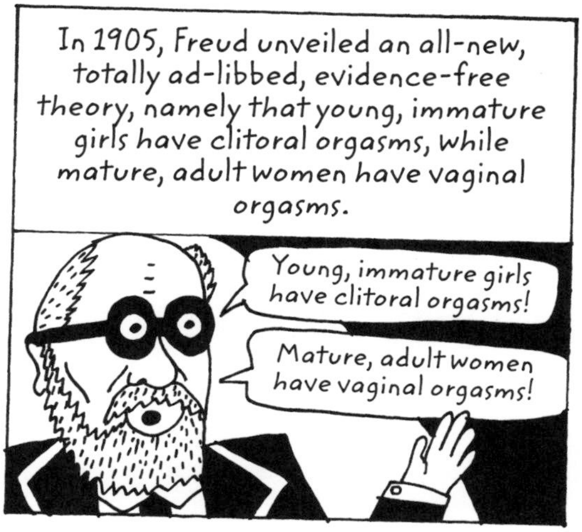
In 1905, Freud unveiled an all-new, totally ad-libbed, evidence-free theory, namely that young, immature girls have clitoral orgasms, while mature, adult women have vaginal orgasms.
Young, immature girls have clitoral orgasms!
Mature, adult women have vaginal orgasms!

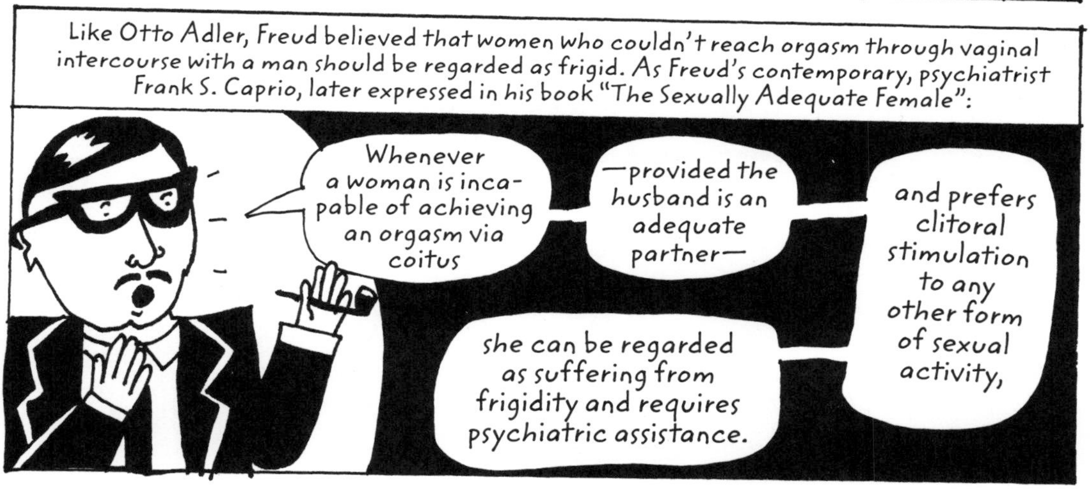
Like Otto Adler, Freud believed that women who couldn't reach orgasm through vaginal intercourse with a man should be regarded as frigid. As Freud's contemporary, psychiatrist Frank S. Caprio, later expressed in his book "The Sexually Adequate Female":
Whenever a woman is incapable of achieving an orgasm via coitus
—provided the husband is an adequate partner—
and prefers clitoral stimulation to any other form of sexual activity,
she can be regarded as suffering from frigidity and requires psychiatric assistance.

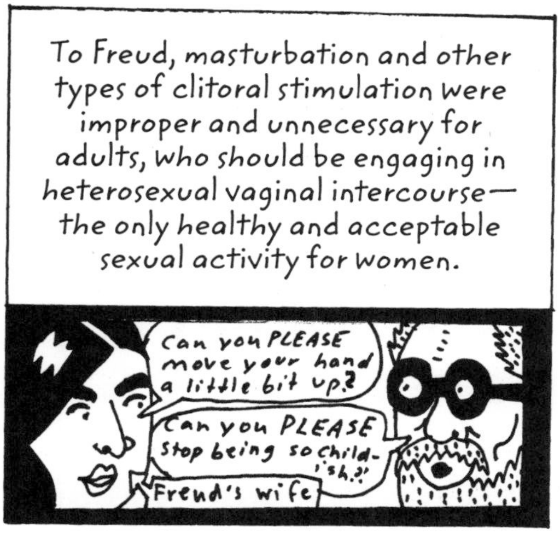
To Freud, masturbation and other types of clitoral stimulation were improper and unnecessary for adults, who should be engaging in heterosexual vaginal intercourse—the only healthy and acceptable sexual activity for women.
Can you PLEASE move your hand a little bit up?
Can you PLEASE Stop being so child-ish?!
Freud's wife

THUS BEGAN A NEW AND EXTREMELY DEPRESSING ERA FOR FEMALE SEXUALITY.

The clitoris, which, "for two millennia, had been regarded as a precious jewel," was now relegated to obscurity. *

TEXTUAL ANALYSES FROM 1900-1950 SHOW THAT THE WORD "CLITORIS" WAS USED VERY INFREQUENTLY DURING THAT PERIOD. →

*Laqueur, Thomas 254

In medical literature, it was quite common not to identify the clitoris in informational images of the genitalia. The hugely popular "Taber's Cyclopedic Medical Dictionary" failed to label the clitoris as recently as its 1981 edition!*

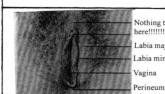

Nothing to see here!!!!!!!!
Labia majora
Labia minora
Vagina
Perineum

*Rebecca Chalker, The Clitoral Truth: The Secret World at Your Finger-tips (New York: Seven Stories Press, 2000), 85.

The clitoris was simply cast aside and expected to be replaced by the vagina as the center point of women's sexuality.

THIS TOO is part of the heteronormative social construct of genders and genitalia as OPPOSITES marked by CONTRASTS. The penis and vagina were set up as natural counterparts, created for each other—and in this natural pairing there was no room for the clitoris!

Mmmm... hand in glove!

Mmmm... soft—hard!

Mmmm... gash—spear!

Mmmm... yin and yang!

PLUS there's a small, erectile organ that—

SHHH!!!

You're killing the mood!!!

Freud also called the clitoris a "male apparatus."

Only young, immature girls reach orgasm via the male apparatus!

THE PROCLAMATION OF THE SUPERIORITY OF VAGINAL ORGASM SUCCEEDED IN MIND-FUCKING GENERATIONS OF WOMEN INTO THINKING THEIR SEXUALITY WAS NONEXISTENT OR DEFECTIVE BECAUSE THEY COULD "ONLY" ACHIEVE CLITORAL ORGASM.

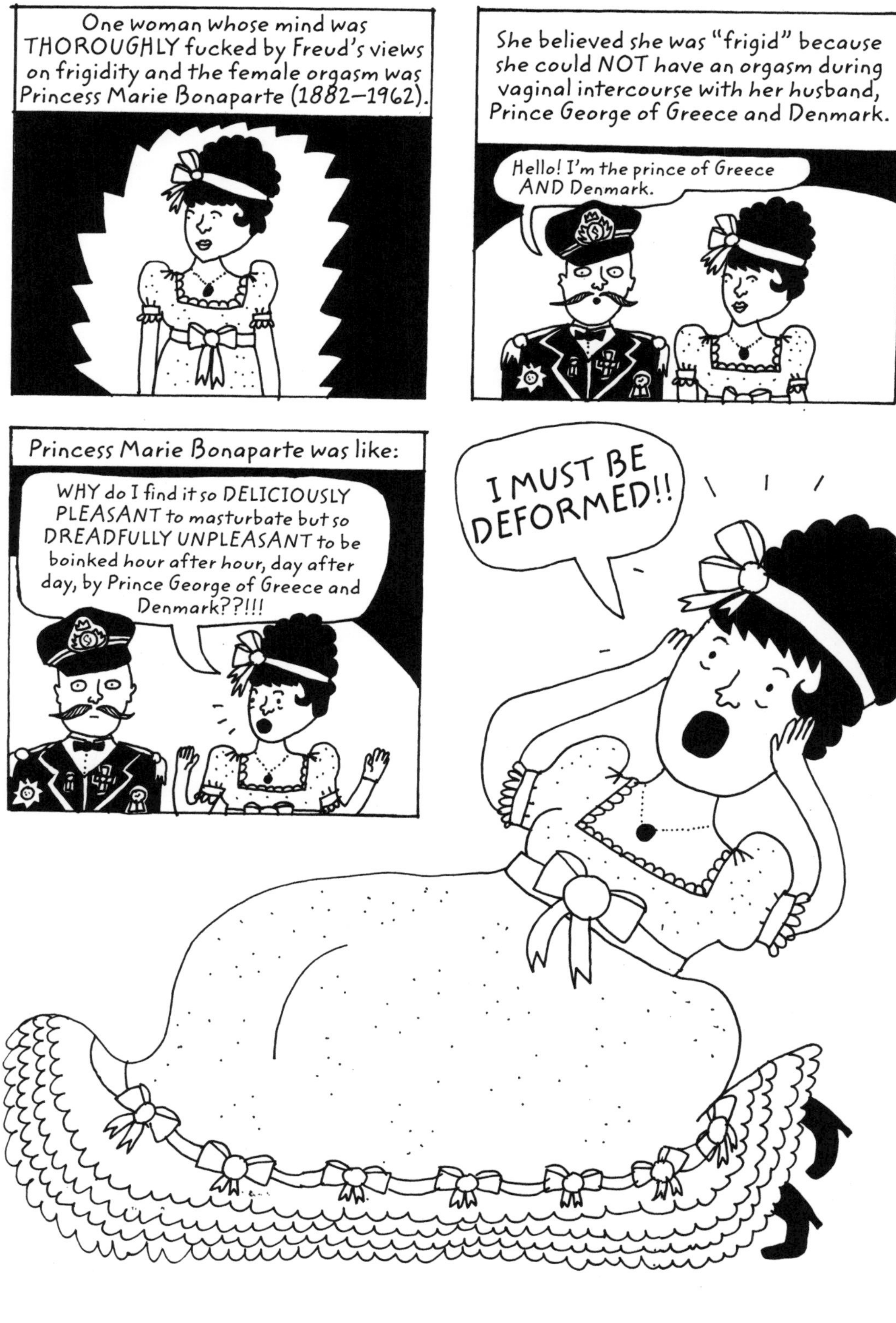
One woman whose mind was THOROUGHLY fucked by Freud's views on frigidity and the female orgasm was Princess Marie Bonaparte (1882–1962).
She believed she was "frigid" because she could NOT have an orgasm during vaginal intercourse with her husband, Prince George of Greece and Denmark.
Hello! I'm the prince of Greece AND Denmark.
Princess Marie Bonaparte was like:
WHY do I find it so DELICIOUSLY PLEASANT to masturbate but so DREADFULLY UNPLEASANT to be boinked hour after hour, day after day, by Prince George of Greece and Denmark??!!!
I MUST BE DEFORMED!!

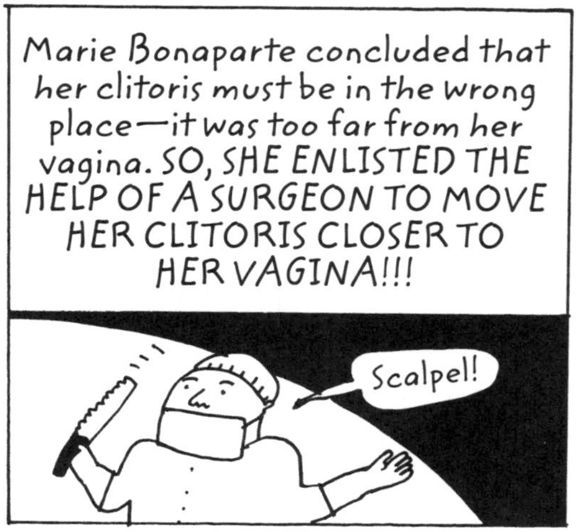
Marie Bonaparte concluded that her clitoris must be in the wrong place—it was too far from her vagina. SO, SHE ENLISTED THE HELP OF A SURGEON TO MOVE HER CLITORIS CLOSER TO HER VAGINA!!!
Scalpel!

PRINCESS MARIE BONAPARTE DECIDED IT WAS EASIER TO SURGICALLY RELOCATE HER OWN CLITORIS THAN TO SIMPLY RELOCATE PRINCE GEORGE'S HAND!!!!

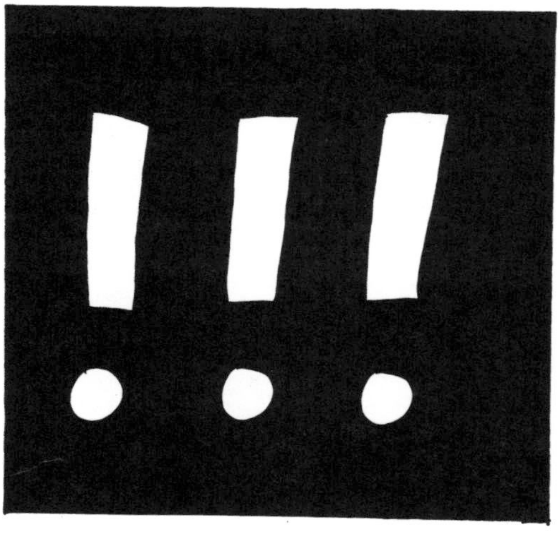
!!!

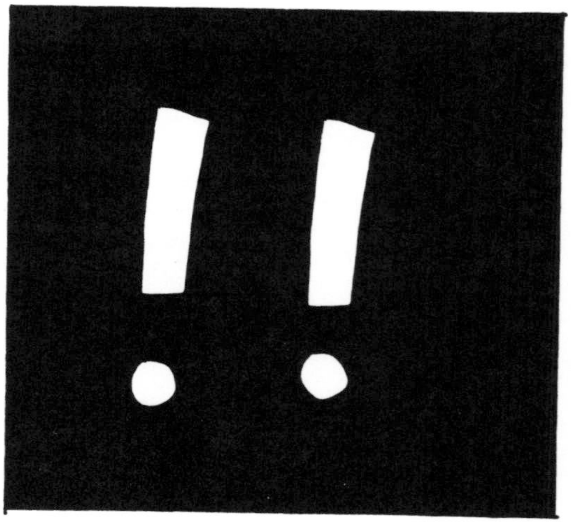
!!

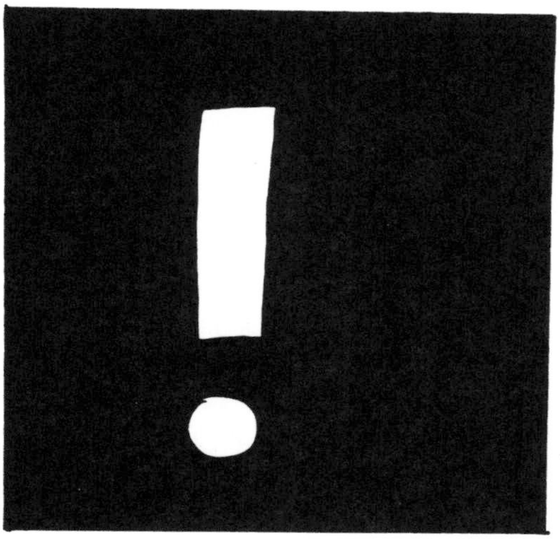
!

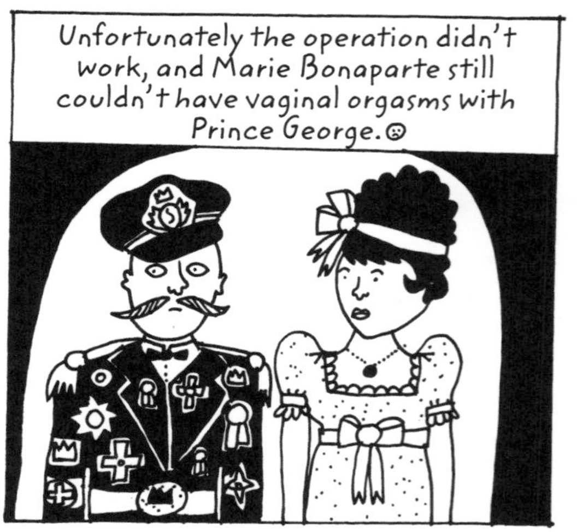
Unfortunately the operation didn't work, and Marie Bonaparte still couldn't have vaginal orgasms with Prince George.☹

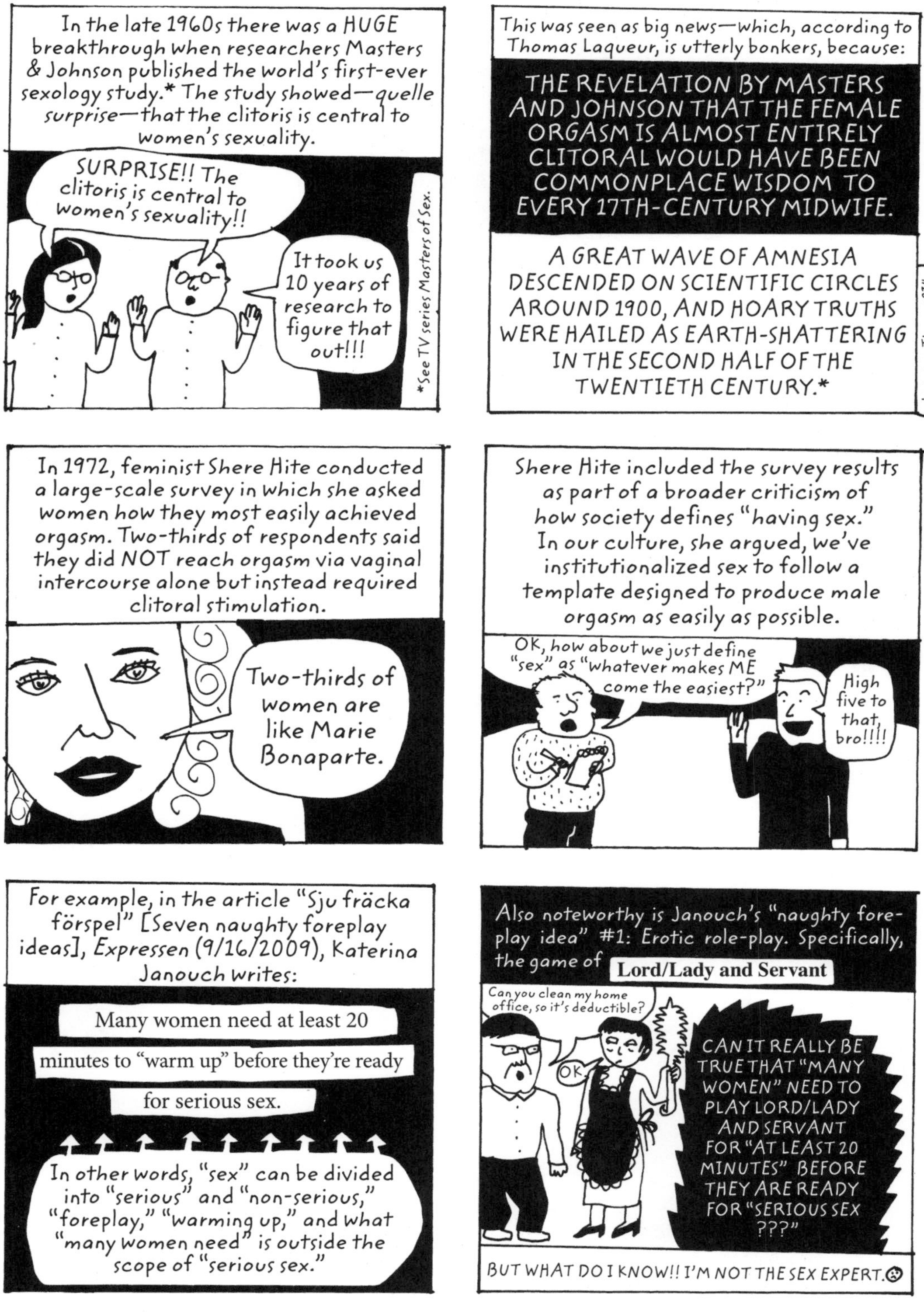
In the late 1960s there was a HUGE breakthrough when researchers Masters & Johnson published the world's first-ever sexology study.* The study showed—quelle surprise—that the clitoris is central to women's sexuality.
SURPRISE!! The clitoris is central to women's sexuality!!
It took us 10 years of research to figure that out!!!
*See TV series Masters of Sex.
This was seen as big news—which, according to Thomas Laqueur, is utterly bonkers, because:
THE REVELATION BY MASTERS AND JOHNSON THAT THE FEMALE ORGASM IS ALMOST ENTIRELY CLITORAL WOULD HAVE BEEN COMMONPLACE WISDOM TO EVERY 17TH-CENTURY MIDWIFE.
A GREAT WAVE OF AMNESIA DESCENDED ON SCIENTIFIC CIRCLES AROUND 1900, AND HOARY TRUTHS WERE HAILED AS EARTH-SHATTERING IN THE SECOND HALF OF THE TWENTIETH CENTURY.*
Laqueur, Thomas 234
In 1972, feminist Shere Hite conducted a large-scale survey in which she asked women how they most easily achieved orgasm. Two-thirds of respondents said they did NOT reach orgasm via vaginal intercourse alone but instead required clitoral stimulation.
Two-thirds of women are like Marie Bonaparte.
Shere Hite included the survey results as part of a broader criticism of how society defines "having sex." In our culture, she argued, we've institutionalized sex to follow a template designed to produce male orgasm as easily as possible.
OK, how about we just define "sex" as "whatever makes ME come the easiest?"
High five to that, bro!!!!
For example, in the article "Sju fräcka förspel" [Seven naughty foreplay ideas], Expressen (9/16/2009), Katerina Janouch writes:
Many women need at least 20
minutes to "warm up" before they're ready
for serious sex.
In other words, "sex" can be divided into "serious" and "non-serious," "foreplay," "warming up," and what "many women need" is outside the scope of "serious sex."
Also noteworthy is Janouch's "naughty foreplay idea" #1: Erotic role-play. Specifically, the game of
Lord/Lady and Servant
Can you clean my home office, so it's deductible?
OK
CAN IT REALLY BE TRUE THAT "MANY WOMEN" NEED TO PLAY LORD/LADY AND SERVANT FOR "AT LEAST 20 MINUTES" BEFORE THEY ARE READY FOR "SERIOUS SEX ???"
BUT WHAT DO I KNOW!! I'M NOT THE SEX EXPERT.

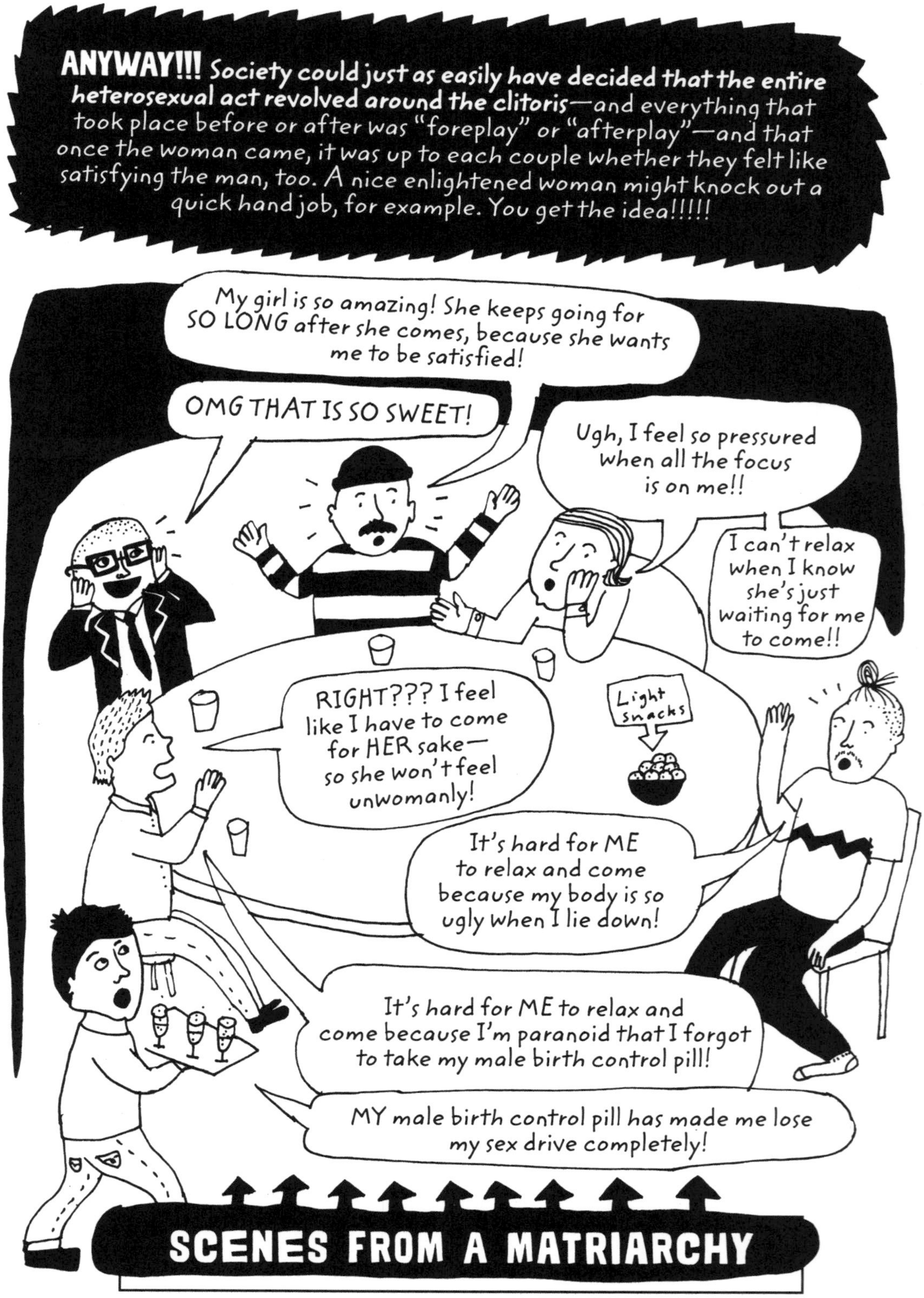
ANYWAY!!! Society could just as easily have decided that the entire heterosexual act revolved around the clitoris—and everything that took place before or after was "foreplay" or "afterplay"—and that once the woman came, it was up to each couple whether they felt like satisfying the man, too. A nice enlightened woman might knock out a quick hand job, for example. You get the idea!!!!!
My girl is so amazing! She keeps going for SO LONG after she comes, because she wants me to be satisfied!
OMG THAT IS SO SWEET!
Ugh, I feel so pressured when all the focus is on me!!
I can't relax when I know she's just waiting for me to come!!
RIGHT??? I feel like I have to come for HER sake—so she won't feel unwomanly!
Light snacks
It's hard for ME to relax and come because my body is so ugly when I lie down!
It's hard for ME to relax and come because I'm paranoid that I forgot to take my male birth control pill!
MY male birth control pill has made me lose my sex drive completely!
SCENES FROM A MATRIARCHY

A few years later, nurse Beverly Whipple came out with a new discovery: the G-spot. That is, a spot partway up the vaginal wall that is said to produce orgasm when stimulated.

THIS BREATHED NEW LIFE INTO THE OLD DISPUTE OVER VAGINAL VS. CLITORAL ORGASM.

According to *Playboy* magazine:

The discovery of the G-spot will relieve men of the clitoral tyranny of Shere Hite.*

*From the 2011 CBC documentary "In Search of the G-spot."

FINALLY, IN 1998—AFTER THOUSANDS OF YEARS OF REALLY, REALLY SHODDY RESEARCH— SOMETHING TRULY INTERESTING HAPPENED.

Urologist Helen O'Connell of The Royal Melbourne Hospital discovered that the visible part of the clitoris is just the tip of the iceberg—the organ itself is about 7–10 centimeters long, with two "legs" that stretch back around the sides of the vagina. The entire organ swells when stimulated.

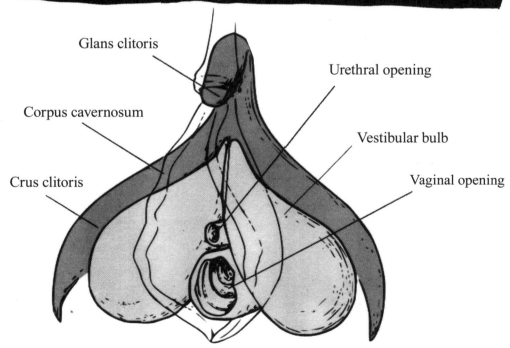

Glans clitoris

Urethral opening

Corpus cavernosum

Vestibular bulb

Crus clitoris

Vaginal opening

RECENT RESEARCH SUGGESTS THAT THE CLITORIS IS EVEN BIGGER— AND ITS NERVE ENDINGS MAY BRANCH OUT OVER A LARGE AREA.

This renders the whole clitoral/vaginal debate meaningless, since all orgasms derive from the clitoral complex.*

SIDE VIEW →

- Uterus
- Bladder
- Urethra
- Clitoral shaft
- Glans clitoris
- Labia majora
- Vestibular bulb
- Crus clitoris
- Vagina

*Kristina Hultman, "Klitoris — The Story," Ottar #2 (2008).

French gynecologist Odile Buisson writes:

The front wall of the vagina is inextricably linked with the internal parts of the clitoris; stimulating the vagina without activating the clitoris may be next to impossible.

Thus, "vaginal" orgasms could be clitoral orgasms by another name.*

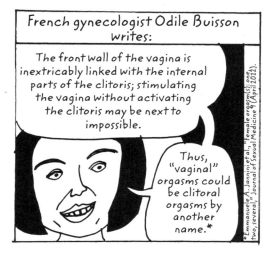

*Emmanuele A. Jannini et al., "Female orgasm(s): one, two, several," Journal of Sexual Medicine 9 (April 2012).

NOTE THAT THE ACTUAL SIZE OF THE CLITORIS WASN'T DISCOVERED UNTIL 1998!

Imagine if another organ— say, the pancreas—had been DESCRIBED COMPLETELY WRONG BY EVERYONE UNTIL 1998!

The pancreas is....ONE centimeter long!!!

Source: a hunch.

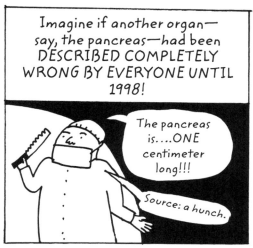

Now, imagine that DECADES AFTER THE DISCOVERY OF THE ORGAN'S ACTUAL SIZE, BIOLOGY TEXTBOOKS WOULD CONTINUE TO GET IT WRONG— TEXTBOOKS PUBLISHED IN 2006 AND STILL IN USE TODAY!!

The sensitive clitoris

At the very front, where the inner labia meet,

is a centimeter-long organ

called the clitoris.*

*Susanne Fabricius, Biologi (Stockholm: LIBER, 2006).

Anyway!!!!!!!

SO, YOU COULD SAY THAT THE MODERN VIEW OF GENDER—THAT GENDER IDENTITY IS TIGHTLY BOUND TO BIOLOGY, THAT THERE ARE TWO GENDERS, AND THAT THE TWO GENDERS ARE MARKED BY OPPOSITION/CONTRAST/COMPLEMENTARITY—WAS BORN IN THE 19TH CENTURY.

The language around sexualitys often emphasizes opposition/complementarity rather than similarity. For example, take the erectile properties of the clitoris/penis. Here's how many biology textbooks describe sexual arousal:

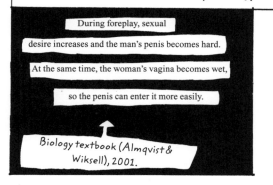

During foreplay, sexual desire increases and the man's penis becomes hard.

At the same time, the woman's vagina becomes wet,

so the penis can enter it more easily.

Biology textbook (Almqvist & Wiksell), 2001.

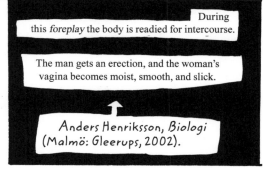

During this *foreplay* the body is readied for intercourse.

The man gets an erection, and the woman's vagina becomes moist, smooth, and slick.

Anders Henriksson, *Biologi* (Malmö: Gleerups, 2002).

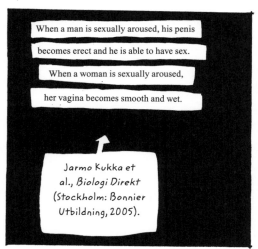

When a man is sexually aroused, his penis becomes erect and he is able to have sex.

When a woman is sexually aroused, her vagina becomes smooth and wet.

Jarmo Kukka et al., *Biologi Direkt* (Stockholm: Bonnier Utbildning, 2005).

OF COURSE, THEY COULD JUST AS EASILY HAVE WRITTEN:

When a man is sexually aroused, his penis becomes erect and he is able to have sex. When a woman is sexually aroused, her clitoris becomes erect and she is able to have sex.

OR:

When a person is sexually aroused, their genitals become erect.

Or something completely different!!!! Which I am too socially conditioned to even think of!!!

Another example of the 200-year focus on DIFFERENCE in construction of gender: Certain similarities between male and female sexuality are ignored—female ejaculation, for instance.

It is described at length in medical books from the 1600s, but then it disappeared from the literature and basically wasn't mentioned again until the 1980s, when nurse Beverly Whipple began studying and writing about it.

Hello! There's such a thing as female ejaculation!

For most of the 20th century, female ejaculation was instead treated as a form of urinary incontinence—and it still is.

I have only one thing to say about female ejaculation!

And that is: It's PEE-PEE!!!

In the UK, for example, censorship laws still prevent porn films from showing female ejaculation, with the rationale that the ejaculate is urine—in the eyes of the law, the combination of urine and sex is obscene.

My point here is that ALL discourse on "female sexuality" and "female orgasm" has ALWAYS been framed in relation to the male body/sexuality/orgasm.

First, you'll recall, as a lesser version—and later as an OPPOSITE.

BUT NEVER IN ITS OWN RIGHT.

End of chapter!!!!!

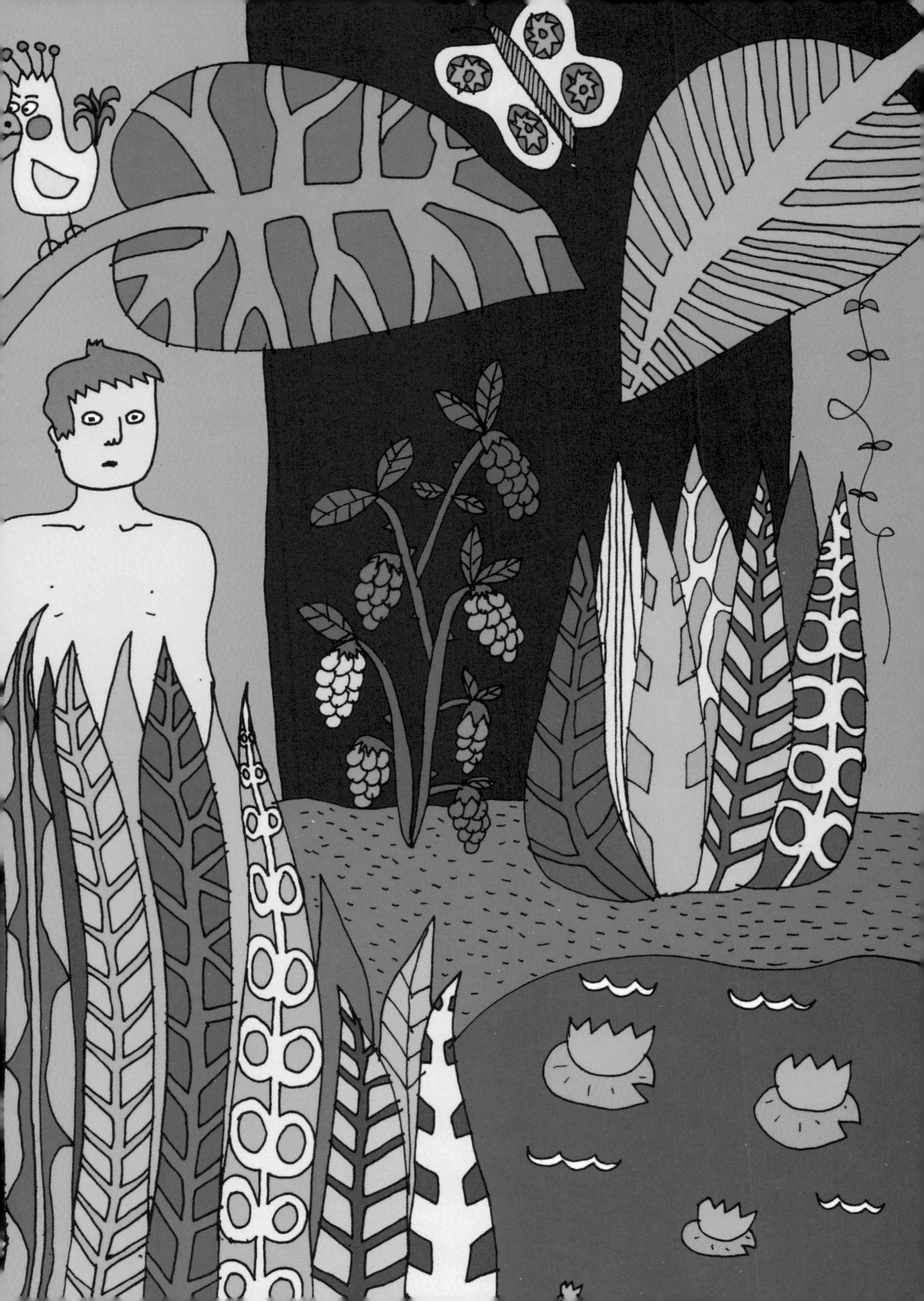

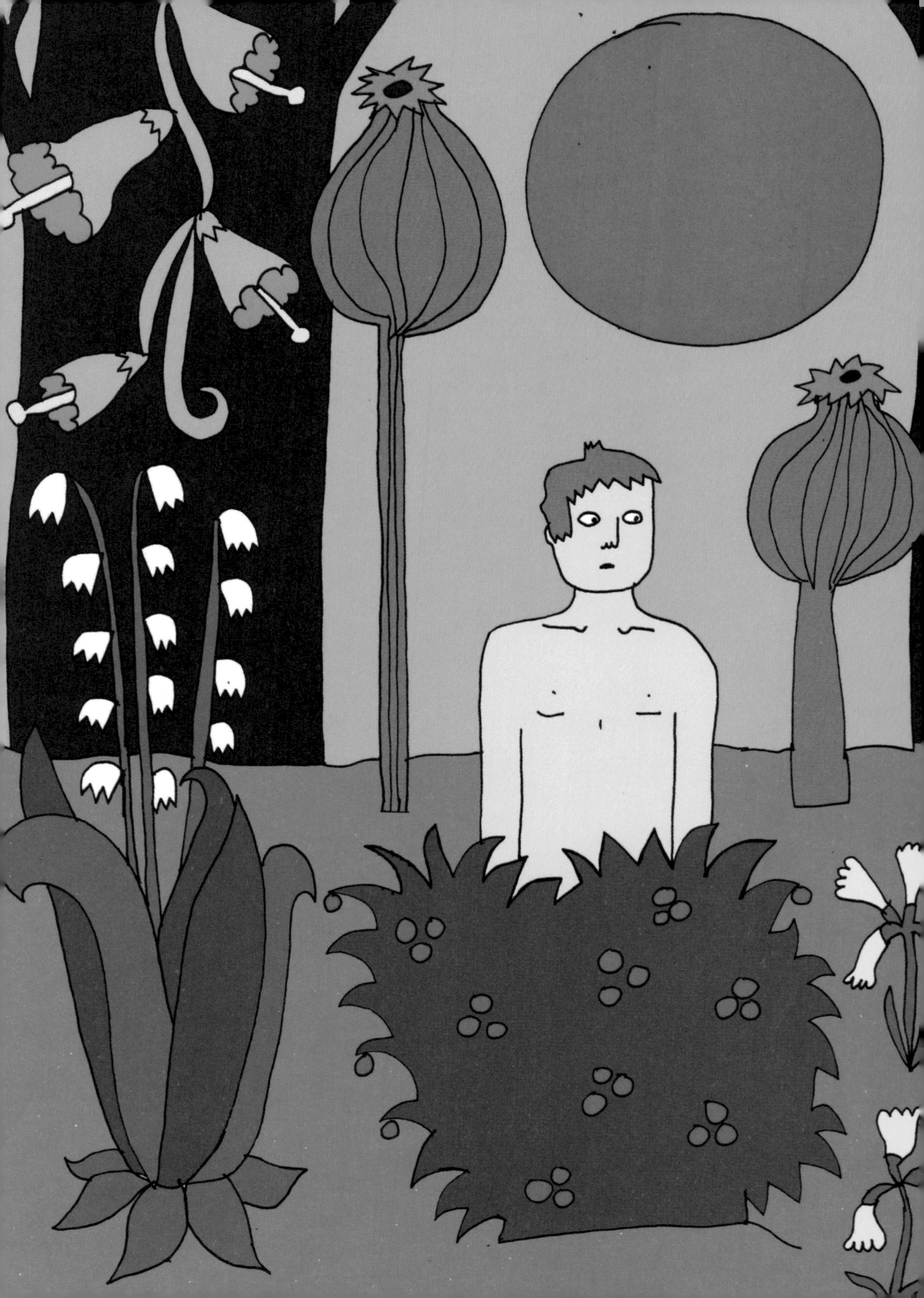

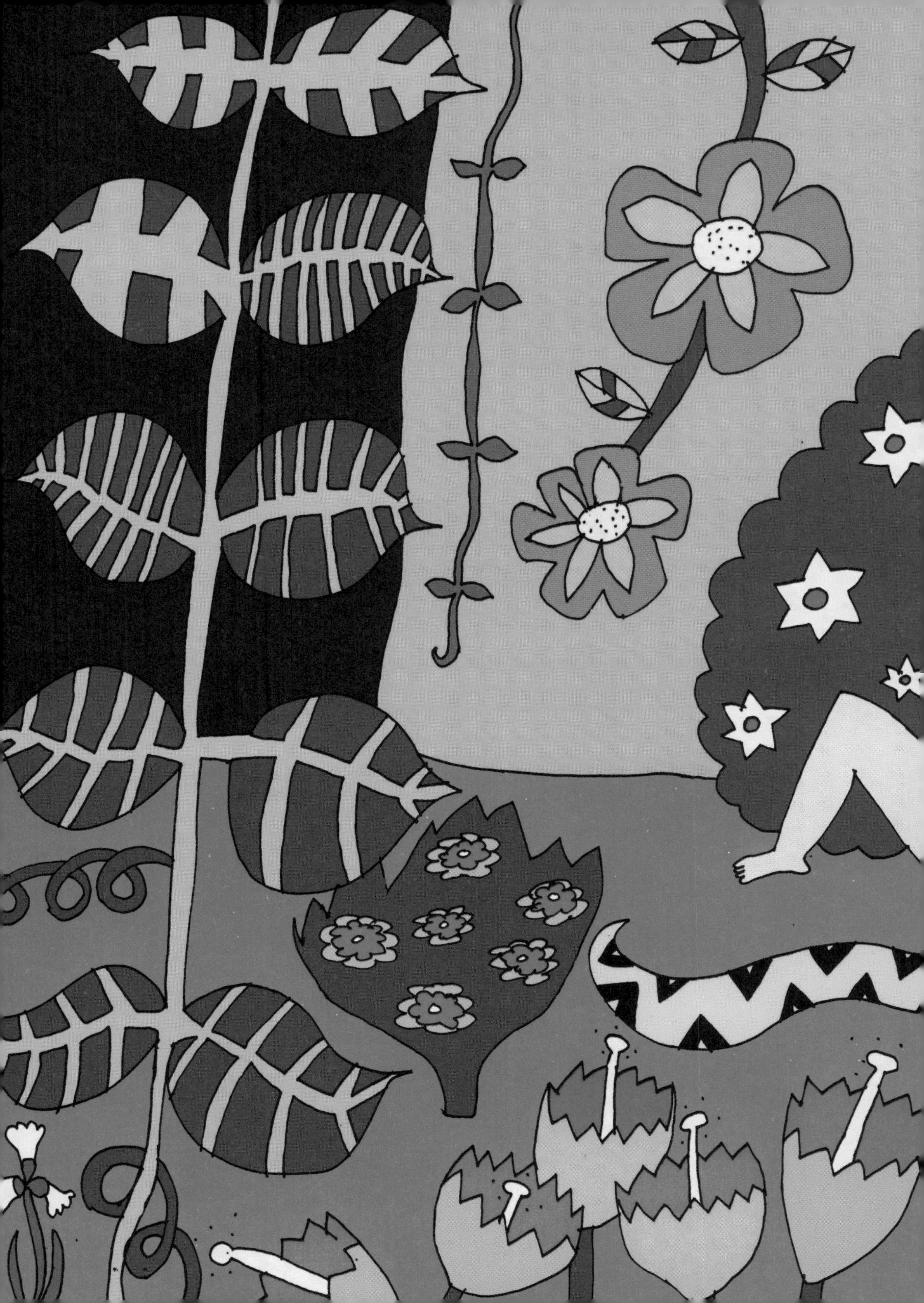

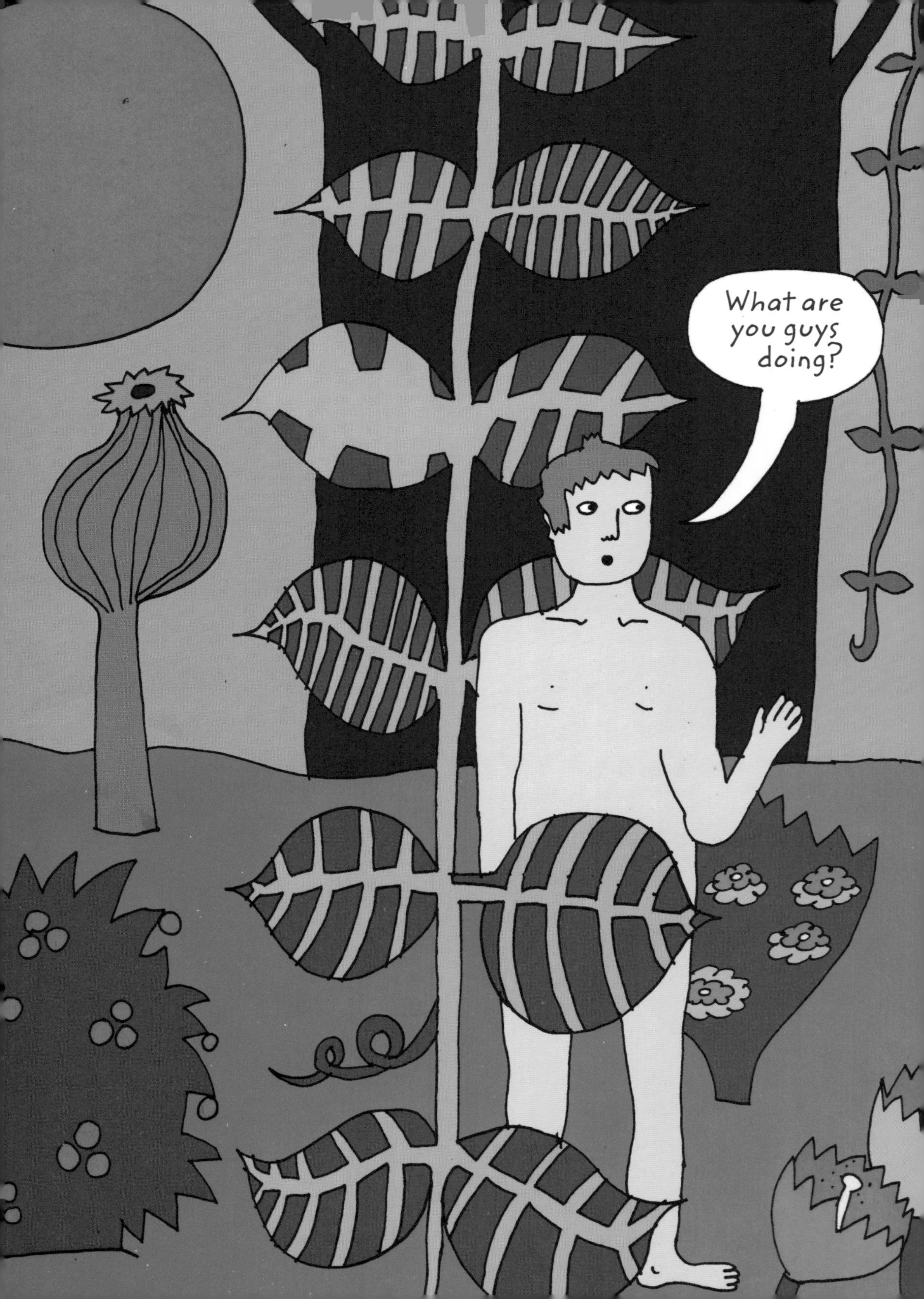
What are you guys doing?

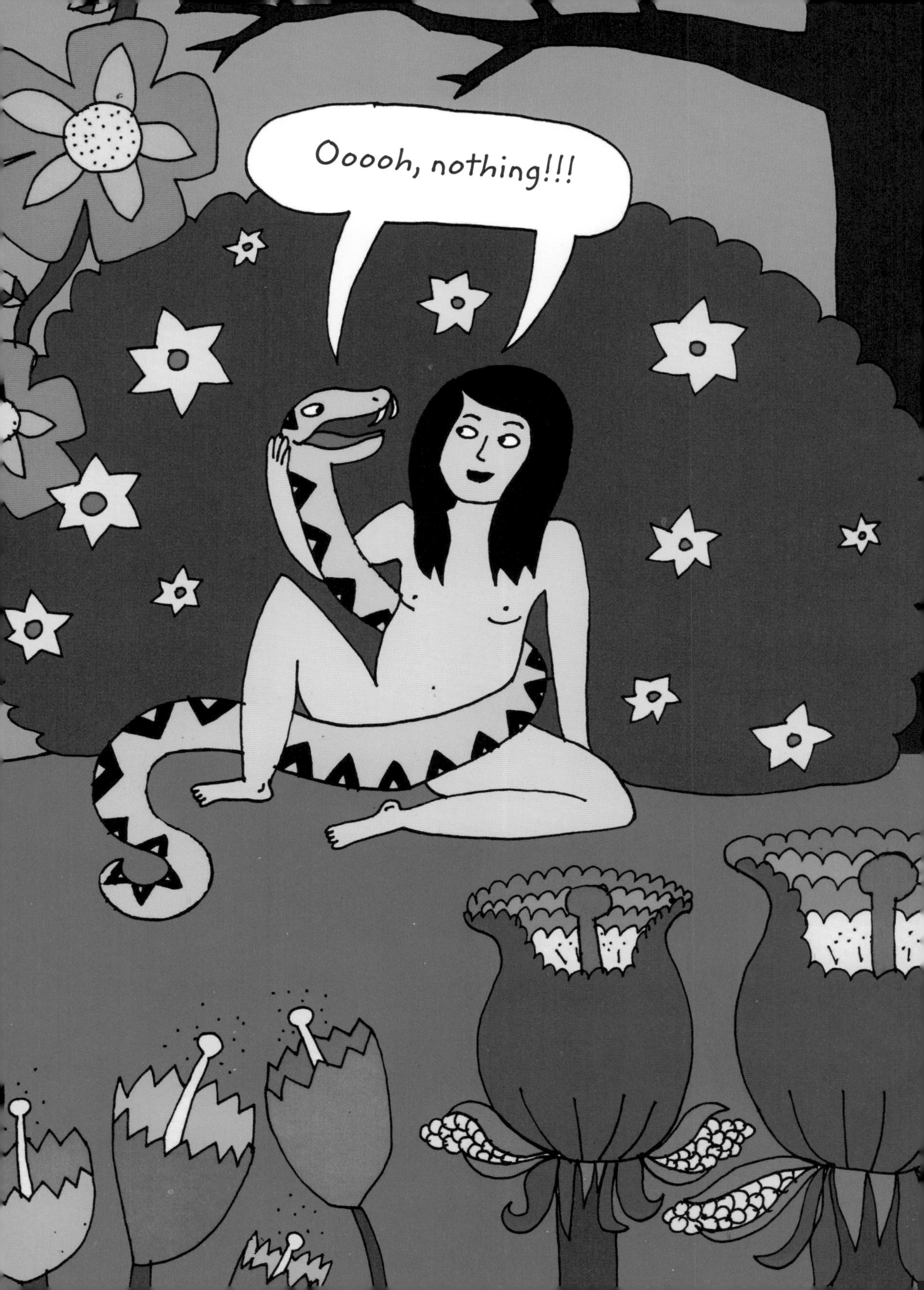
Ooooh, nothing!!!

FEELING EVE

OR:

IN SEARCH OF OUR MOTHERS' GARDENS

I ONCE READ THAT THE DIFFERENCE BETWEEN GUILT AND SHAME IS THAT WE FEEL GUILT FOR SOMETHING WE'VE DONE, BUT WE FEEL SHAME FOR WHAT WE ARE.

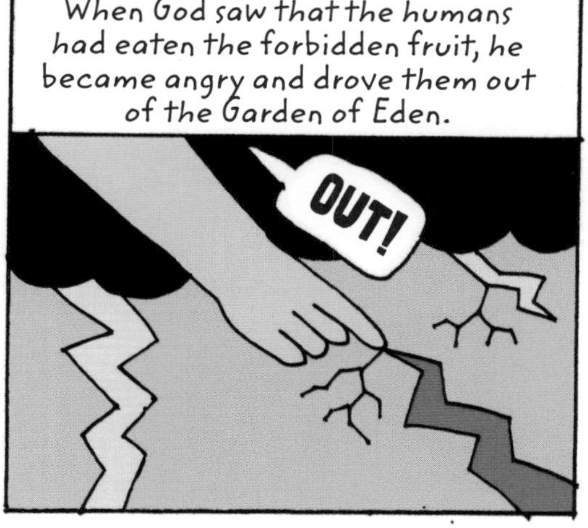

When God saw that the humans had eaten the forbidden fruit, he became angry and drove them out of the Garden of Eden.
OUT!

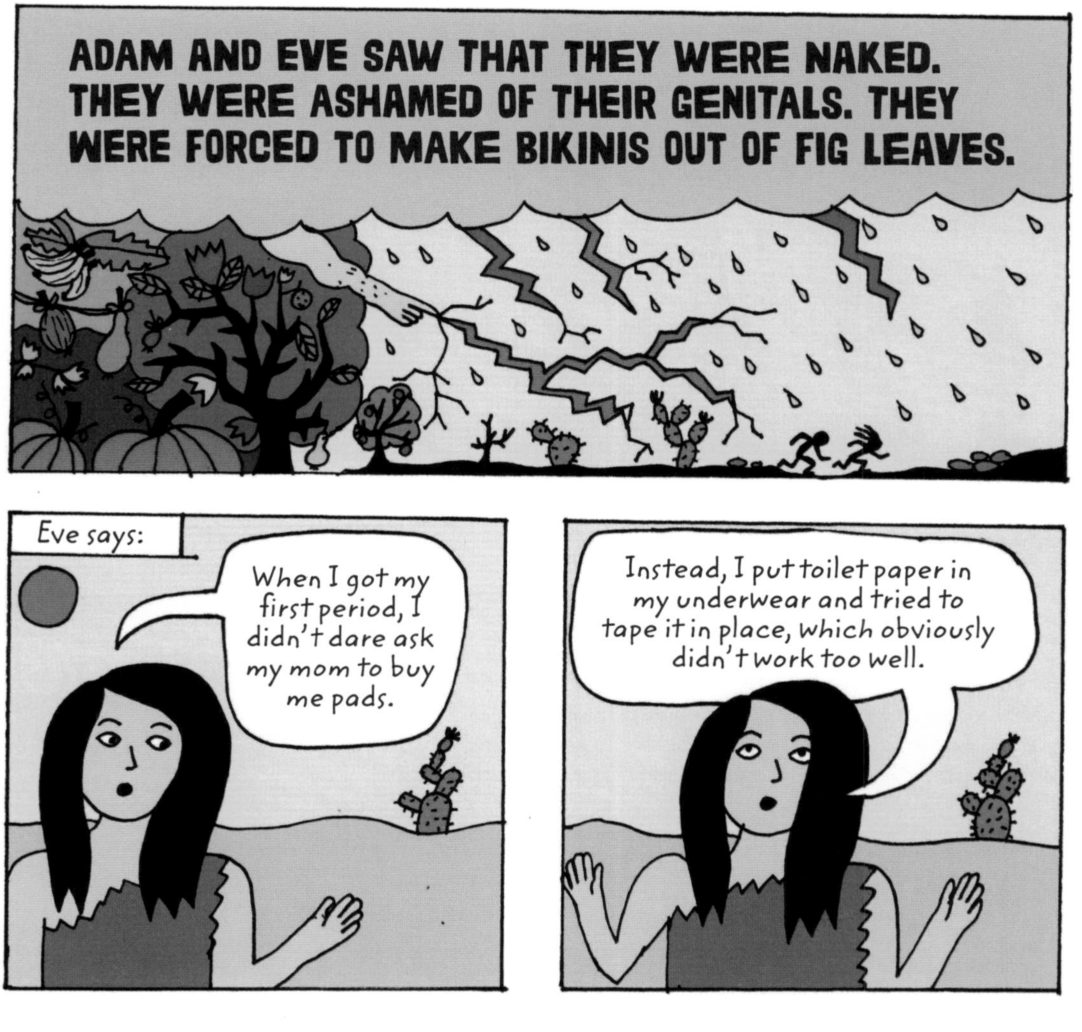

ADAM AND EVE SAW THAT THEY WERE NAKED. THEY WERE ASHAMED OF THEIR GENITALS. THEY WERE FORCED TO MAKE BIKINIS OUT OF FIG LEAVES.
Eve says:
When I got my first period, I didn't dare ask my mom to buy me pads.
Instead, I put toilet paper in my underwear and tried to tape it in place, which obviously didn't work too well.

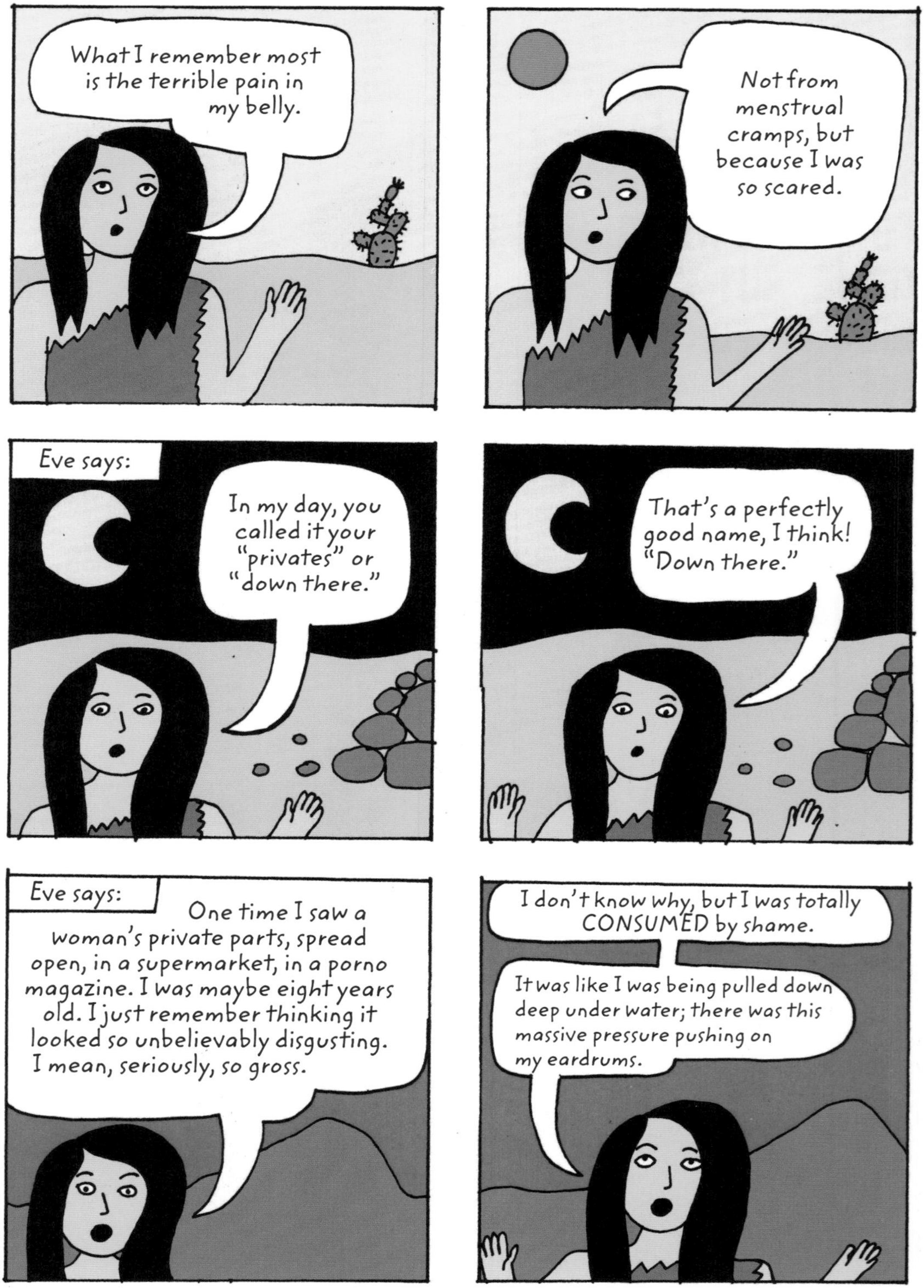
What I remember most is the terrible pain in my belly.
Not from menstrual cramps, but because I was so scared.
Eve says:
In my day, you called it your "privates" or "down there."
That's a perfectly good name, I think! "Down there."
Eve says:
One time I saw a woman's private parts, spread open, in a supermarket, in a porno magazine. I was maybe eight years old. I just remember thinking it looked so unbelievably disgusting. I mean, seriously, so gross.
I don't know why, but I was totally CONSUMED by shame.
It was like I was being pulled down deep under water; there was this massive pressure pushing on my eardrums.

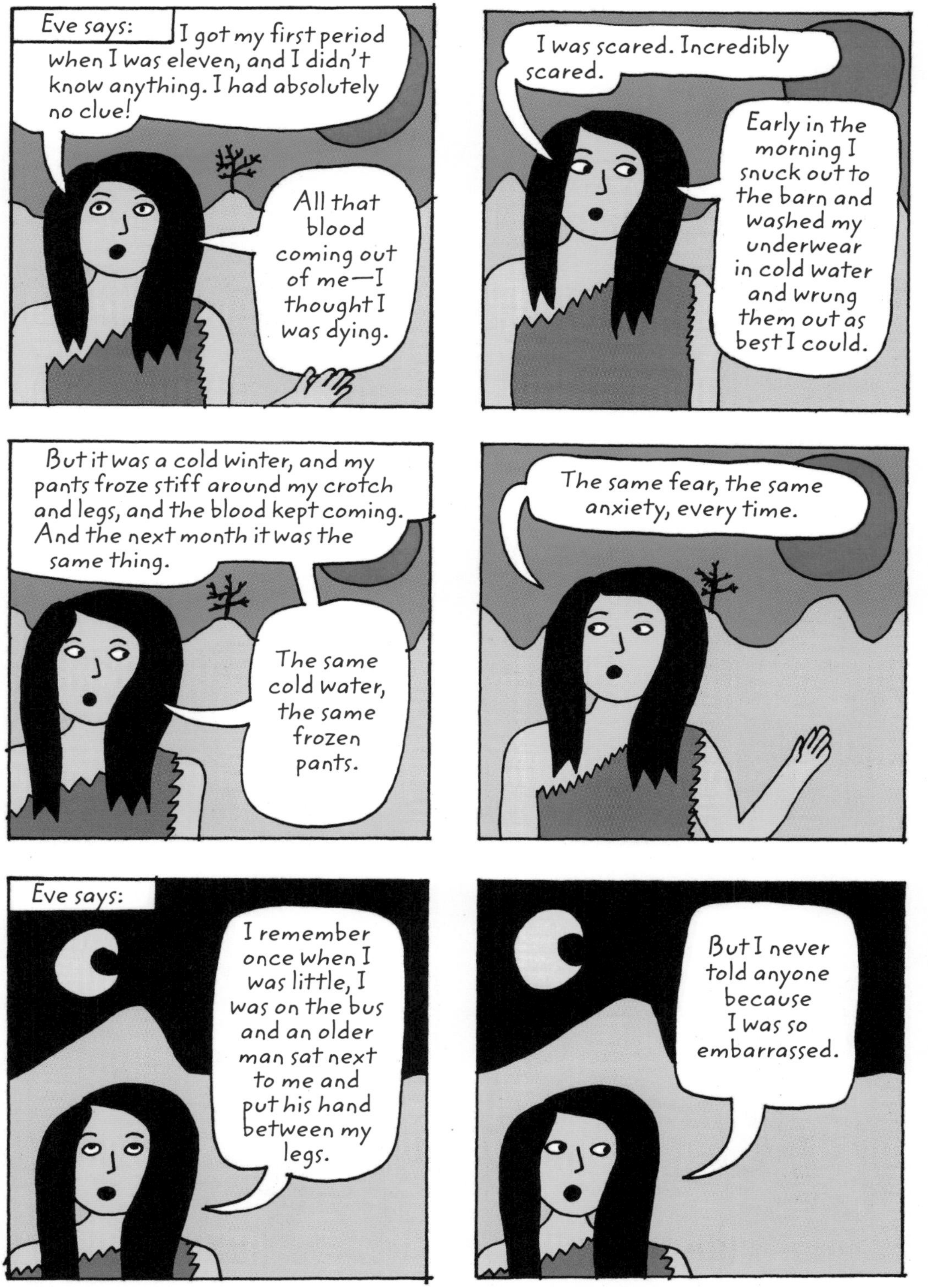
Eve says:
I got my first period when I was eleven, and I didn't know anything. I had absolutely no clue!
All that blood coming out of me—I thought I was dying.
I was scared. Incredibly scared.
Early in the morning I snuck out to the barn and washed my underwear in cold water and wrung them out as best I could.
But it was a cold winter, and my pants froze stiff around my crotch and legs, and the blood kept coming. And the next month it was the same thing.
The same cold water, the same frozen pants.
The same fear, the same anxiety, every time.
Eve says:
I remember once when I was little, I was on the bus and an older man sat next to me and put his hand between my legs.
But I never told anyone because I was so embarrassed.

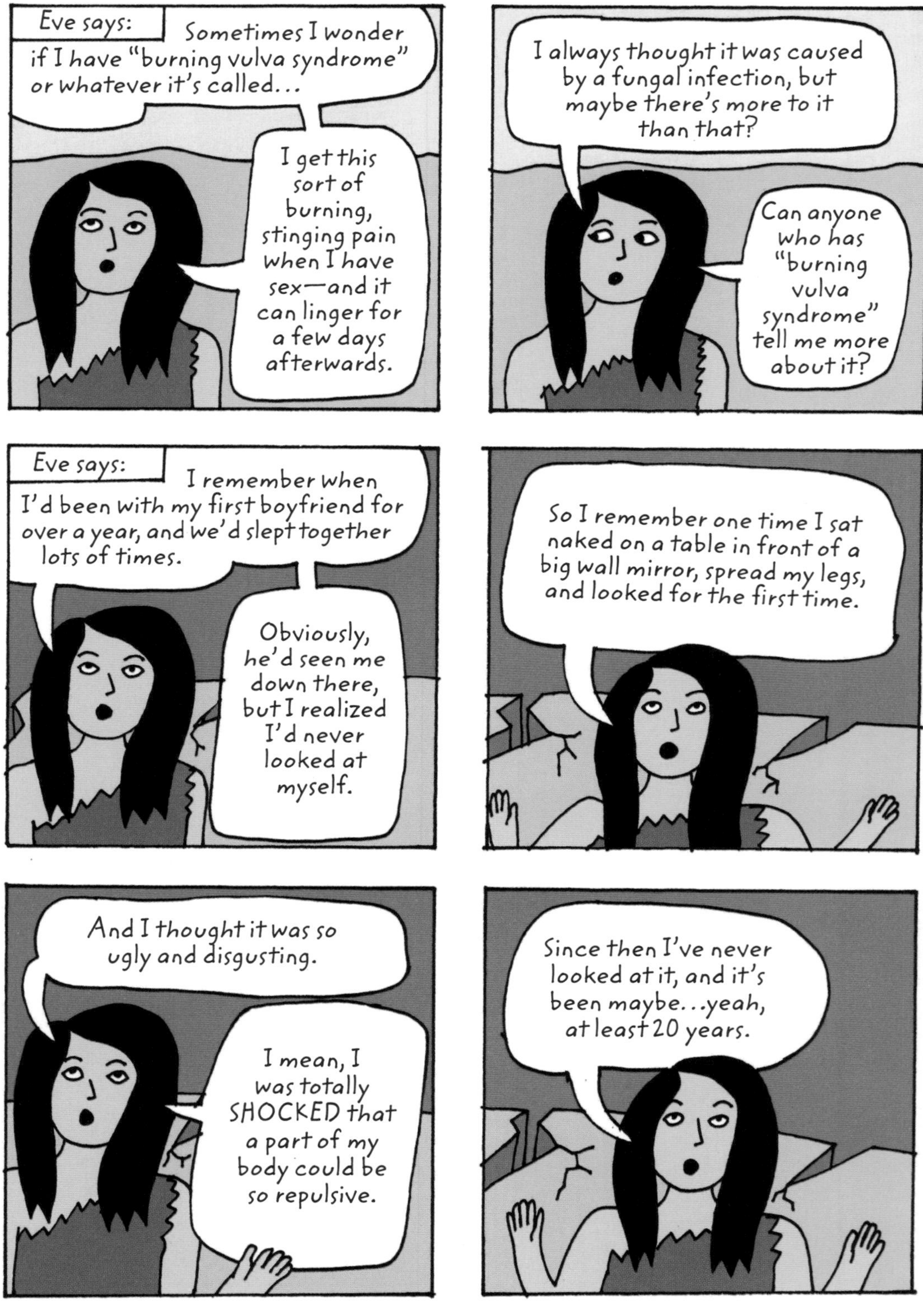
Eve says:
Sometimes I wonder if I have "burning vulva syndrome" or whatever it's called...
I get this sort of burning, stinging pain when I have sex—and it can linger for a few days afterwards.
I always thought it was caused by a fungal infection, but maybe there's more to it than that?
Can anyone who has "burning vulva syndrome" tell me more about it?
Eve says:
I remember when I'd been with my first boyfriend for over a year, and we'd slept together lots of times.
Obviously, he'd seen me down there, but I realized I'd never looked at myself.
So I remember one time I sat naked on a table in front of a big wall mirror, spread my legs, and looked for the first time.
And I thought it was so ugly and disgusting.
I mean, I was totally SHOCKED that a part of my body could be so repulsive.
Since then I've never looked at it, and it's been maybe...yeah, at least 20 years.

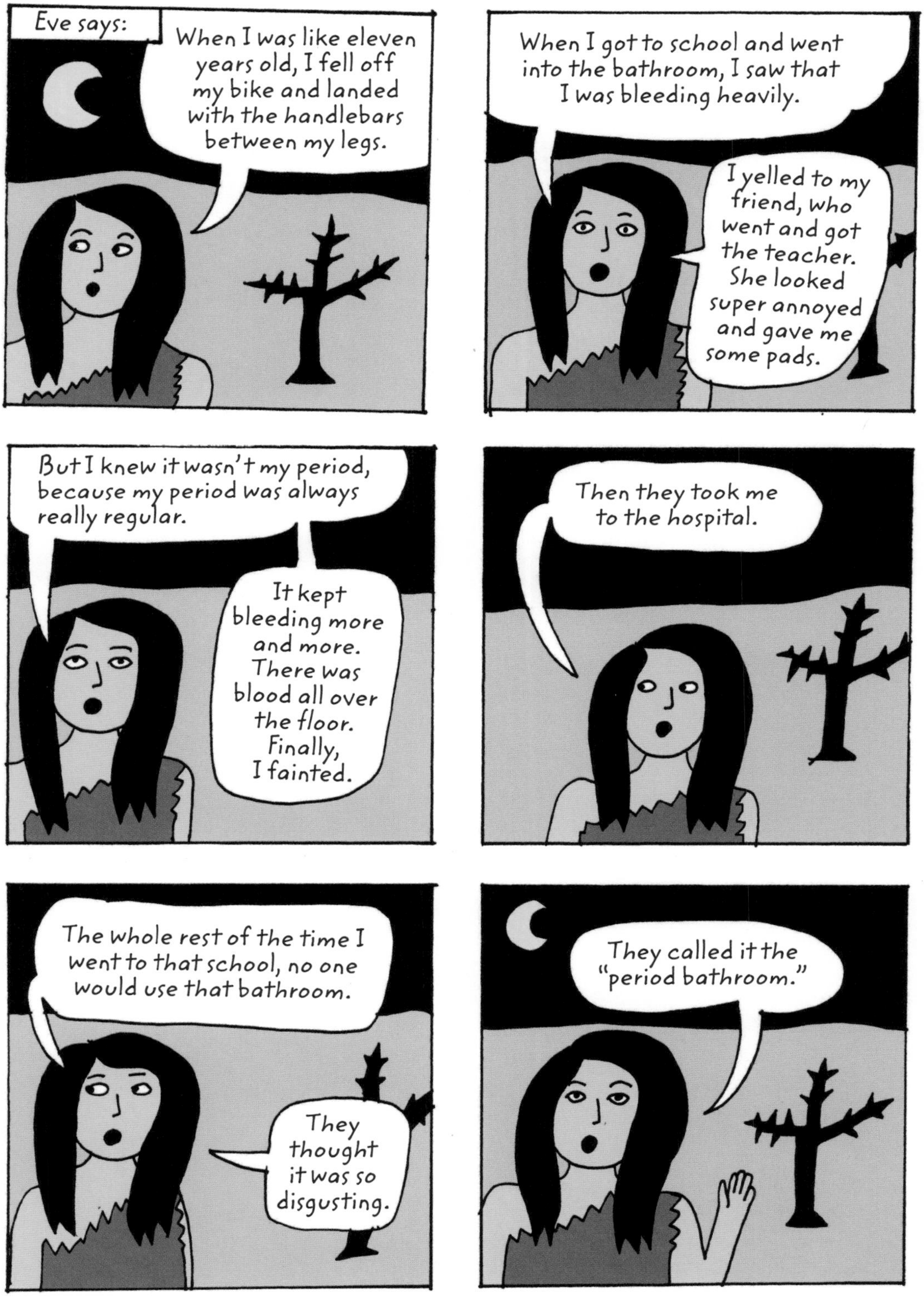
Eve says:
When I was like eleven years old, I fell off my bike and landed with the handlebars between my legs.
When I got to school and went into the bathroom, I saw that I was bleeding heavily.
I yelled to my friend, who went and got the teacher. She looked super annoyed and gave me some pads.
But I knew it wasn't my period, because my period was always really regular.
It kept bleeding more and more. There was blood all over the floor. Finally, I fainted.
Then they took me to the hospital.
The whole rest of the time I went to that school, no one would use that bathroom.
They thought it was so disgusting.
They called it the "period bathroom."

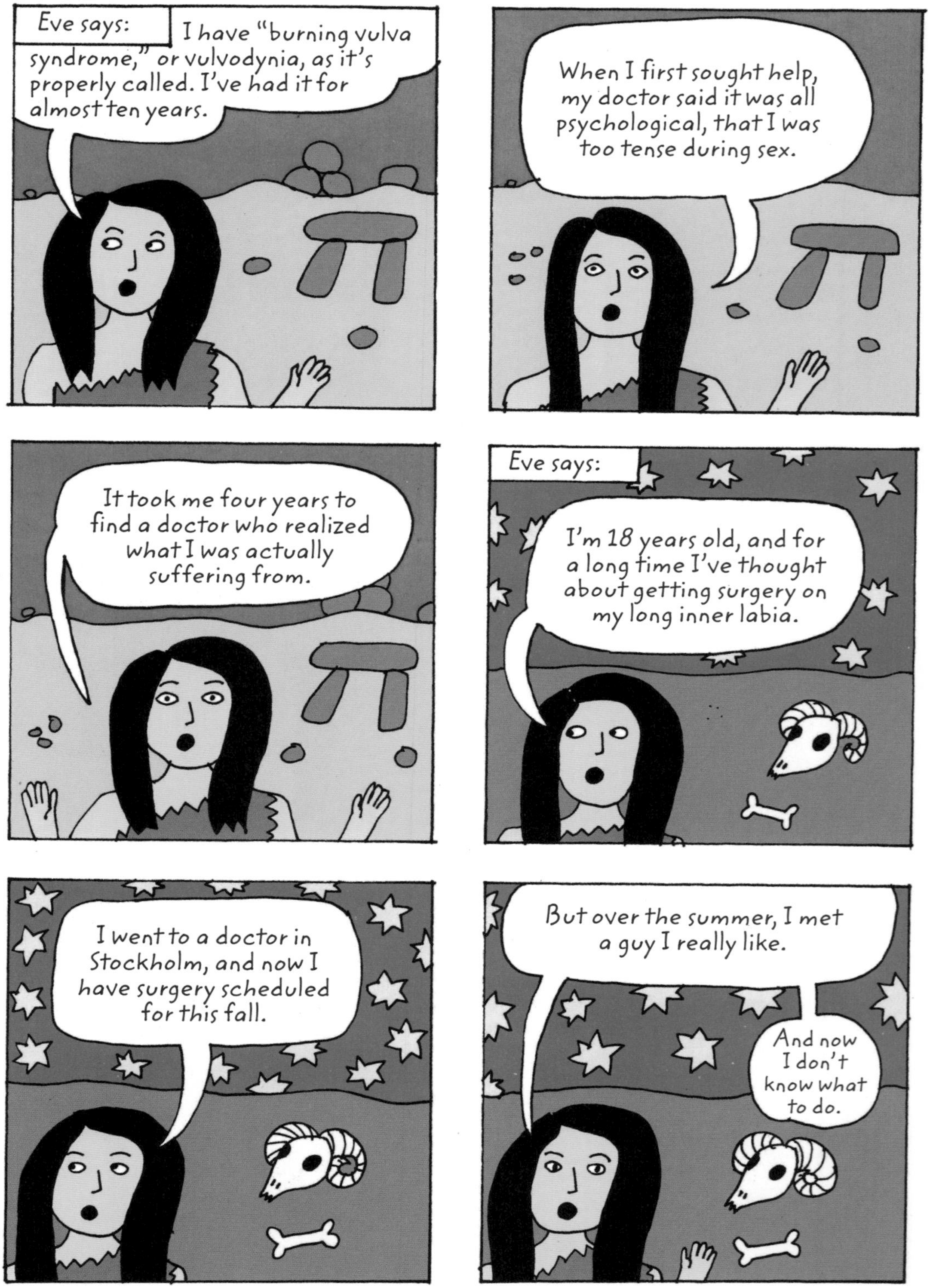
Eve says:
I have "burning vulva syndrome," or vulvodynia, as it's properly called. I've had it for almost ten years.
When I first sought help, my doctor said it was all psychological, that I was too tense during sex.
It took me four years to find a doctor who realized what I was actually suffering from.
Eve says:
I'm 18 years old, and for a long time I've thought about getting surgery on my long inner labia.
I went to a doctor in Stockholm, and now I have surgery scheduled for this fall.
But over the summer, I met a guy I really like.
And now I don't know what to do.

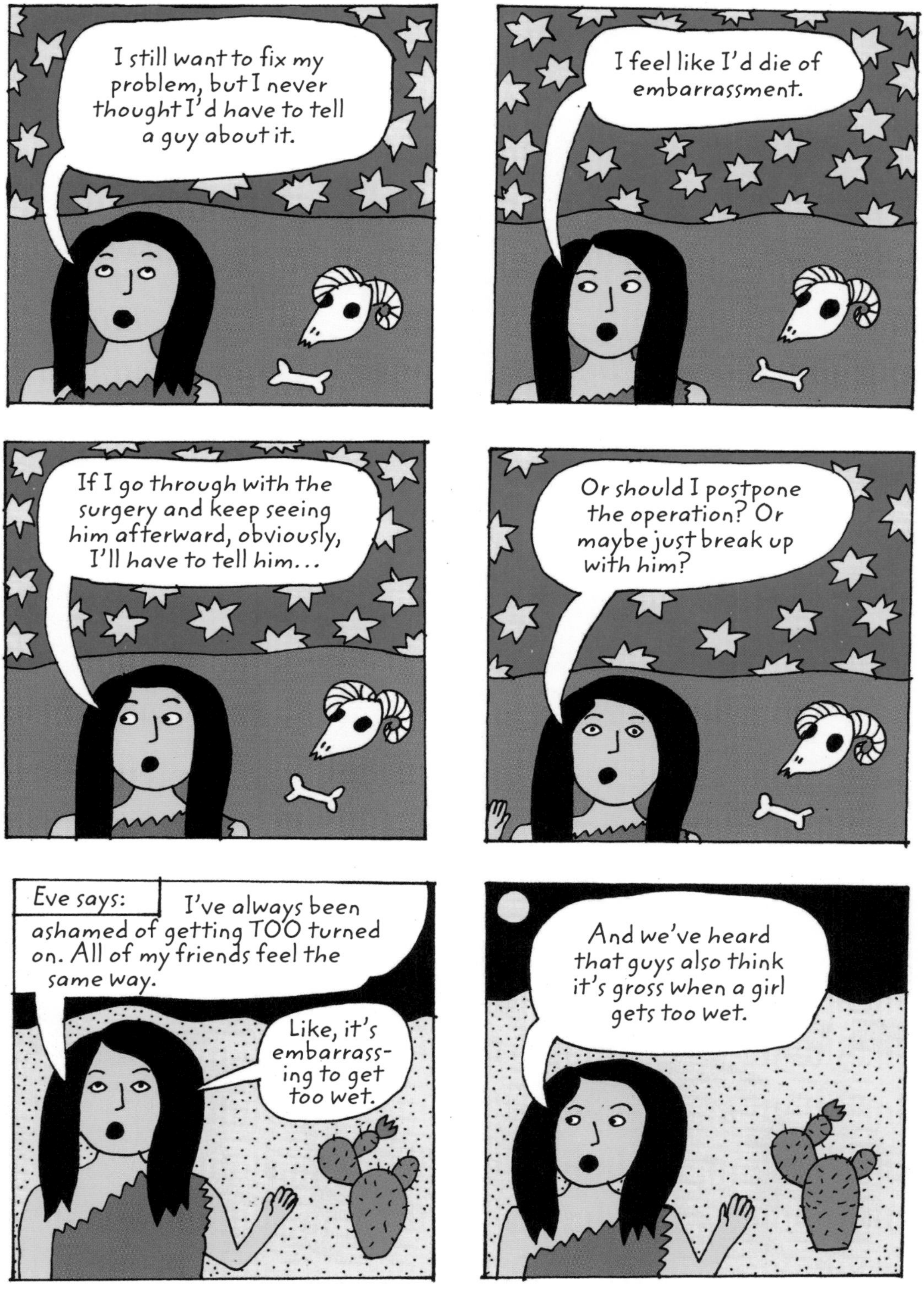
I still want to fix my problem, but I never thought I'd have to tell a guy about it.
I feel like I'd die of embarrassment.
If I go through with the surgery and keep seeing him afterward, obviously, I'll have to tell him...
Or should I postpone the operation? Or maybe just break up with him?
Eve says:
I've always been ashamed of getting TOO turned on. All of my friends feel the same way.
Like, it's embarrass-ing to get too wet.
And we've heard that guys also think it's gross when a girl gets too wet.

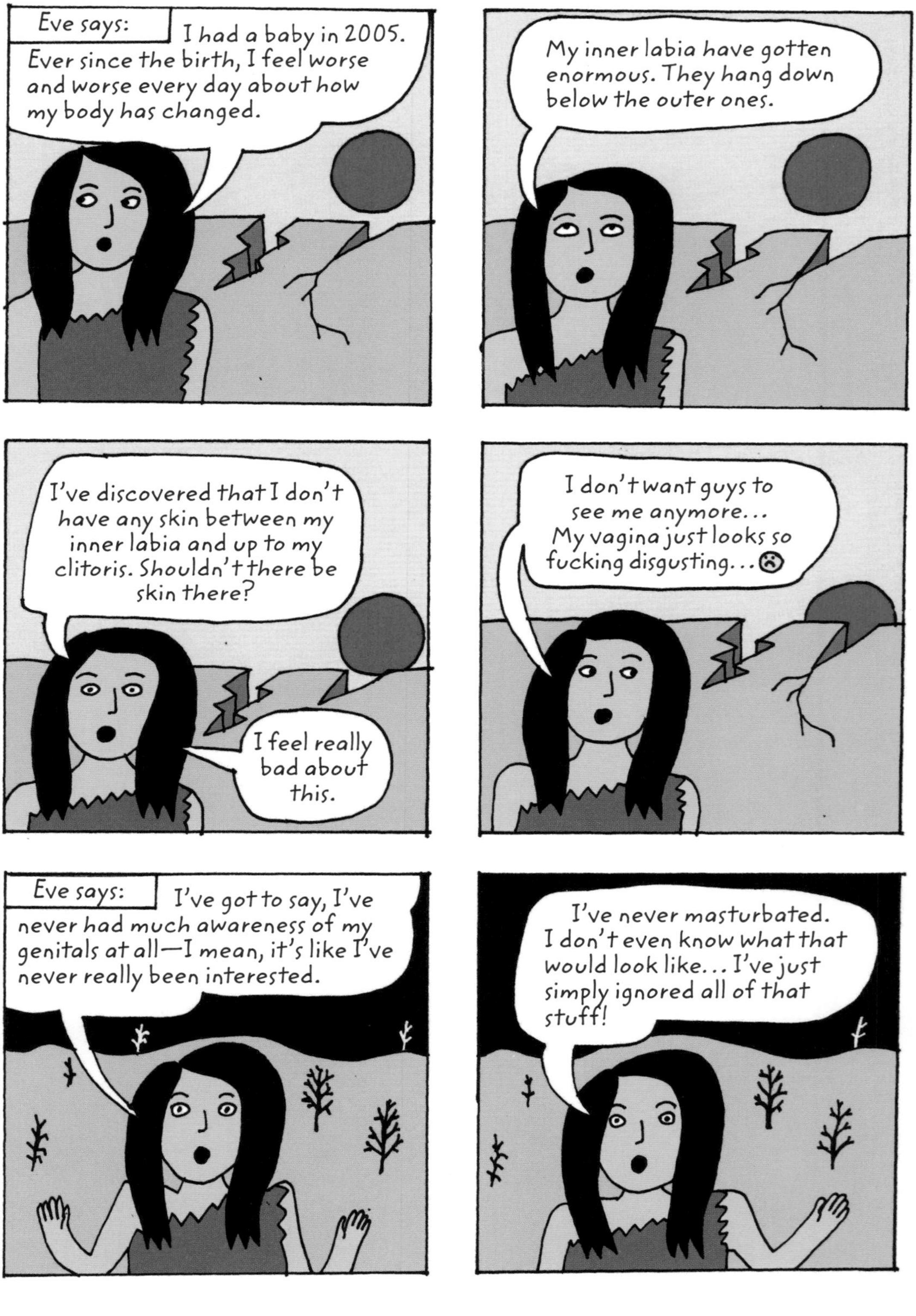
Eve says:
I had a baby in 2005. Ever since the birth, I feel worse and worse every day about how my body has changed.
My inner labia have gotten enormous. They hang down below the outer ones.
I've discovered that I don't have any skin between my inner labia and up to my clitoris. Shouldn't there be skin there?
I feel really bad about this.
I don't want guys to see me anymore... My vagina just looks so fucking disgusting...
Eve says:
I've got to say, I've never had much awareness of my genitals at all—I mean, it's like I've never really been interested.
I've never masturbated. I don't even know what that would look like... I've just simply ignored all of that stuff!

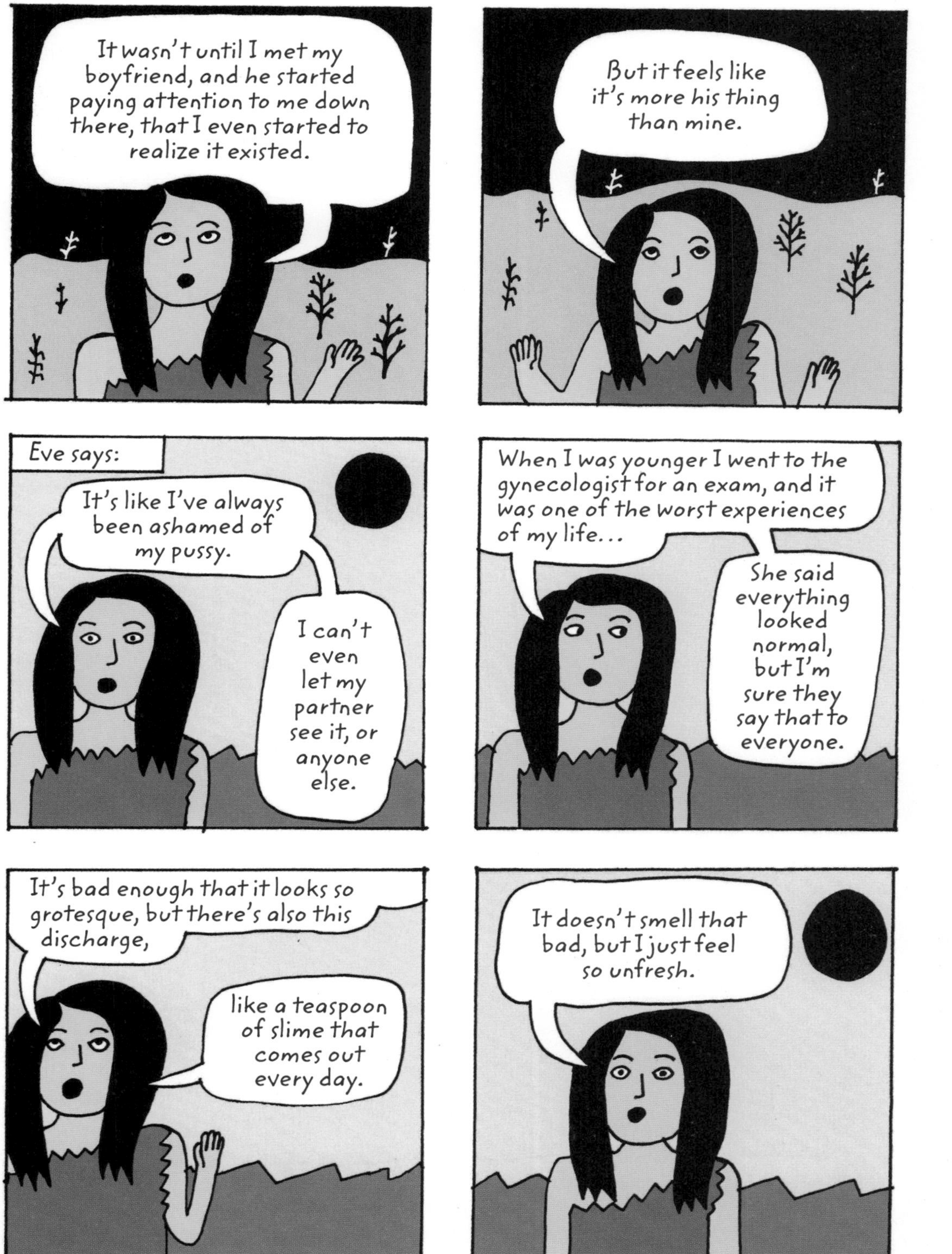

It wasn't until I met my boyfriend, and he started paying attention to me down there, that I even started to realize it existed.
But it feels like it's more his thing than mine.
Eve says:
It's like I've always been ashamed of my pussy.
I can't even let my partner see it, or anyone else.
When I was younger I went to the gynecologist for an exam, and it was one of the worst experiences of my life...
She said everything looked normal, but I'm sure they say that to everyone.
It's bad enough that it looks so grotesque, but there's also this discharge,
like a teaspoon of slime that comes out every day.
It doesn't smell that bad, but I just feel so unfresh.

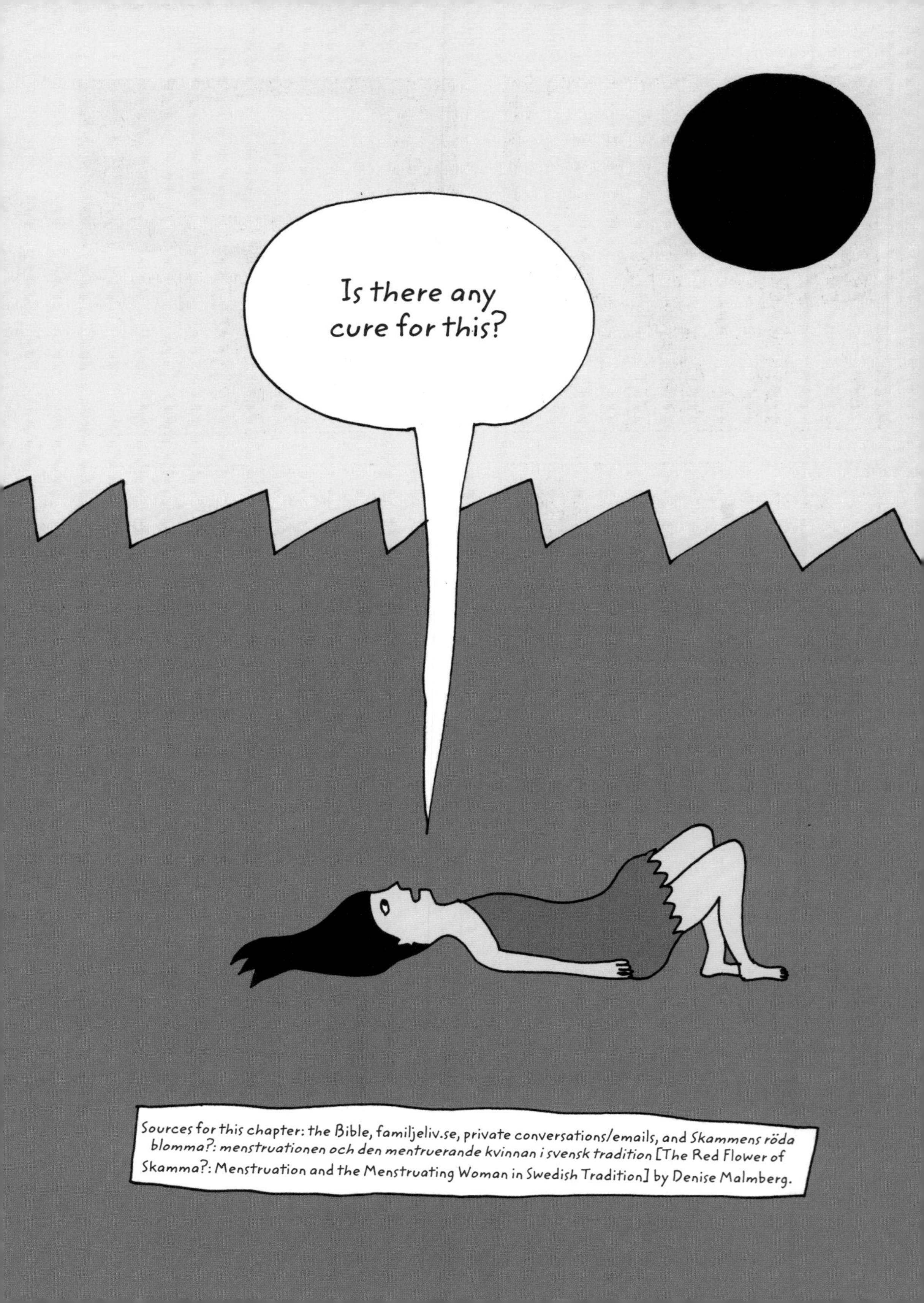
Is there any cure for this?
Sources for this chapter: the Bible, familjeliv.se, private conversations/emails, and Skammens röda blomma?: menstruationen och den mentruerande kvinnan i svensk tradition [The Red Flower of Skamma?: Menstruation and the Menstruating Woman in Swedish Tradition] by Denise Malmberg.

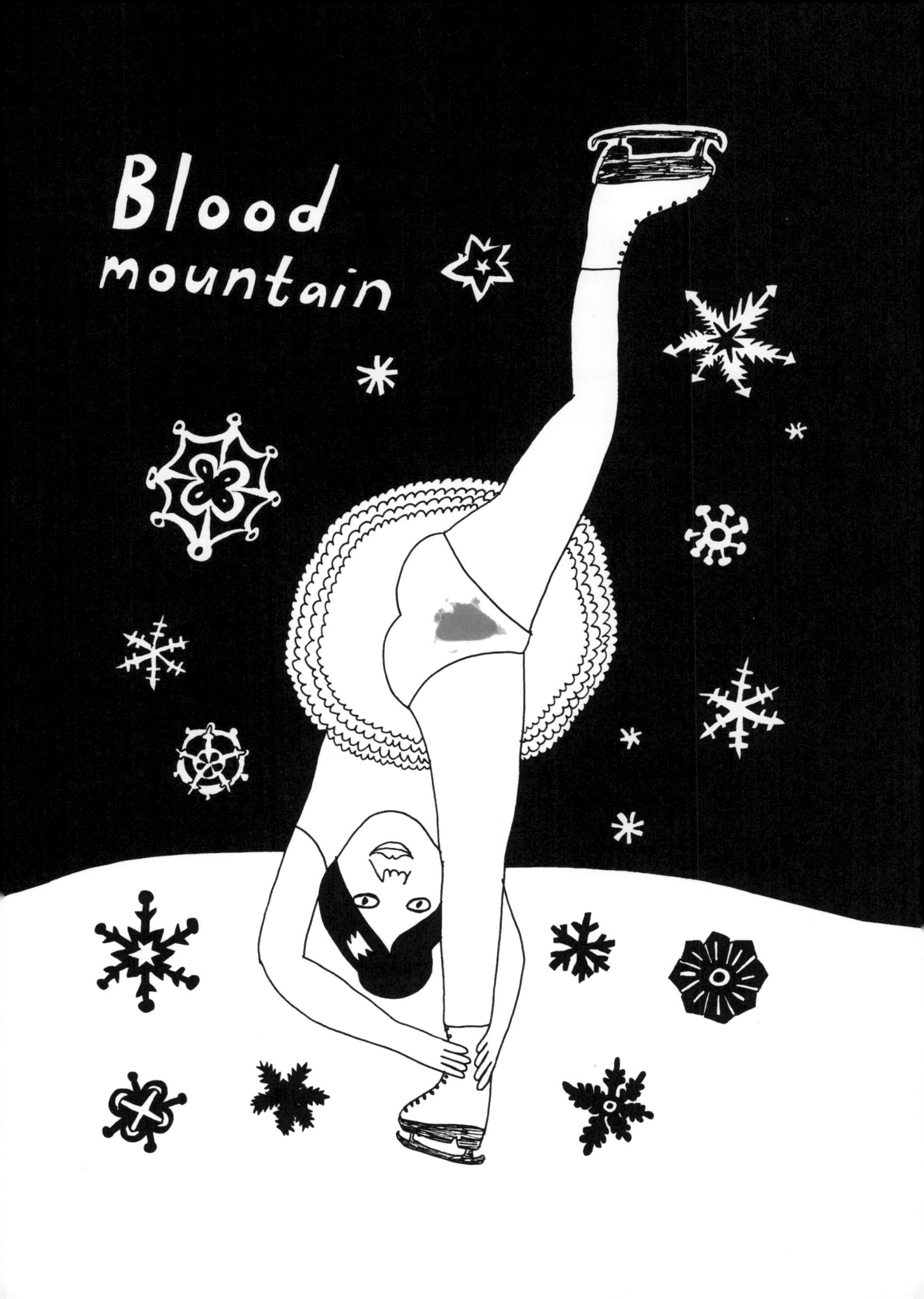
Blood
mountain

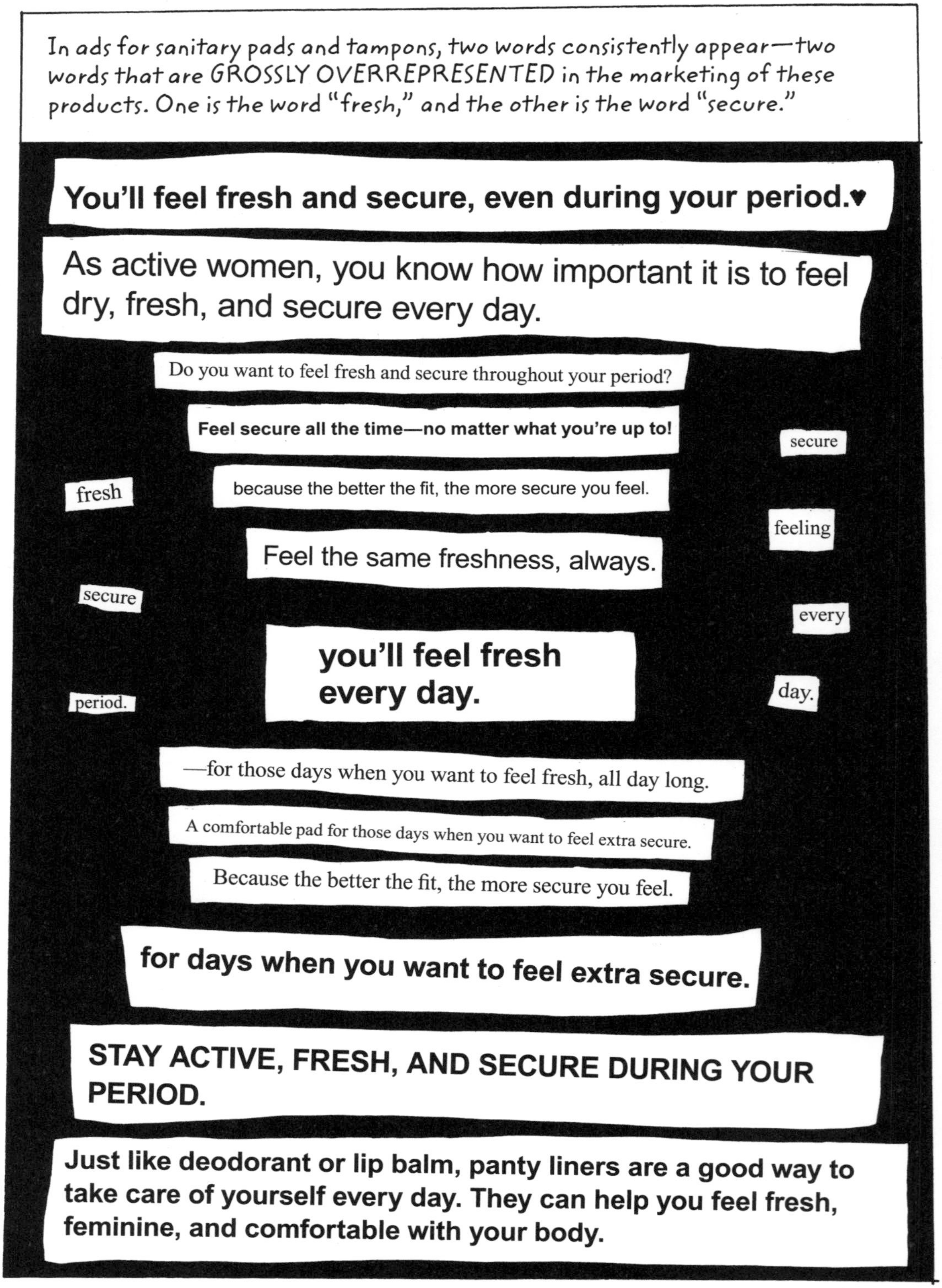
In ads for sanitary pads and tampons, two words consistently appear—two words that are GROSSLY OVERREPRESENTED in the marketing of these products. One is the word "fresh," and the other is the word "secure."
You'll feel fresh and secure, even during your period.♥
As active women, you know how important it is to feel dry, fresh, and secure every day.
Do you want to feel fresh and secure throughout your period?
Feel secure all the time—no matter what you're up to!
secure
fresh
because the better the fit, the more secure you feel.
feeling
Feel the same freshness, always.
secure
every
you'll feel fresh every day.
period.
day.
—for those days when you want to feel fresh, all day long.
A comfortable pad for those days when you want to feel extra secure.
Because the better the fit, the more secure you feel.
for days when you want to feel extra secure.
STAY ACTIVE, FRESH, AND SECURE DURING YOUR PERIOD.
Just like deodorant or lip balm, panty liners are a good way to take care of yourself every day. They can help you feel fresh, feminine, and comfortable with your body.

BUT WHY THOSE TWO WORDS IN PARTICULAR? WHAT DO WE NEED TO FEEL SECURE ABOUT DURING OUR PERIOD? WHAT THREAT MUST WE BE PROTECTED AGAINST?

Well, obviously, the threat that our menstrual products will leak and blood will run down our inner thighs and stain our underwear, our sheets, and maybe—in extreme cases—sofas, chairs or other items in the public space.

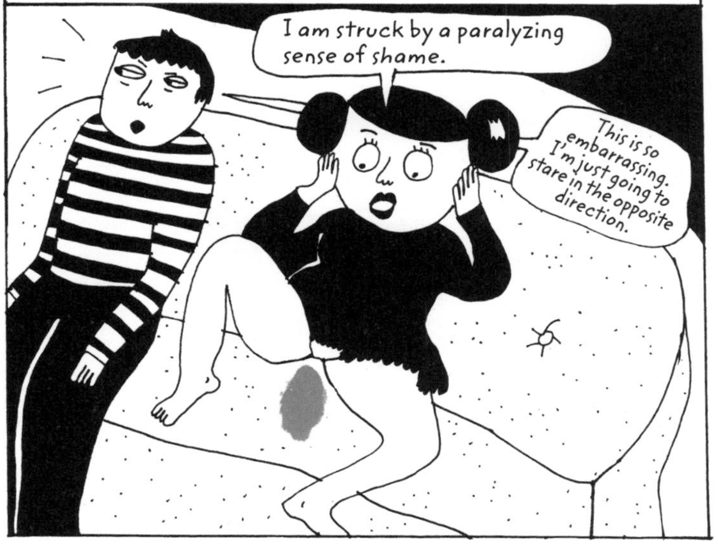
I am struck by a paralyzing sense of shame.
This is so embarrassing. I'm just going to stare in the opposite direction.

Now, compare this with some other situation where you risk soiling the furniture—for example, sitting on the sofa, drunk on red wine, merrily splashing Two Buck Chuck on yourself and your companions. You wouldn't use the word "insecure" to describe this situation, would you?

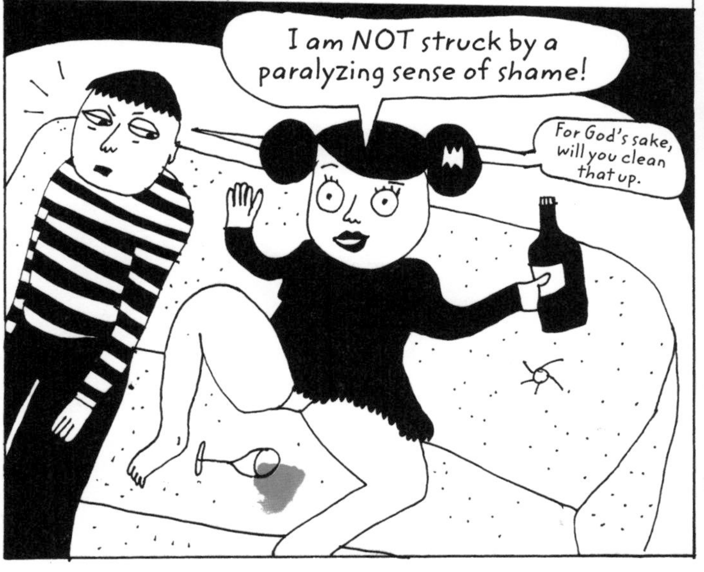
I am NOT struck by a paralyzing sense of shame!
For God's sake, will you clean that up.

SO, WHAT WE'RE AFRAID OF DURING OUR PERIOD IS NOT THAT WE'LL BE FORCED TO DO SOME EXTRA HOUSEWORK. WE'RE AFRAID OTHER PEOPLE WILL DISCOVER THAT WE HAVE OUR PERIOD.

One tampon company even says on its website:	Another says:
 tampons fit right in your jeans pocket, and you can hold one in your hand on your way to the bathroom without anyone seeing what you're carrying.	No one will suspect that you have your period, and you won't have to be afraid of leaks.

BUT WHY MUST NO ONE SEE WHAT YOU'RE CARRYING? WHY CAN'T ANYONE KNOW YOU'RE ON YOUR PERIOD?

BECAUSE, OF COURSE, MENSTRUATION IS TABOO—A TABOO THAT HAS PLAYED OUT DIFFERENTLY IN DIFFERENT CULTURES BUT HAS NONETHELESS REMAINED SURPRISINGLY CONSTANT OVER THE LAST FEW THOUSAND YEARS.

EVEN THE WORD "TABOO" IS THOUGHT TO COME FROM THE POLYNESIAN WORD "TUPUA," WHICH ALSO MEANS MENSTRUATION*

*Janice Delaney, Mary Jane Lupton, and Emily Toth, The Curse: A Cultural History of Menstruation (New York: Dutton, 1976), 1.

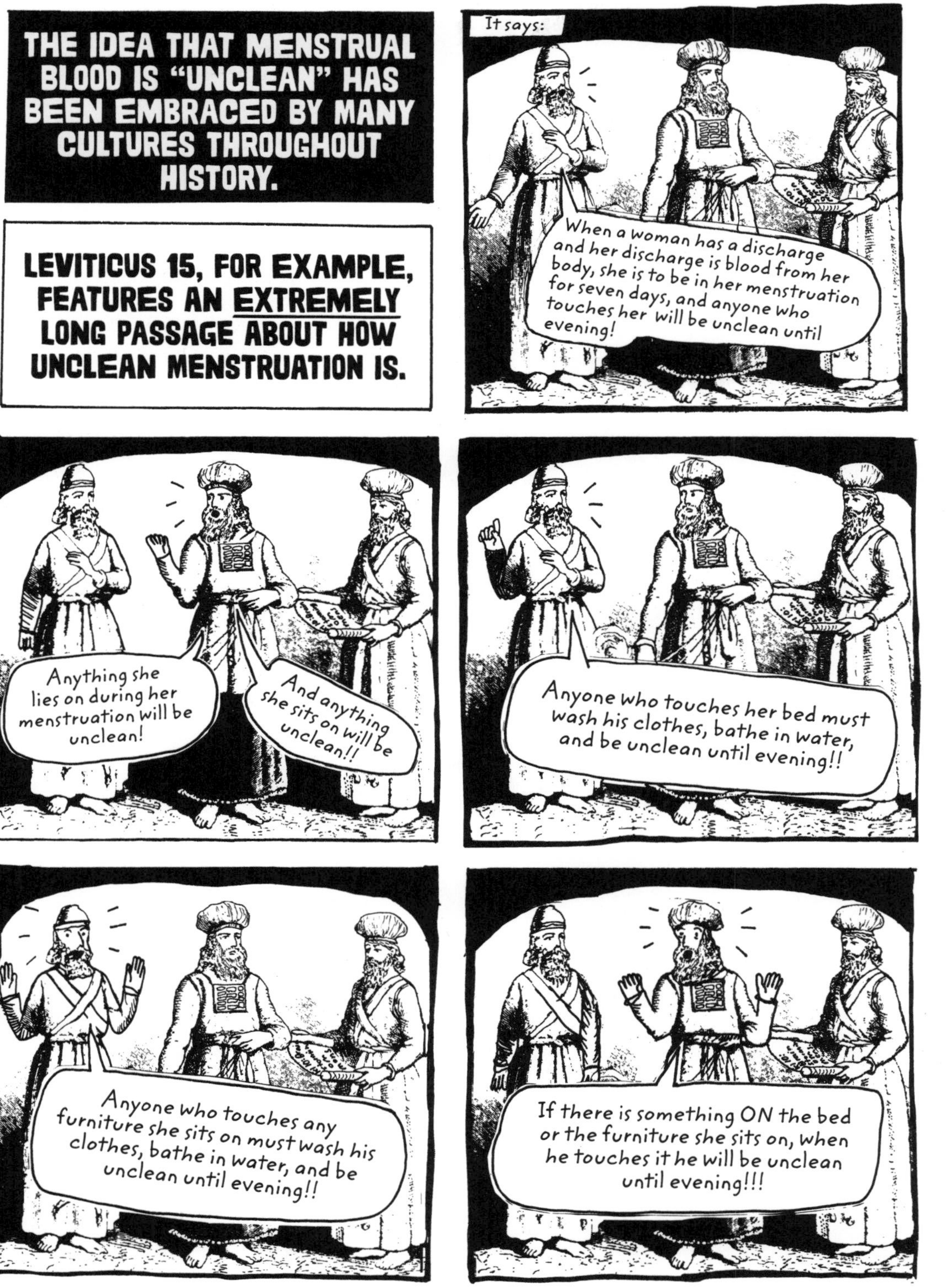
THE IDEA THAT MENSTRUAL BLOOD IS "UNCLEAN" HAS BEEN EMBRACED BY MANY CULTURES THROUGHOUT HISTORY.
It says:
When a woman has a discharge and her discharge is blood from her body, she is to be in her menstruation for seven days, and anyone who touches her will be unclean until evening!
LEVITICUS 15, FOR EXAMPLE, FEATURES AN EXTREMELY LONG PASSAGE ABOUT HOW UNCLEAN MENSTRUATION IS.
Anything she lies on during her menstruation will be unclean!
And anything she sits on will be unclean!!
Anyone who touches her bed must wash his clothes, bathe in water, and be unclean until evening!!
Anyone who touches any furniture she sits on must wash his clothes, bathe in water, and be unclean until evening!!
If there is something ON the bed or the furniture she sits on, when he touches it he will be unclean until evening!!!

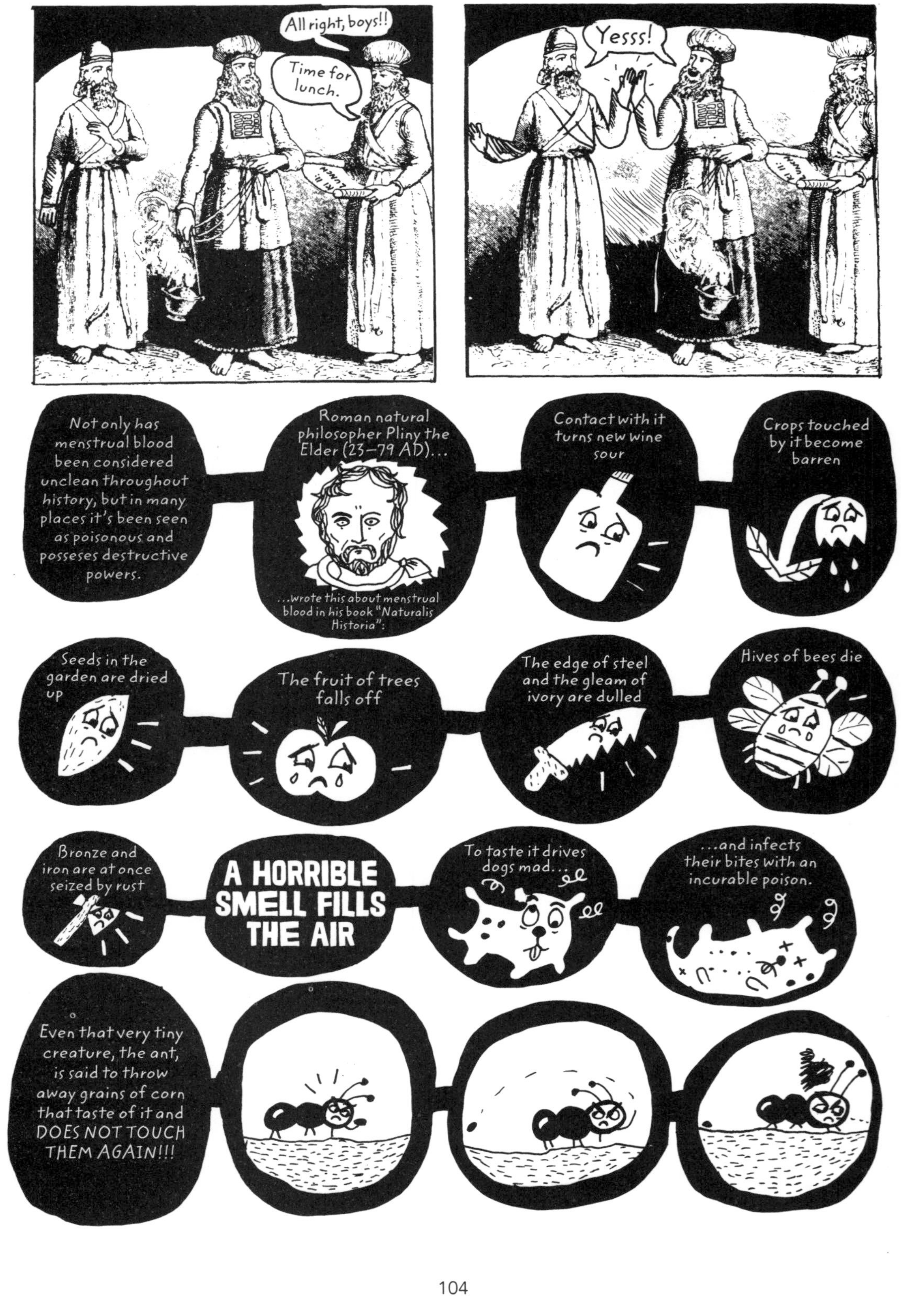
All right, boys!!
Time for lunch.
Yesss!
Not only has menstrual blood been considered unclean throughout history, but in many places it's been seen as poisonous and posseses destructive powers.
Roman natural philosopher Pliny the Elder (23–79 AD)...
...wrote this about menstrual blood in his book "Naturalis Historia":
Contact with it turns new wine sour
Crops touched by it become barren
Seeds in the garden are dried up
The fruit of trees falls off
The edge of steel and the gleam of ivory are dulled
Hives of bees die
Bronze and iron are at once seized by rust
A HORRIBLE SMELL FILLS THE AIR
To taste it drives dogs mad...
...and infects their bites with an incurable poison.
Even that very tiny creature, the ant, is said to throw away grains of corn that taste of it and DOES NOT TOUCH THEM AGAIN!!!

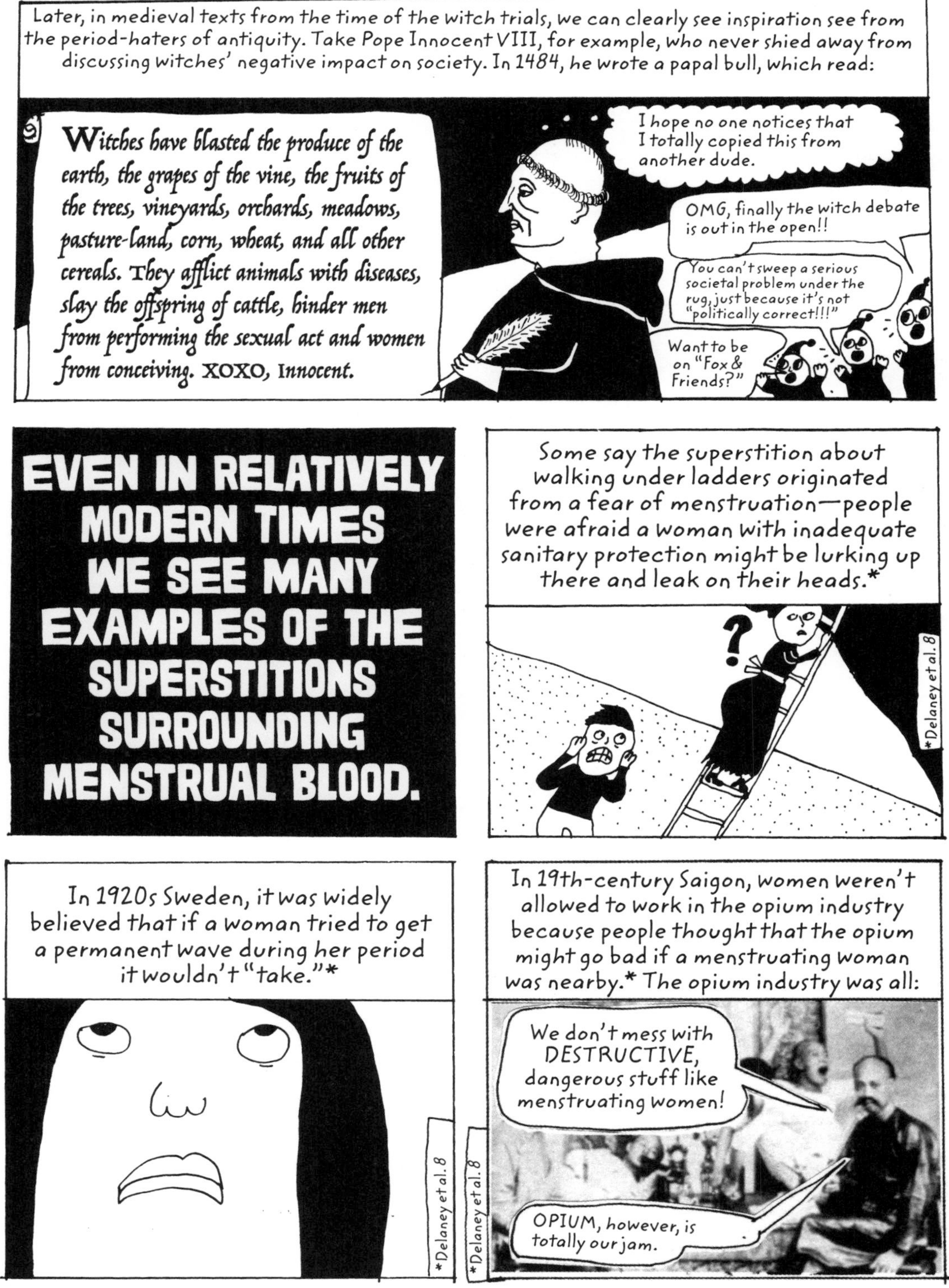
Later, in medieval texts from the time of the witch trials, we can clearly see inspiration see from the period-haters of antiquity. Take Pope Innocent VIII, for example, who never shied away from discussing witches' negative impact on society. In 1484, he wrote a papal bull, which read:
Witches have blasted the produce of the earth, the grapes of the vine, the fruits of the trees, vineyards, orchards, meadows, pasture-land, corn, wheat, and all other cereals. They afflict animals with diseases, slay the offspring of cattle, hinder men from performing the sexual act and women from conceiving. XOXO, Innocent.
I hope no one notices that I totally copied this from another dude.
OMG, finally the witch debate is out in the open!!
You can't sweep a serious societal problem under the rug, just because it's not "politically correct!!!"
Want to be on "Fox & Friends?"
EVEN IN RELATIVELY MODERN TIMES WE SEE MANY EXAMPLES OF THE SUPERSTITIONS SURROUNDING MENSTRUAL BLOOD.
Some say the superstition about walking under ladders originated from a fear of menstruation—people were afraid a woman with inadequate sanitary protection might be lurking up there and leak on their heads.*
?
*Delaney et al. 8
In 1920s Sweden, it was widely believed that if a woman tried to get a permanent wave during her period it wouldn't "take."*
*Delaney et al. 8
In 19th-century Saigon, women weren't allowed to work in the opium industry because people thought that the opium might go bad if a menstruating woman was nearby.* The opium industry was all:
We don't mess with DESTRUCTIVE, dangerous stuff like menstruating women!
OPIUM, however, is totally our jam.
*Delaney et al. 8

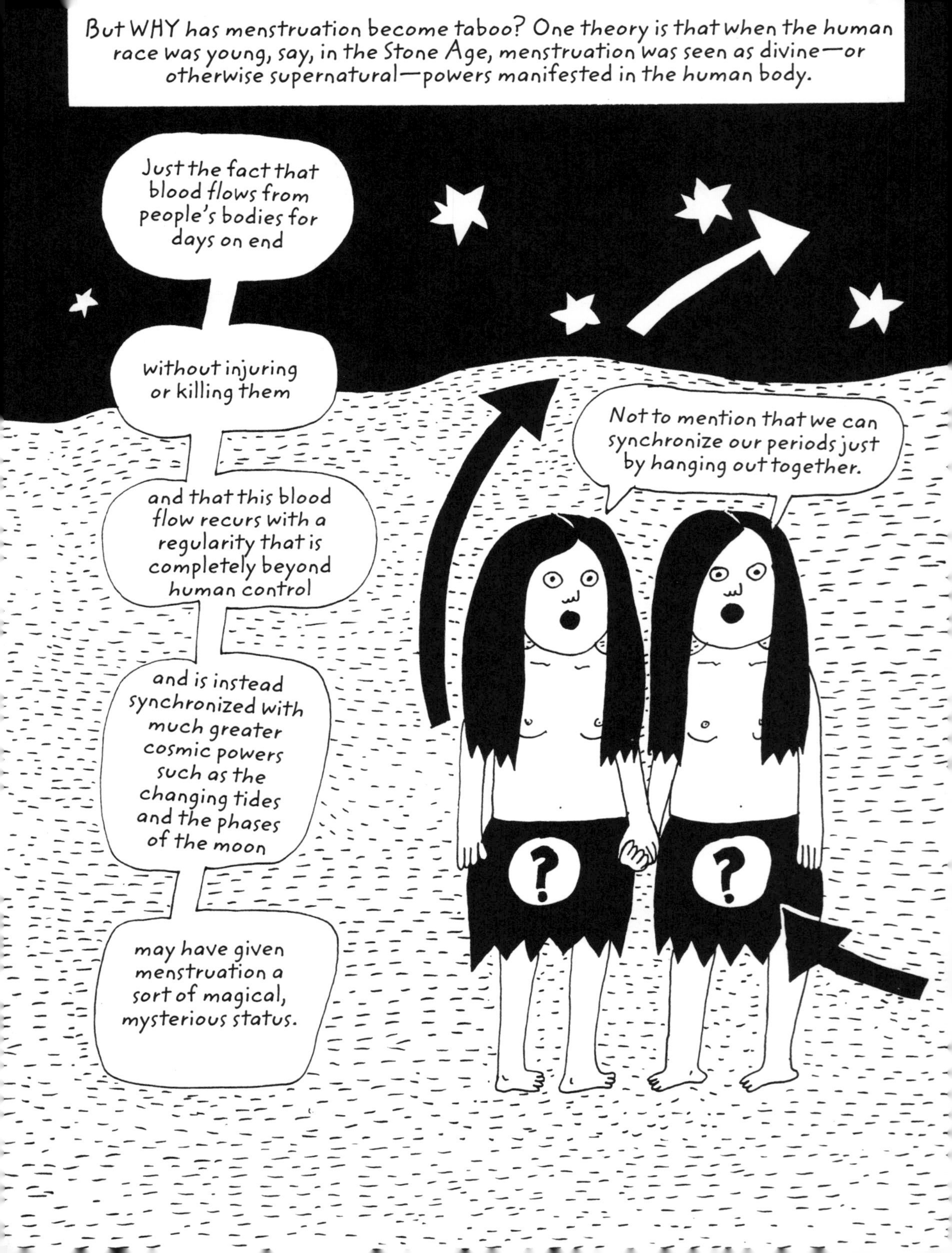
But WHY has menstruation become taboo? One theory is that when the human race was young, say, in the Stone Age, menstruation was seen as divine—or otherwise supernatural—powers manifested in the human body.
Just the fact that blood flows from people's bodies for days on end
without injuring or killing them
and that this blood flow recurs with a regularity that is completely beyond human control
and is instead synchronized with much greater cosmic powers such as the changing tides and the phases of the moon
may have given menstruation a sort of magical, mysterious status.
Not to mention that we can synchronize our periods just by hanging out together.
?
?

You'd imagine this perceived divine/supernatural/holy/dangerous power would lead to all kinds of taboos around menstruation. (*The Curse*, p. 7)

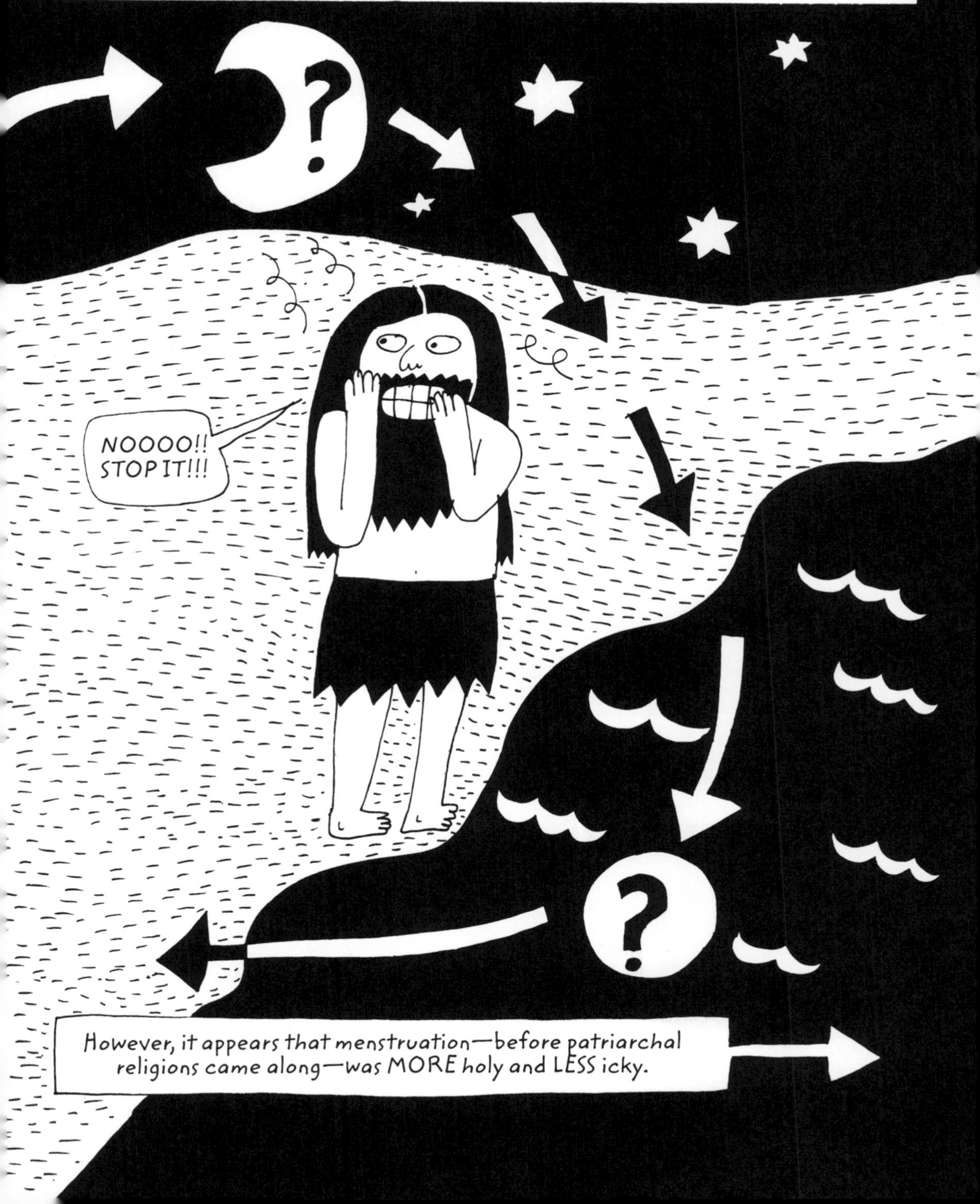
NOOOO!! STOP IT!!!

However, it appears that menstruation—before patriarchal religions came along—was MORE holy and LESS icky.

This image was found in a temple at the world's oldest known religious cult site, Turkey's Göbekli Tepe, which is ca. 12,000 years old (i.e., 7,000 years older than Stonehenge!!!):

(Sketched from an image in the 2012 BBC documentary "Divine Women: When God Was a Girl!")

Archaeologists think this 15,000-year-old dotted pattern on stone, found in Hohle Fels cave in Germany, is some form of menstruation calendar (*Der Spiegel*, 11/9/2011).

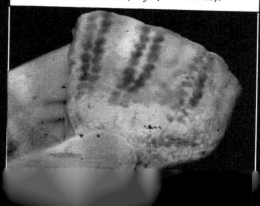

Polytheistic religions such as Hinduism, which still incorporate female incarnations of the divine, also portray menstruating women in a religious context.

Wood carving, southern India. From Sanyal, *Vulva*, p. 79.

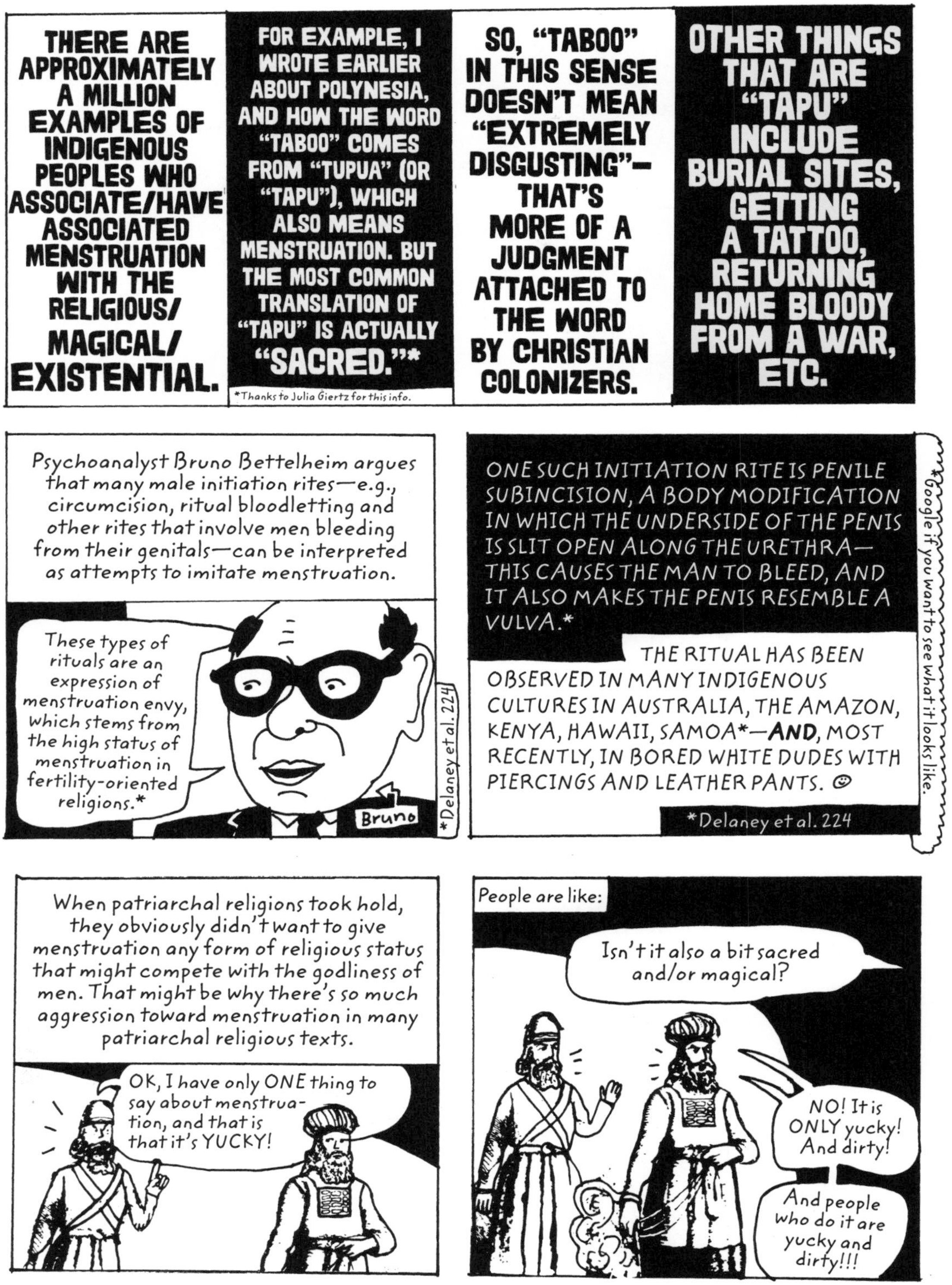
THERE ARE APPROXIMATELY A MILLION EXAMPLES OF INDIGENOUS PEOPLES WHO ASSOCIATE/HAVE ASSOCIATED MENSTRUATION WITH THE RELIGIOUS/ MAGICAL/ EXISTENTIAL.
FOR EXAMPLE, I WROTE EARLIER ABOUT POLYNESIA, AND HOW THE WORD "TABOO" COMES FROM "TUPUA" (OR "TAPU"), WHICH ALSO MEANS MENSTRUATION. BUT THE MOST COMMON TRANSLATION OF "TAPU" IS ACTUALLY "SACRED."*
*Thanks to Julia Giertz for this info.
SO, "TABOO" IN THIS SENSE DOESN'T MEAN "EXTREMELY DISGUSTING"—THAT'S MORE OF A JUDGMENT ATTACHED TO THE WORD BY CHRISTIAN COLONIZERS.
OTHER THINGS THAT ARE "TAPU" INCLUDE BURIAL SITES, GETTING A TATTOO, RETURNING HOME BLOODY FROM A WAR, ETC.
Psychoanalyst Bruno Bettelheim argues that many male initiation rites—e.g., circumcision, ritual bloodletting and other rites that involve men bleeding from their genitals—can be interpreted as attempts to imitate menstruation.
These types of rituals are an expression of menstruation envy, which stems from the high status of menstruation in fertility-oriented religions.*
Bruno
*Delaney et al. 224
ONE SUCH INITIATION RITE IS PENILE SUBINCISION, A BODY MODIFICATION IN WHICH THE UNDERSIDE OF THE PENIS IS SLIT OPEN ALONG THE URETHRA—THIS CAUSES THE MAN TO BLEED, AND IT ALSO MAKES THE PENIS RESEMBLE A VULVA.*
THE RITUAL HAS BEEN OBSERVED IN MANY INDIGENOUS CULTURES IN AUSTRALIA, THE AMAZON, KENYA, HAWAII, SAMOA*—**AND**, MOST RECENTLY, IN BORED WHITE DUDES WITH PIERCINGS AND LEATHER PANTS. ☺
*Delaney et al. 224
*Google if you want to see what it looks like.
When patriarchal religions took hold, they obviously didn't want to give menstruation any form of religious status that might compete with the godliness of men. That might be why there's so much aggression toward menstruation in many patriarchal religious texts.
OK, I have only ONE thing to say about menstruation, and that is that it's YUCKY!
People are like:
Isn't it also a bit sacred and/or magical?
NO! It is ONLY yucky! And dirty!
And people who do it are yucky and dirty!!!

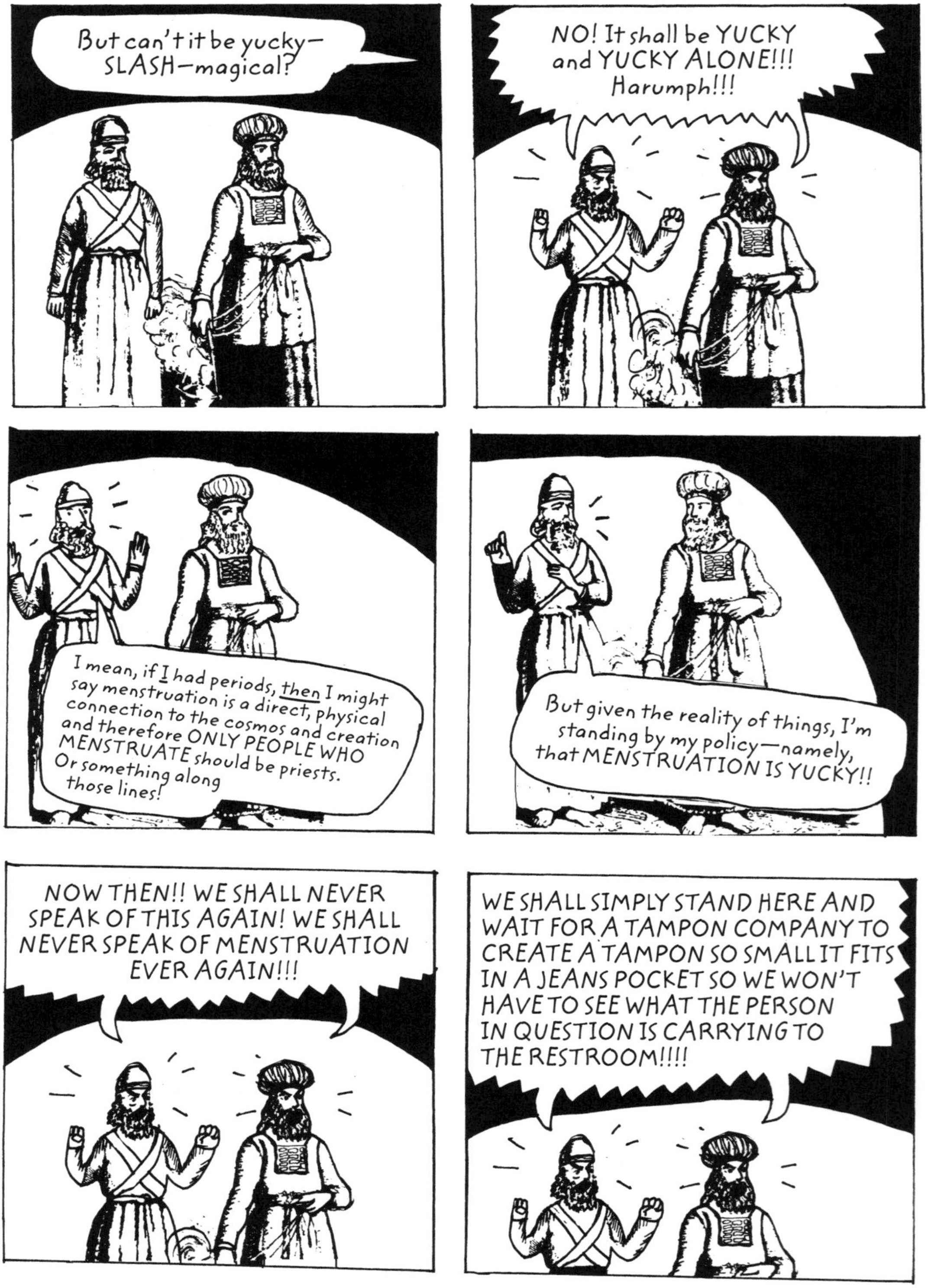
But can't it be yucky—SLASH—magical?
NO! It shall be YUCKY and YUCKY ALONE!!! Harumph!!!
I mean, if I had periods, then I might say menstruation is a direct, physical connection to the cosmos and creation and therefore ONLY PEOPLE WHO MENSTRUATE should be priests. Or something along those lines!
But given the reality of things, I'm standing by my policy—namely, that MENSTRUATION IS YUCKY!!
NOW THEN!! WE SHALL NEVER SPEAK OF THIS AGAIN! WE SHALL NEVER SPEAK OF MENSTRUATION EVER AGAIN!!!
WE SHALL SIMPLY STAND HERE AND WAIT FOR A TAMPON COMPANY TO CREATE A TAMPON SO SMALL IT FITS IN A JEANS POCKET SO WE WON'T HAVE TO SEE WHAT THE PERSON IN QUESTION IS CARRYING TO THE RESTROOM!!!!

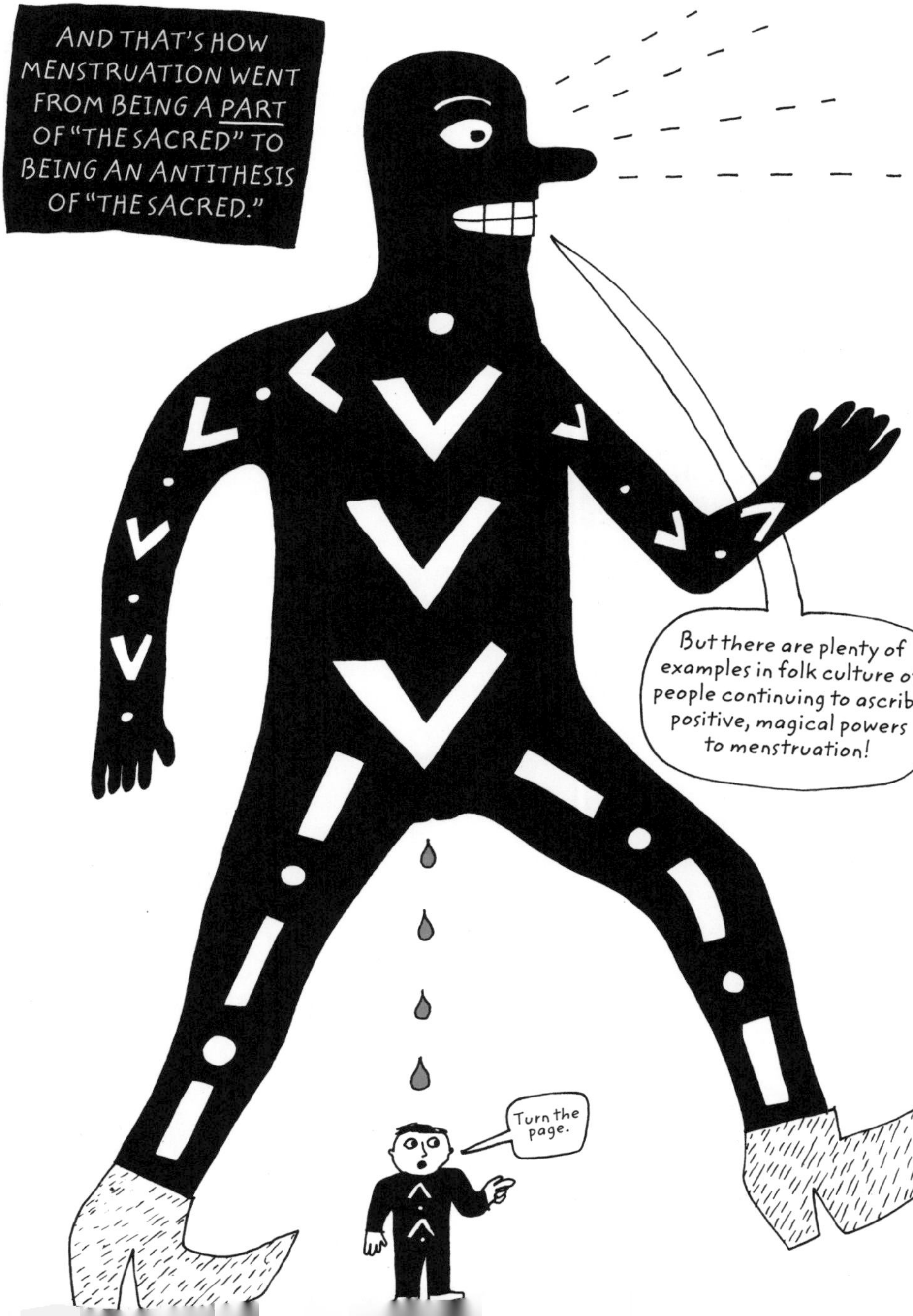
AND THAT'S HOW MENSTRUATION WENT FROM BEING A PART OF "THE SACRED" TO BEING AN ANTITHESIS OF "THE SACRED."
But there are plenty of examples in folk culture of people continuing to ascribe positive, magical powers to menstruation!
Turn the page.

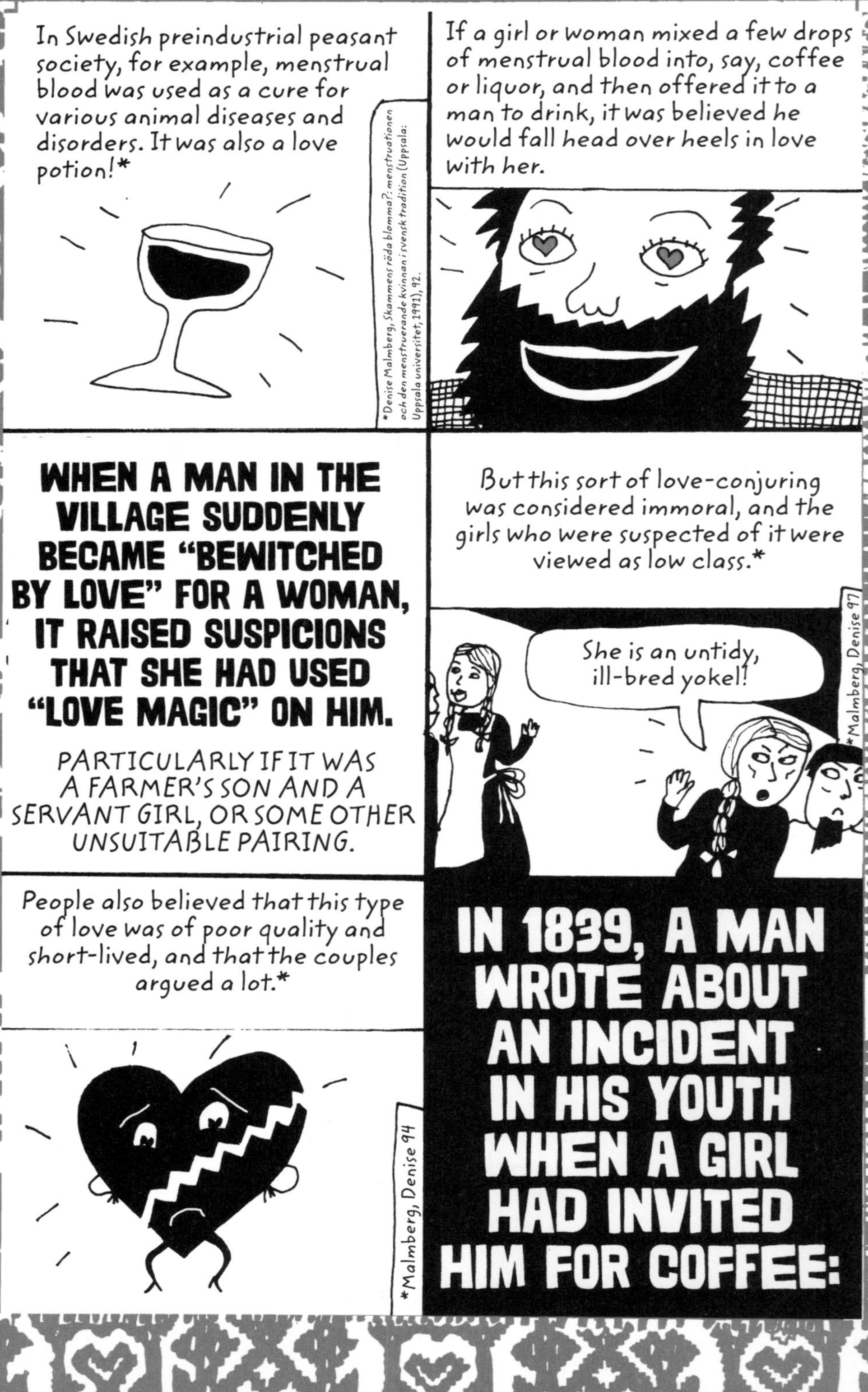
In Swedish preindustrial peasant society, for example, menstrual blood was used as a cure for various animal diseases and disorders. It was also a love potion!*
*Denise Malmberg, Skammens röda blomma?: menstruationen och den menstruerande kvinnan i svensk tradition (Uppsala: Uppsala universitet, 1991), 92.
If a girl or woman mixed a few drops of menstrual blood into, say, coffee or liquor, and then offered it to a man to drink, it was believed he would fall head over heels in love with her.
WHEN A MAN IN THE VILLAGE SUDDENLY BECAME "BEWITCHED BY LOVE" FOR A WOMAN, IT RAISED SUSPICIONS THAT SHE HAD USED "LOVE MAGIC" ON HIM.
PARTICULARLY IF IT WAS A FARMER'S SON AND A SERVANT GIRL, OR SOME OTHER UNSUITABLE PAIRING.
But this sort of love-conjuring was considered immoral, and the girls who were suspected of it were viewed as low class.*
*Malmberg, Denise 97
She is an untidy, ill-bred yokel!
People also believed that this type of love was of poor quality and short-lived, and that the couples argued a lot.*
*Malmberg, Denise 94
IN 1839, A MAN WROTE ABOUT AN INCIDENT IN HIS YOUTH WHEN A GIRL HAD INVITED HIM FOR COFFEE:

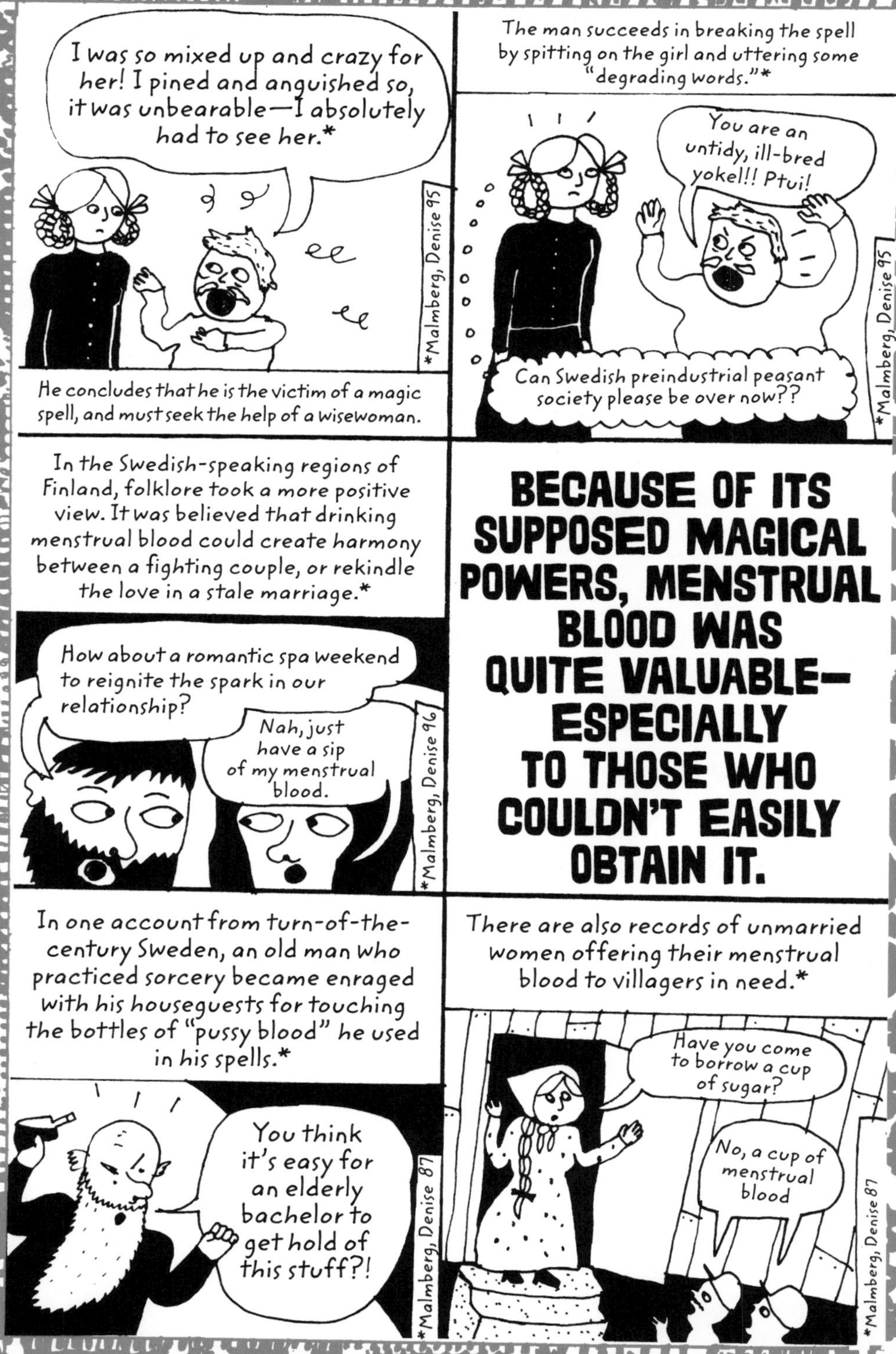
I was so mixed up and crazy for her! I pined and anguished so, it was unbearable—I absolutely had to see her.*
*Malmberg, Denise 95
He concludes that he is the victim of a magic spell, and must seek the help of a wisewoman.
The man succeeds in breaking the spell by spitting on the girl and uttering some "degrading words."*
You are an untidy, ill-bred yokel!! Ptui!
Can Swedish preindustrial peasant society please be over now??
*Malmberg, Denise 95
In the Swedish-speaking regions of Finland, folklore took a more positive view. It was believed that drinking menstrual blood could create harmony between a fighting couple, or rekindle the love in a stale marriage.*
How about a romantic spa weekend to reignite the spark in our relationship?
Nah, just have a sip of my menstrual blood.
*Malmberg, Denise 96
BECAUSE OF ITS SUPPOSED MAGICAL POWERS, MENSTRUAL BLOOD WAS QUITE VALUABLE—ESPECIALLY TO THOSE WHO COULDN'T EASILY OBTAIN IT.
In one account from turn-of-the-century Sweden, an old man who practiced sorcery became enraged with his houseguests for touching the bottles of "pussy blood" he used in his spells.*
You think it's easy for an elderly bachelor to get hold of this stuff?!
*Malmberg, Denise 87
There are also records of unmarried women offering their menstrual blood to villagers in need.*
Have you come to borrow a cup of sugar?
No, a cup of menstrual blood
*Malmberg, Denise 87

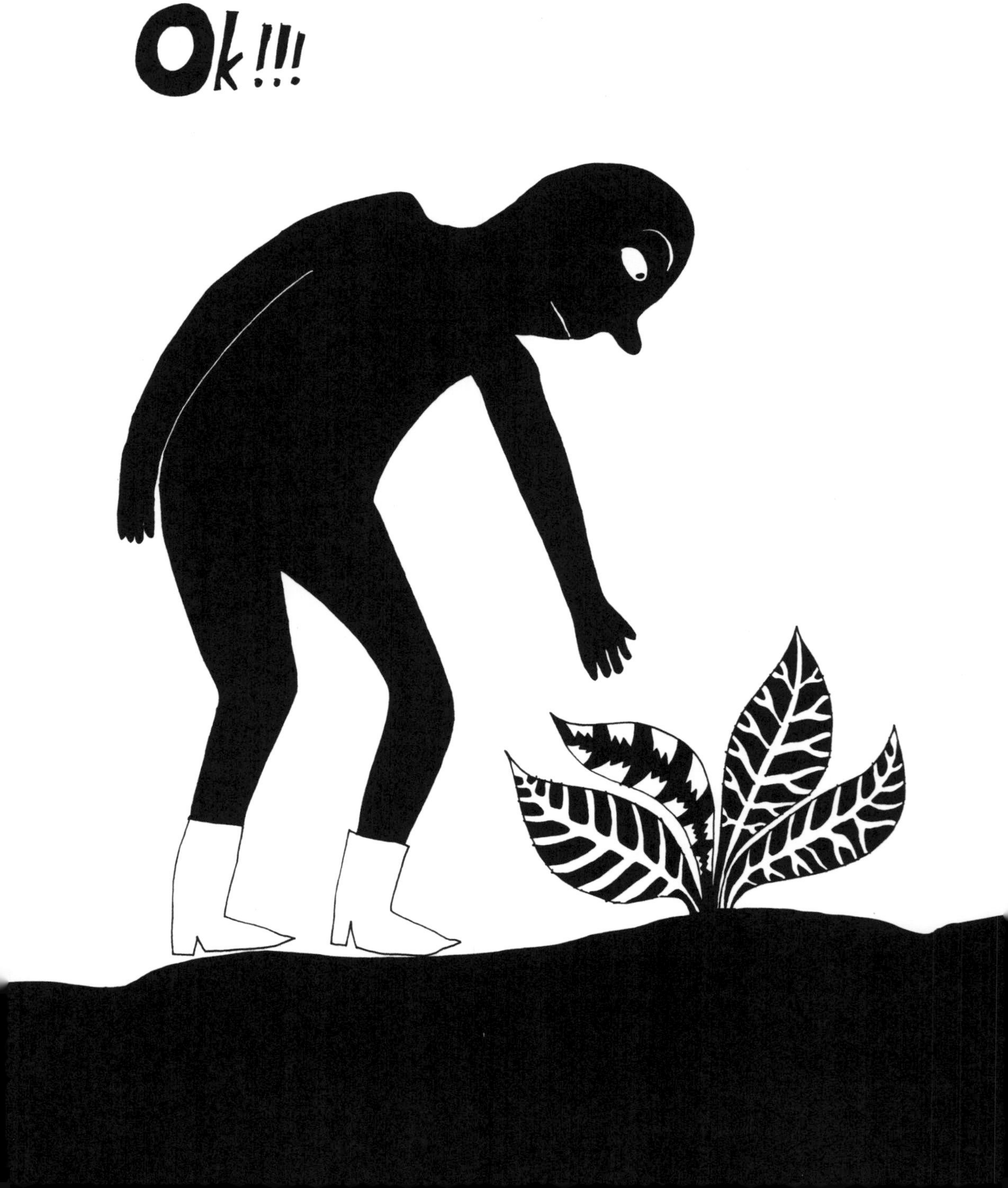
Ok!!!

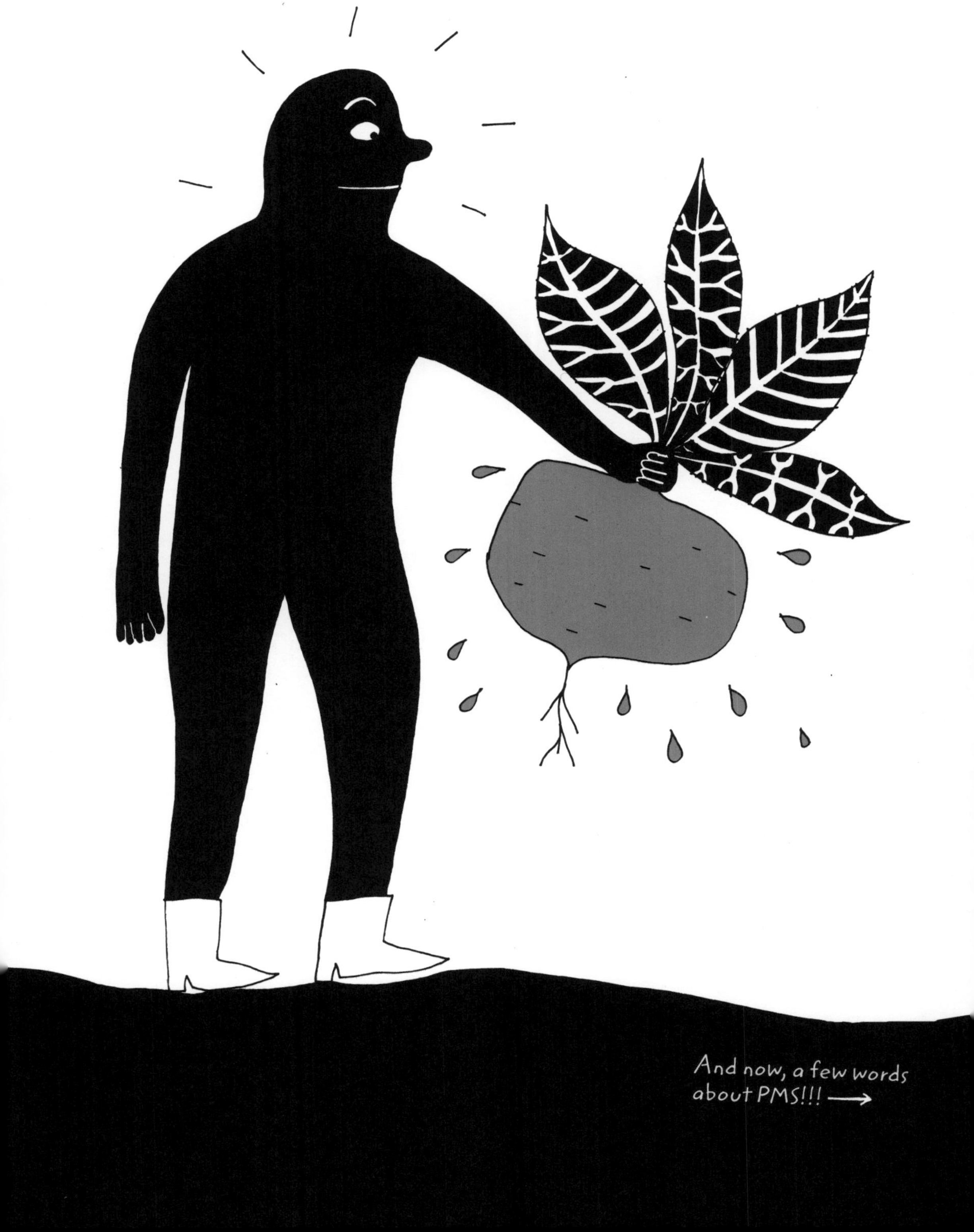
And now, a few words
about PMS!!! →

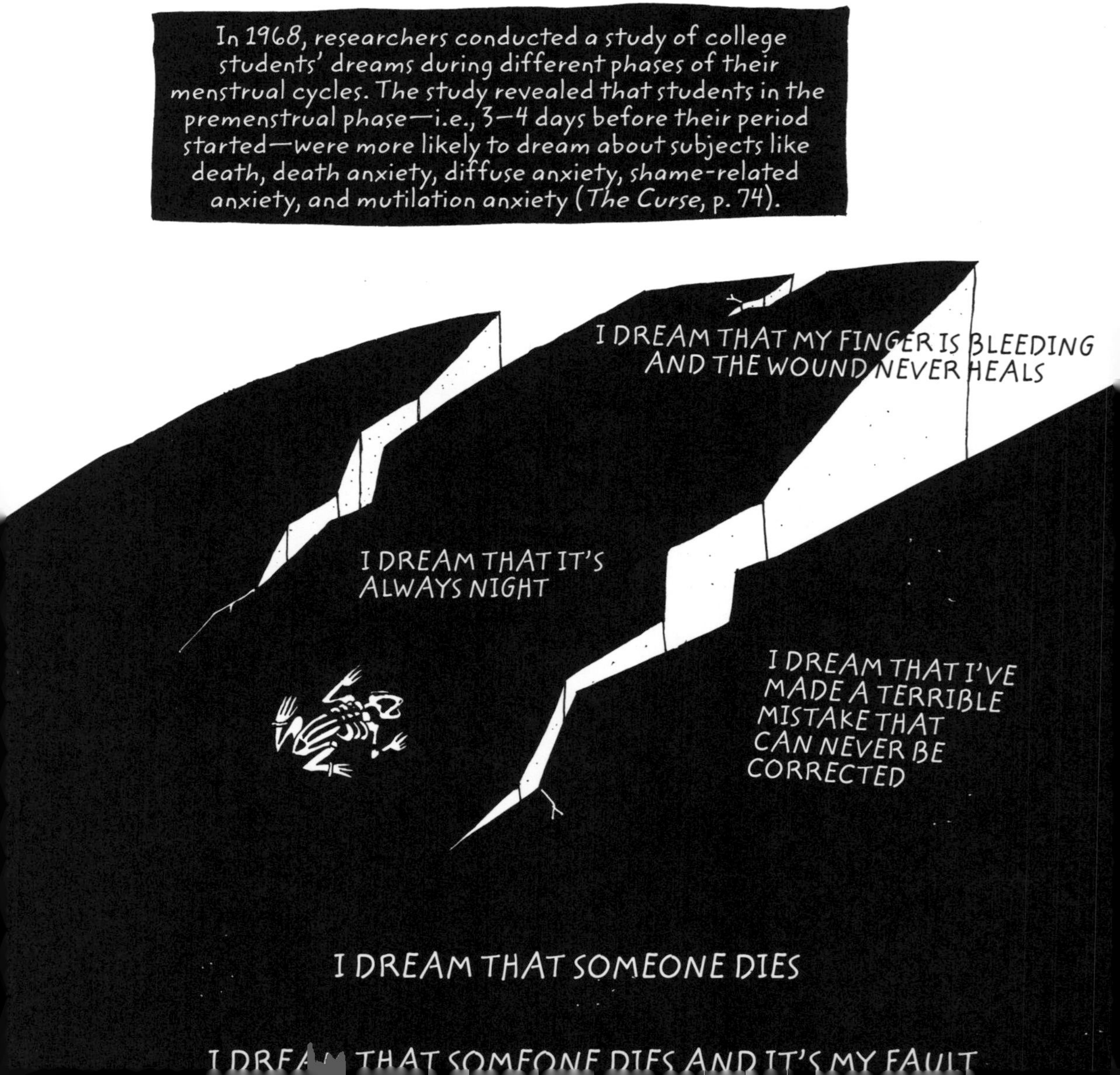
In 1968, researchers conducted a study of college students' dreams during different phases of their menstrual cycles. The study revealed that students in the premenstrual phase—i.e., 3–4 days before their period started—were more likely to dream about subjects like death, death anxiety, diffuse anxiety, shame-related anxiety, and mutilation anxiety (*The Curse*, p. 74).
I DREAM THAT MY FINGER IS BLEEDING AND THE WOUND NEVER HEALS
I DREAM THAT IT'S ALWAYS NIGHT
I DREAM THAT I'VE MADE A TERRIBLE MISTAKE THAT CAN NEVER BE CORRECTED
I DREAM THAT SOMEONE DIES
I DREAM THAT SOMEONE DIES AND IT'S MY FAULT

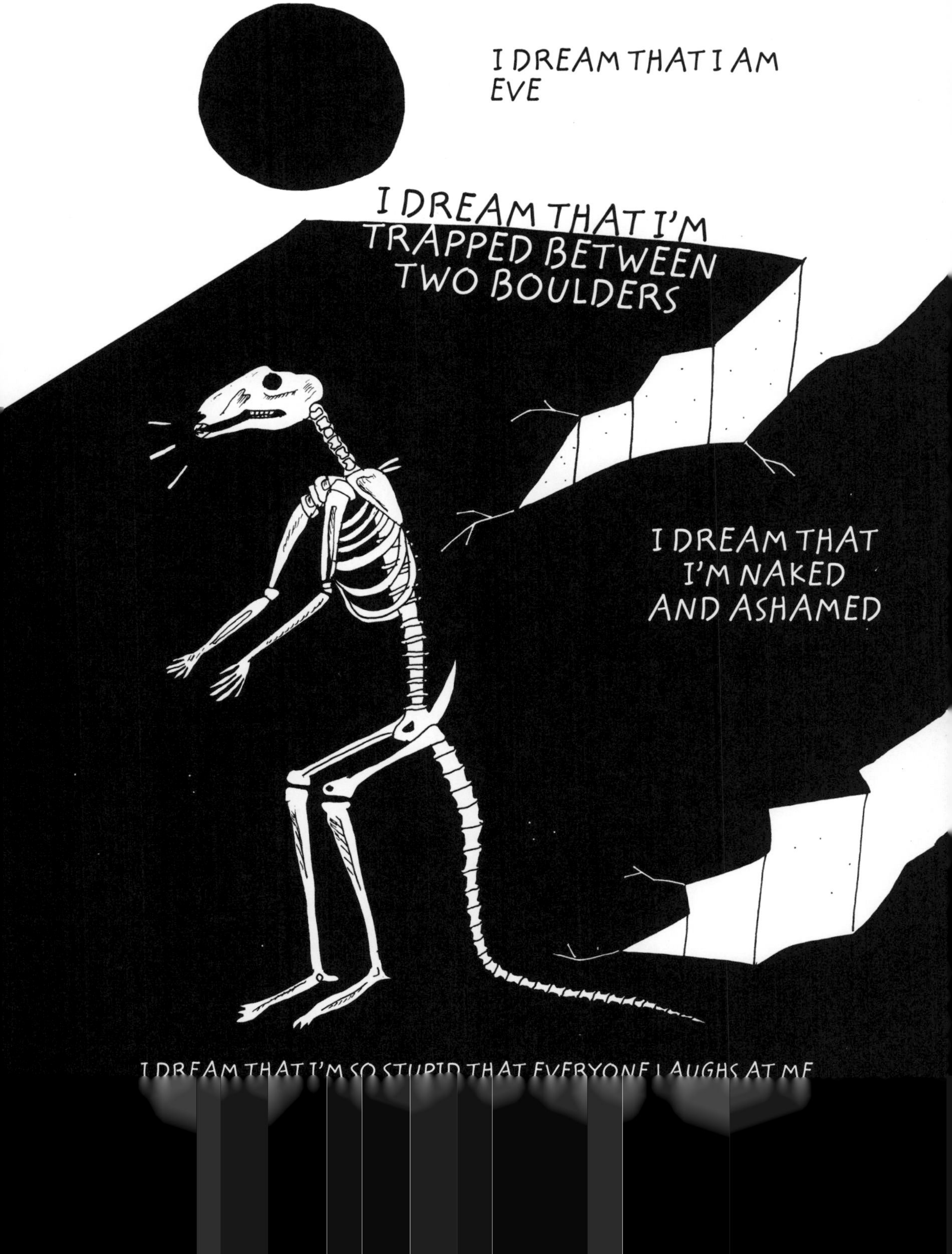
I DREAM THAT I AM EVE
I DREAM THAT I'M TRAPPED BETWEEN TWO BOULDERS
I DREAM THAT I'M NAKED AND ASHAMED
I DREAM THAT I'M SO STUPID THAT EVERYONE LAUGHS AT ME

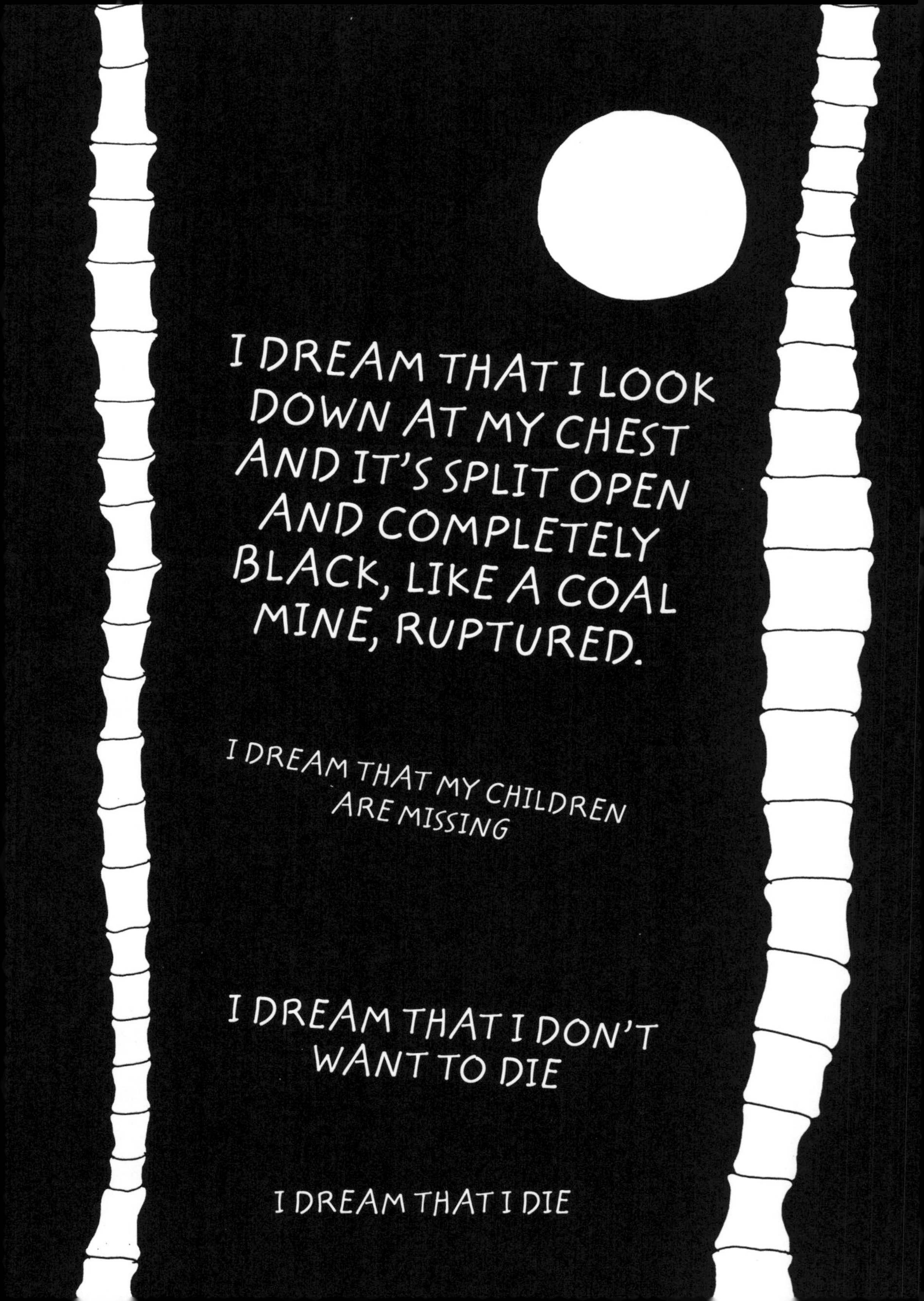
I DREAM THAT I LOOK DOWN AT MY CHEST AND IT'S SPLIT OPEN AND COMPLETELY BLACK, LIKE A COAL MINE, RUPTURED.
I DREAM THAT MY CHILDREN ARE MISSING
I DREAM THAT I DON'T WANT TO DIE
I DREAM THAT I DIE

IN THE STUDY, DREAMS WERE SORTED INTO DIFFERENT "PREMENSTRUAL THEMES." FOR EXAMPLE:

INADEQUACY

i.e., feeling "less than" in some way.

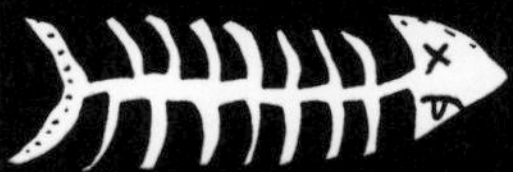

HOSTILITY

i.e., hating something/someone.

I hate it when thunderclouds symbolize anger! It's so goddamned cliché!!

DEATH

i.e. (possibly), feeling a profound existential pain over the transience of creation, a sort of GRIEF over the utter meaninglessness of life.

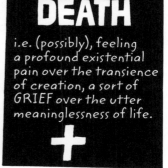

REGARDLESS OF WHAT WE THINK ABOUT THIS STUDY, IF WE JUST LOOK AROUND US WE SEE THAT MANY WOMEN GO THROUGH THESE KINDS OF EMOTIONS IN THE DAYS LEADING UP TO THEIR PERIOD. NOT ALL, BUT MANY.

IT'S AS IF THESE FEW DAYS—FOR SOME WOMEN—OPEN A SORT OF CHANNEL, OR INCREASED SUSCEPTIBILITY, TO THE "DARK SIDE."

FOR SOME WOMEN, THIS PHASE IN THEIR MENSTRUAL CYCLE IS A TIME OF HEIGHTENED SENSITIVITY AND PERCEPTIVENESS—WHICH CAN BE DIFFICULT, OF COURSE, BUT ALSO INTERESTING AND REWARDING, E.G., FROM A CREATIVE STANDPOINT.

I spoke with one musician/songwriter who told me that every month, in the two days just before her period, she has a shitload of anxiety—but she uses those days to write songs, because her creative urge is so strong.

I lead an otherwise very peaceful and happy life, so without that sort of PMS-induced mental anguish, I wouldn't have any drive to create at all.

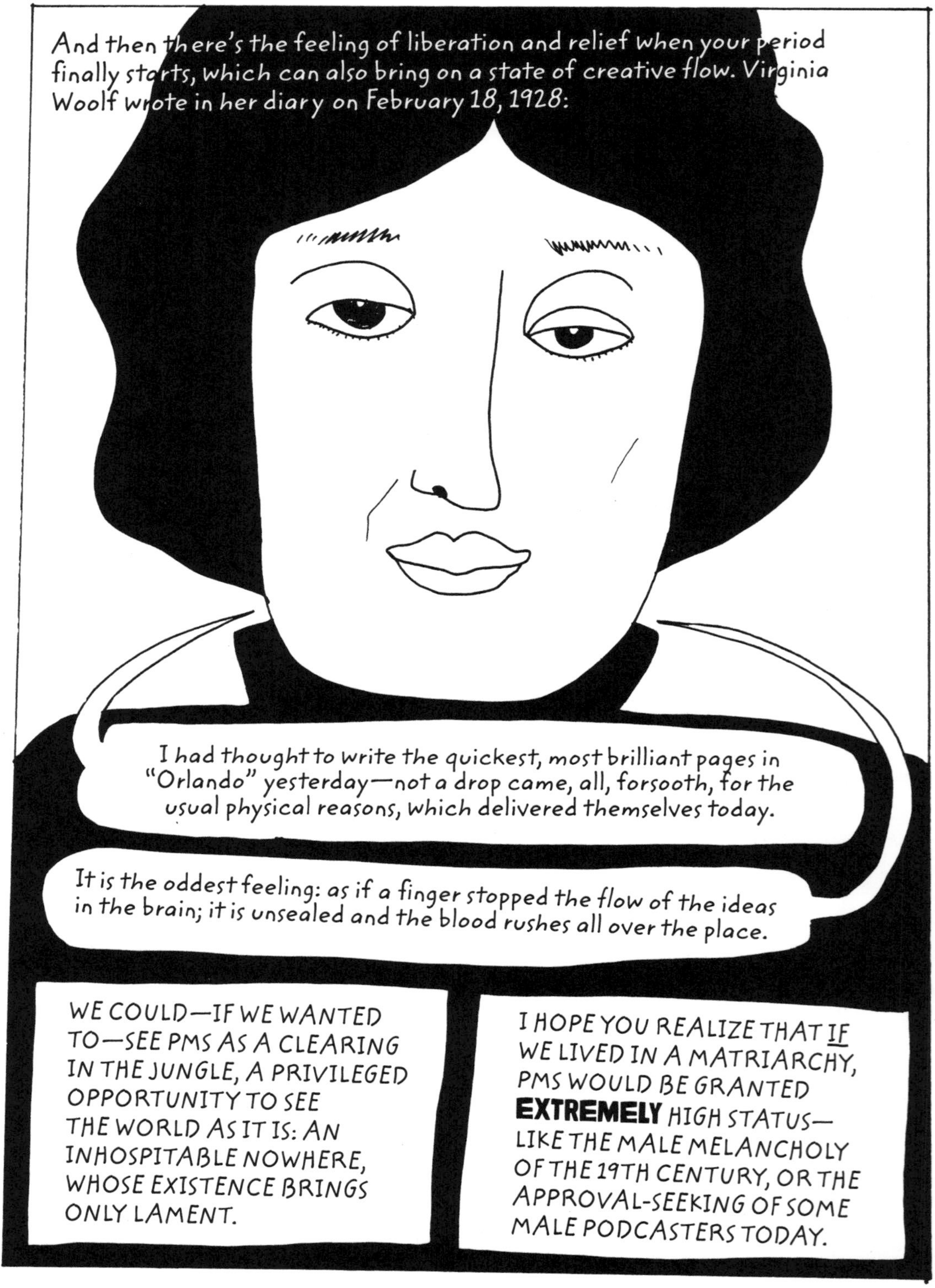
And then there's the feeling of liberation and relief when your period finally starts, which can also bring on a state of creative flow. Virginia Woolf wrote in her diary on February 18, 1928:
I had thought to write the quickest, most brilliant pages in "Orlando" yesterday—not a drop came, all, forsooth, for the usual physical reasons, which delivered themselves today.
It is the oddest feeling: as if a finger stopped the flow of the ideas in the brain; it is unsealed and the blood rushes all over the place.
WE COULD—IF WE WANTED TO—SEE PMS AS A CLEARING IN THE JUNGLE, A PRIVILEGED OPPORTUNITY TO SEE THE WORLD AS IT IS: AN INHOSPITABLE NOWHERE, WHOSE EXISTENCE BRINGS ONLY LAMENT.
I HOPE YOU REALIZE THAT IF WE LIVED IN A MATRIARCHY, PMS WOULD BE GRANTED EXTREMELY HIGH STATUS—LIKE THE MALE MELANCHOLY OF THE 19TH CENTURY, OR THE APPROVAL-SEEKING OF SOME MALE PODCASTERS TODAY.

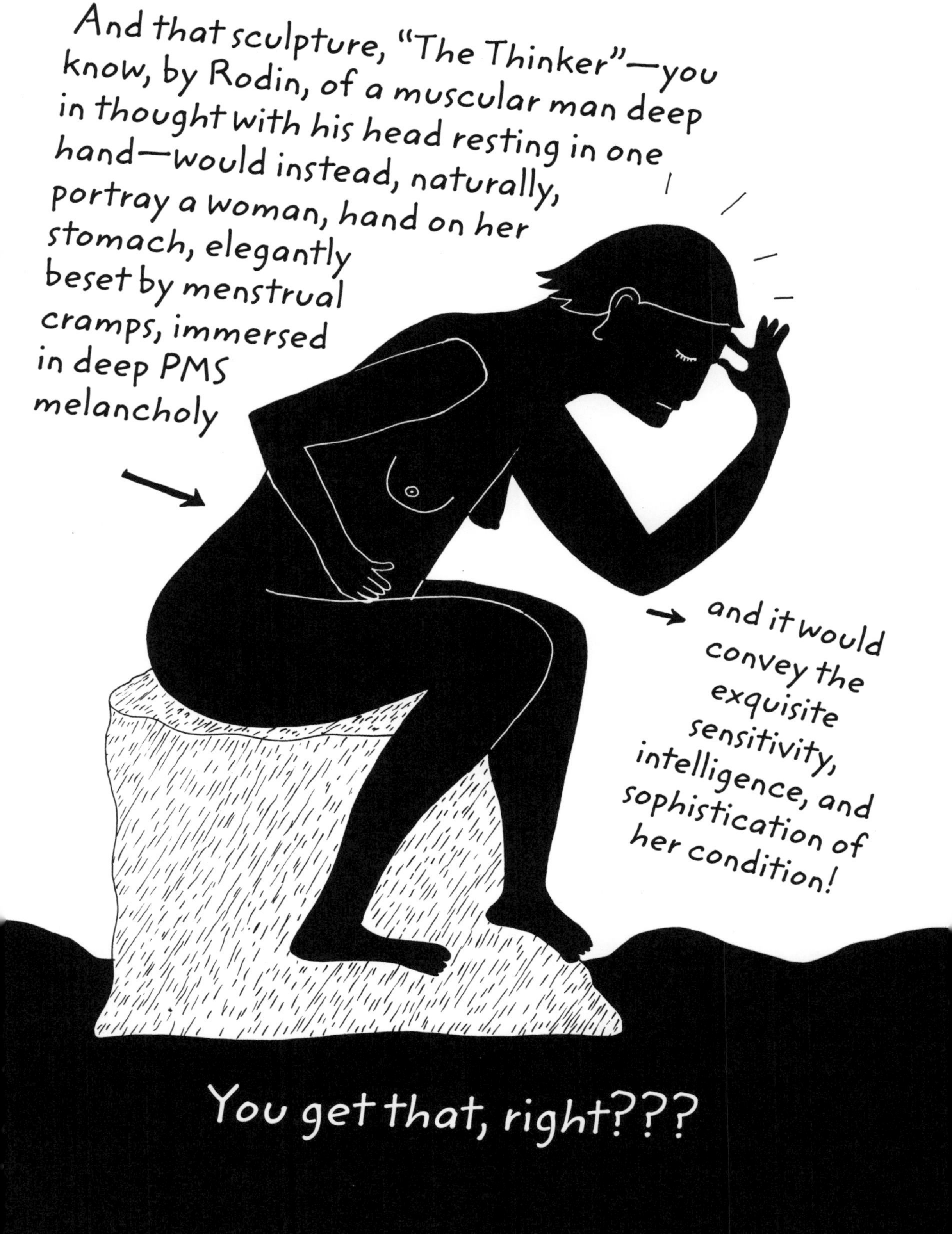
And that sculpture, "The Thinker"—you know, by Rodin, of a muscular man deep in thought with his head resting in one hand—would instead, naturally, portray a woman, hand on her stomach, elegantly beset by menstrual cramps, immersed in deep PMS melancholy
and it would convey the exquisite sensitivity, intelligence, and sophistication of her condition!
You get that, right???

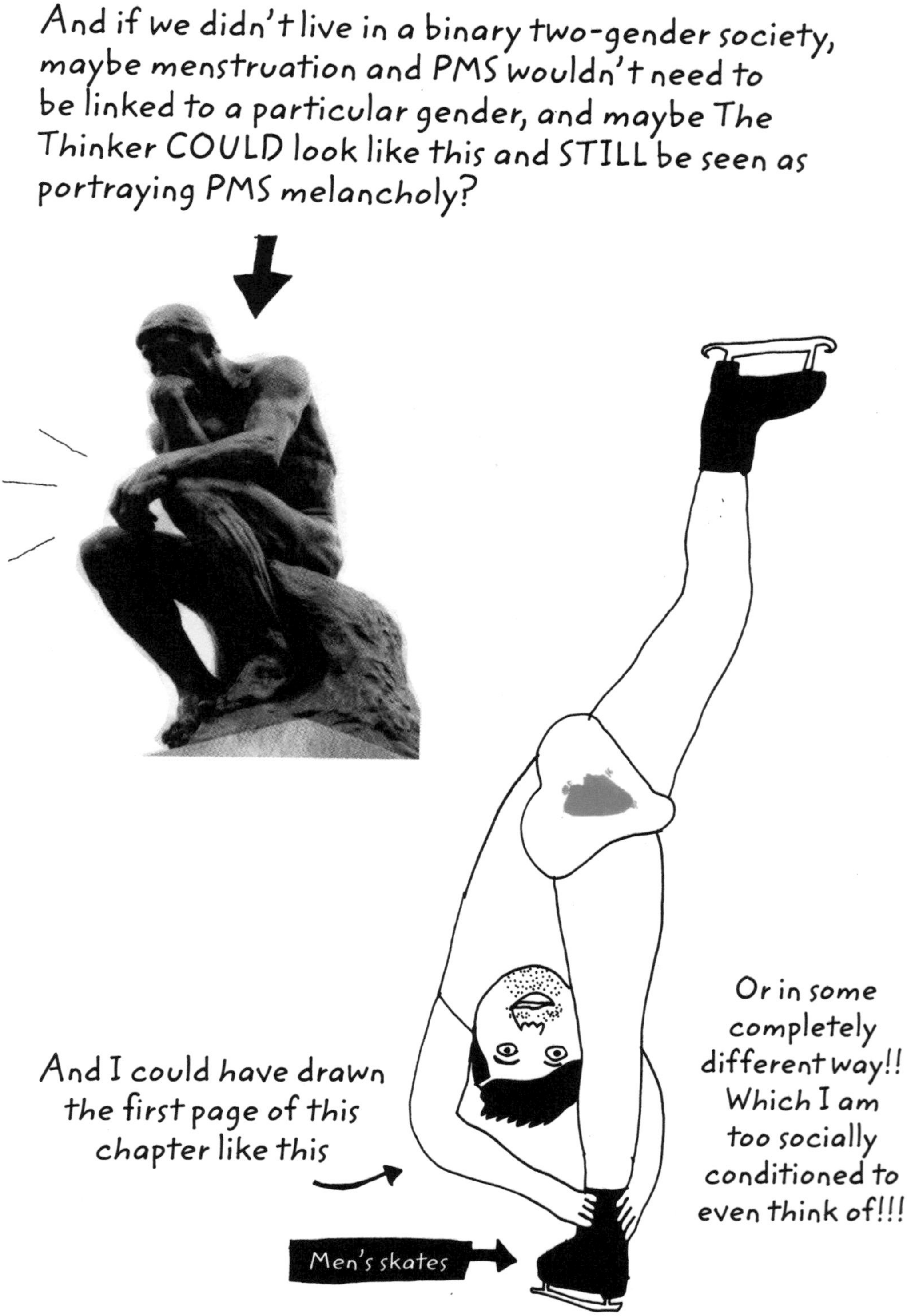
And if we didn't live in a binary two-gender society, maybe menstruation and PMS wouldn't need to be linked to a particular gender, and maybe The Thinker COULD look like this and STILL be seen as portraying PMS melancholy?
And I could have drawn the first page of this chapter like this
Men's skates
Or in some completely different way!! Which I am too socially conditioned to even think of!!!

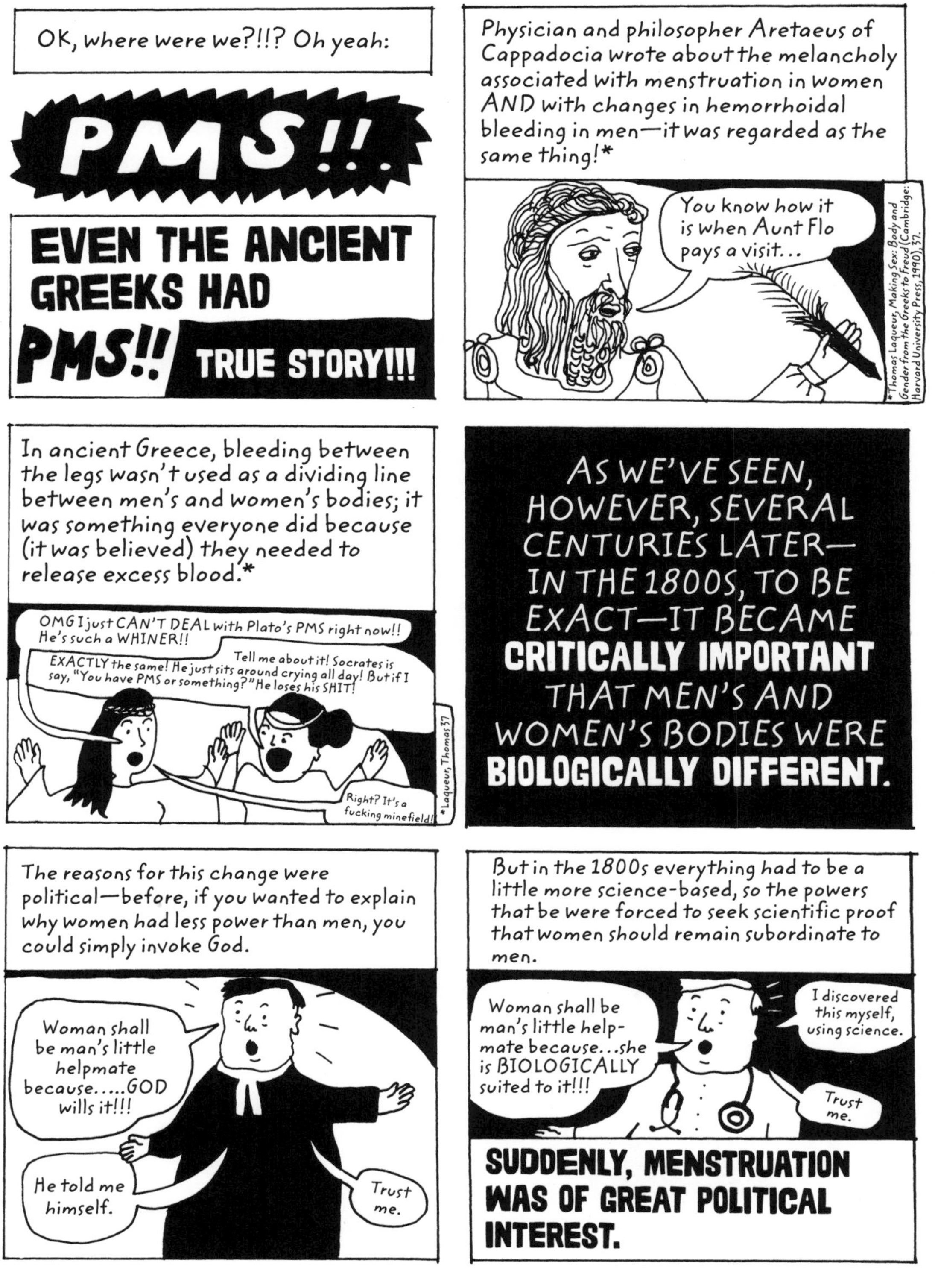

OK, where were we?!!? Oh yeah:
PMS!!
EVEN THE ANCIENT GREEKS HAD PMS!! TRUE STORY!!!
Physician and philosopher Aretaeus of Cappadocia wrote about the melancholy associated with menstruation in women AND with changes in hemorrhoidal bleeding in men—it was regarded as the same thing!*
You know how it is when Aunt Flo pays a visit...
*Thomas Laqueur, Making Sex: Body and Gender from the Greeks to Freud (Cambridge: Harvard University Press, 1990), 37.
In ancient Greece, bleeding between the legs wasn't used as a dividing line between men's and women's bodies; it was something everyone did because (it was believed) they needed to release excess blood.*
OMG I just CAN'T DEAL with Plato's PMS right now!! He's such a WHINER!!
Tell me about it! Socrates is EXACTLY the same! He just sits around crying all day! But if I say, "You have PMS or something?" He loses his SHIT!
Right? It's a fucking minefield!!
*Laqueur, Thomas 37
AS WE'VE SEEN, HOWEVER, SEVERAL CENTURIES LATER—IN THE 1800S, TO BE EXACT—IT BECAME CRITICALLY IMPORTANT THAT MEN'S AND WOMEN'S BODIES WERE BIOLOGICALLY DIFFERENT.
The reasons for this change were political—before, if you wanted to explain why women had less power than men, you could simply invoke God.
Woman shall be man's little helpmate because.....GOD wills it!!!
He told me himself.
Trust me.
But in the 1800s everything had to be a little more science-based, so the powers that be were forced to seek scientific proof that women should remain subordinate to men.
Woman shall be man's little help-mate because...she is BIOLOGICALLY suited to it!!!
I discovered this myself, using science.
Trust me.
SUDDENLY, MENSTRUATION WAS OF GREAT POLITICAL INTEREST.

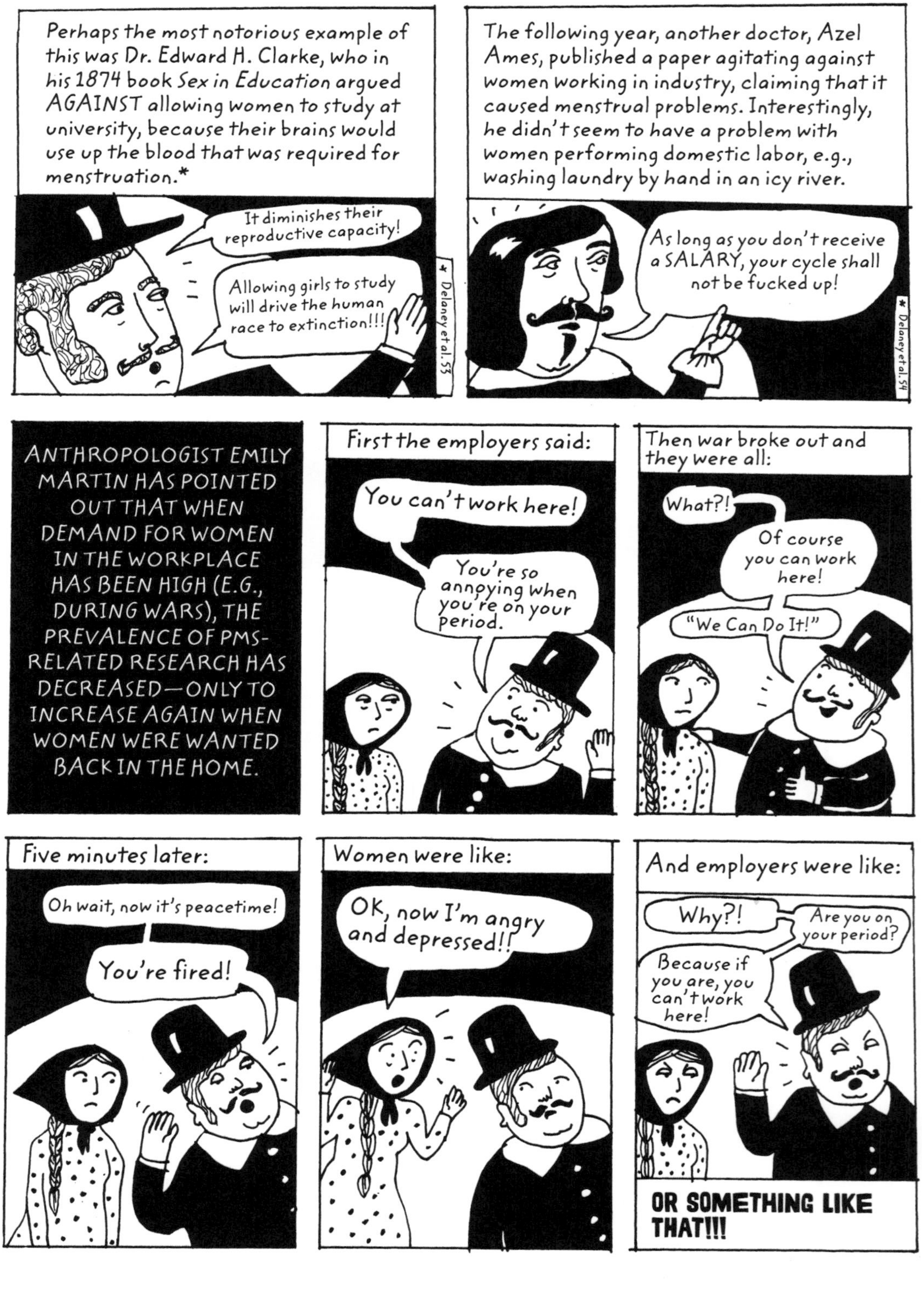
Perhaps the most notorious example of this was Dr. Edward H. Clarke, who in his 1874 book Sex in Education argued AGAINST allowing women to study at university, because their brains would use up the blood that was required for menstruation.*
It diminishes their reproductive capacity!
Allowing girls to study will drive the human race to extinction!!!
* Delaney et al. 53
The following year, another doctor, Azel Ames, published a paper agitating against women working in industry, claiming that it caused menstrual problems. Interestingly, he didn't seem to have a problem with women performing domestic labor, e.g., washing laundry by hand in an icy river.
As long as you don't receive a SALARY, your cycle shall not be fucked up!
* Delaney et al. 54
ANTHROPOLOGIST EMILY MARTIN HAS POINTED OUT THAT WHEN DEMAND FOR WOMEN IN THE WORKPLACE HAS BEEN HIGH (E.G., DURING WARS), THE PREVALENCE OF PMS-RELATED RESEARCH HAS DECREASED—ONLY TO INCREASE AGAIN WHEN WOMEN WERE WANTED BACK IN THE HOME.
First the employers said:
You can't work here!
You're so annoying when you're on your period.
Then war broke out and they were all:
What?!
Of course you can work here!
"We Can Do It!"
Five minutes later:
Oh wait, now it's peacetime!
You're fired!
Women were like:
OK, now I'm angry and depressed!!
And employers were like:
Why?!
Are you on your period?
Because if you are, you can't work here!
OR SOMETHING LIKE THAT!!!

Oddly enough, I haven't found one researcher or doctor in history who has concluded, for example, that women's dangerous mood swings make them unfit to care for children.

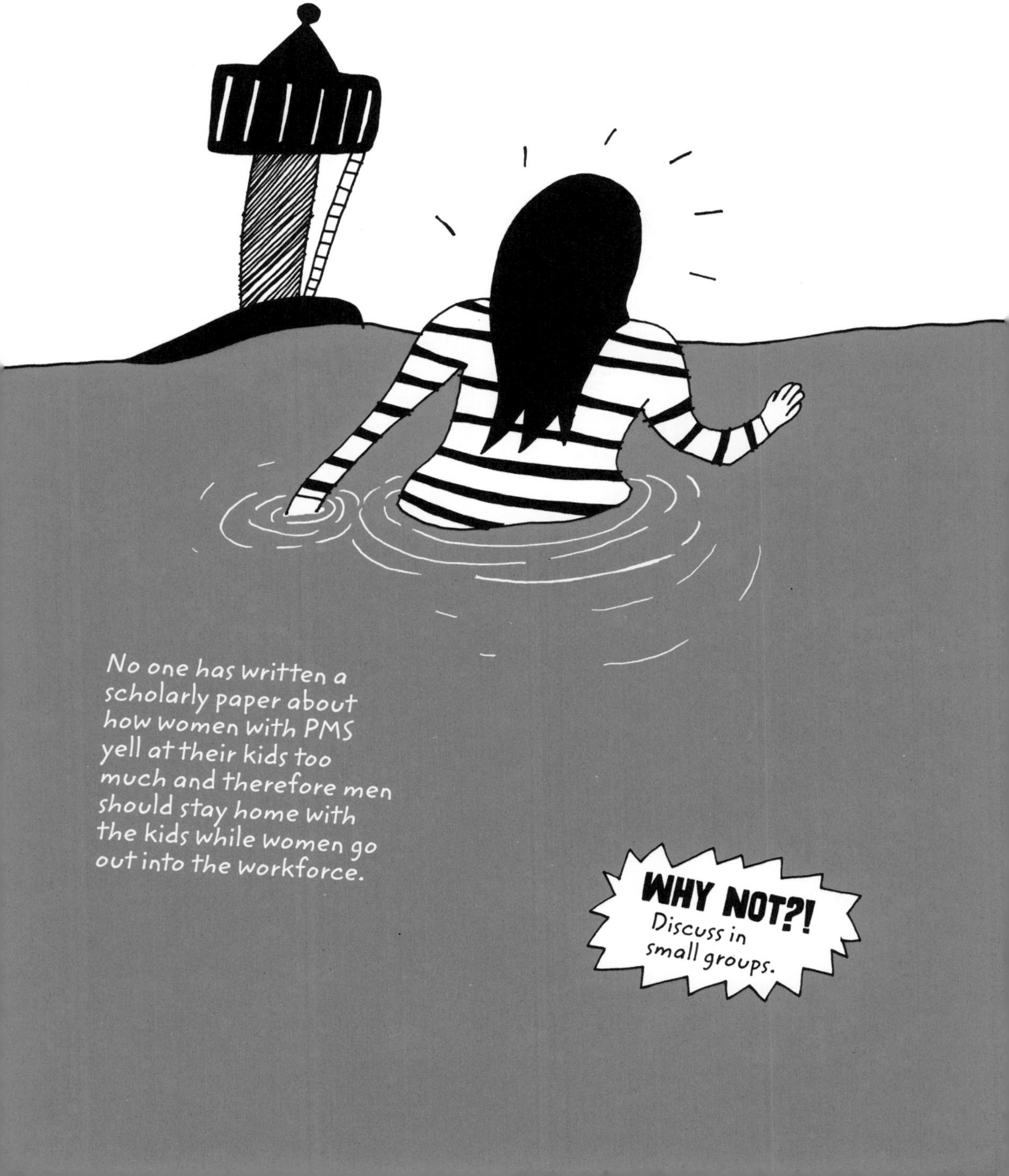
No one has written a scholarly paper about how women with PMS yell at their kids too much and therefore men should stay home with the kids while women go out into the workforce.
WHY NOT?!
Discuss in small groups.

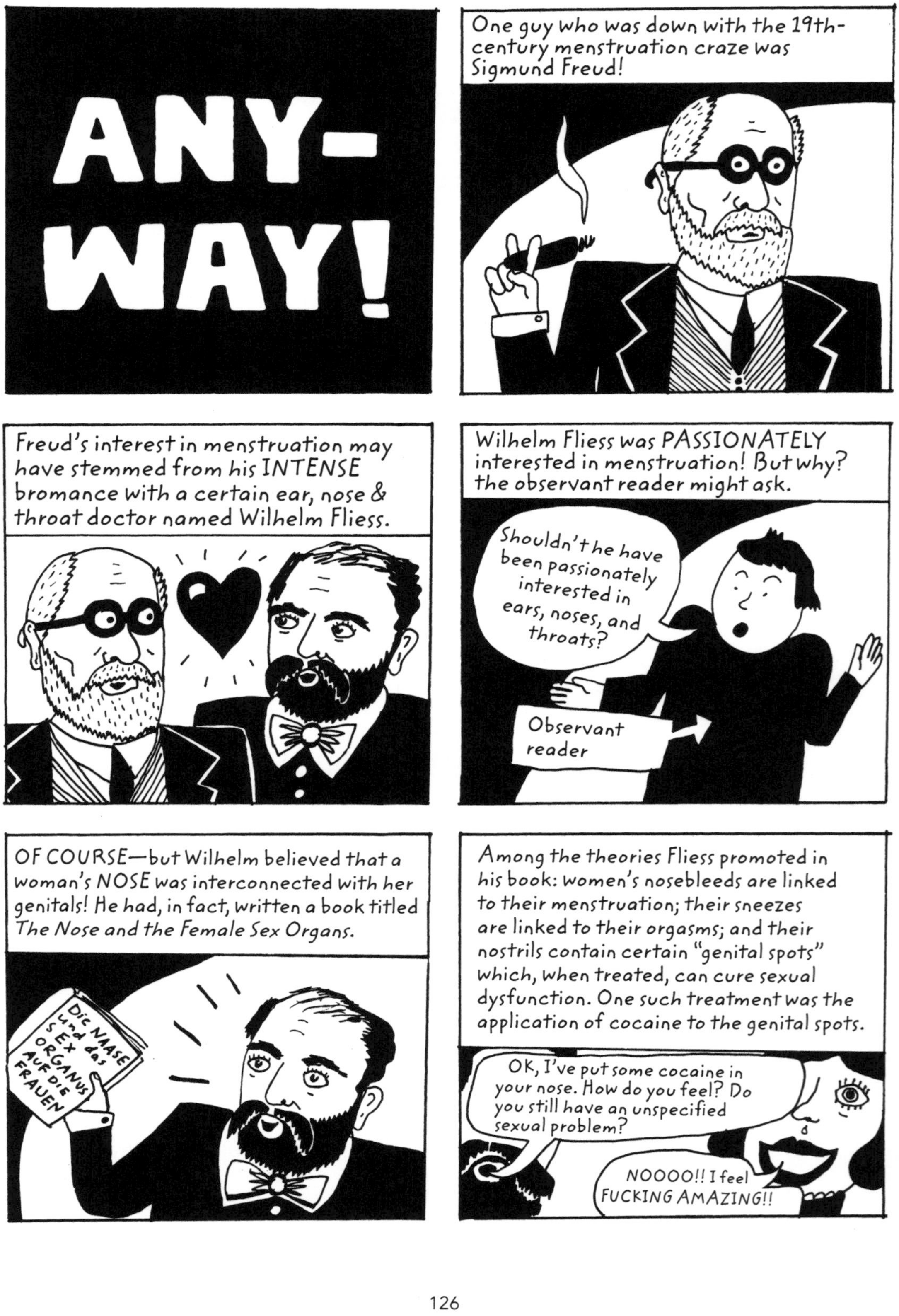
ANY-WAY!
One guy who was down with the 19th-century menstruation craze was Sigmund Freud!
Freud's interest in menstruation may have stemmed from his INTENSE bromance with a certain ear, nose & throat doctor named Wilhelm Fliess.
Wilhelm Fliess was PASSIONATELY interested in menstruation! But why? the observant reader might ask.
Shouldn't he have been passionately interested in ears, noses, and throats?
Observant reader
OF COURSE—but Wilhelm believed that a woman's NOSE was interconnected with her genitals! He had, in fact, written a book titled *The Nose and the Female Sex Organs.*
Die NAASE und das SEX ORGANUS AUF DIE FRAUEN
Among the theories Fliess promoted in his book: women's nosebleeds are linked to their menstruation; their sneezes are linked to their orgasms; and their nostrils contain certain "genital spots" which, when treated, can cure sexual dysfunction. One such treatment was the application of cocaine to the genital spots.
OK, I've put some cocaine in your nose. How do you feel? Do you still have an unspecified sexual problem?
NOOOO!! I feel FUCKING AMAZING!!

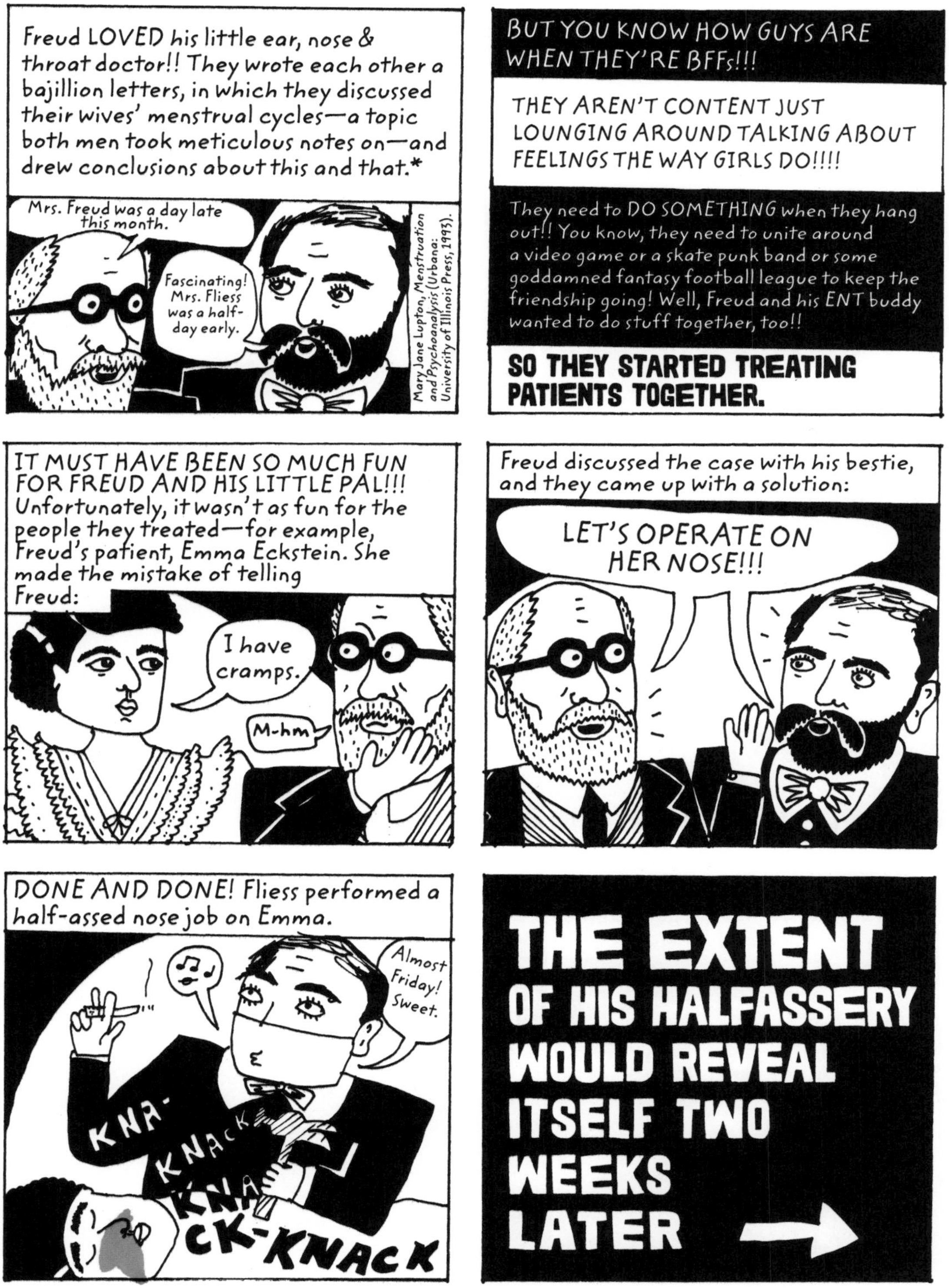
Freud LOVED his little ear, nose & throat doctor!! They wrote each other a bajillion letters, in which they discussed their wives' menstrual cycles—a topic both men took meticulous notes on—and drew conclusions about this and that.*
Mrs. Freud was a day late this month.
Fascinating! Mrs. Fliess was a half-day early.
Mary Jane Lupton, Menstruation and Psychoanalysis (Urbana: University of Illinois Press, 1993).
BUT YOU KNOW HOW GUYS ARE WHEN THEY'RE BFFs!!!
THEY AREN'T CONTENT JUST LOUNGING AROUND TALKING ABOUT FEELINGS THE WAY GIRLS DO!!!!
They need to DO SOMETHING when they hang out!! You know, they need to unite around a video game or a skate punk band or some goddamned fantasy football league to keep the friendship going! Well, Freud and his ENT buddy wanted to do stuff together, too!!
SO THEY STARTED TREATING PATIENTS TOGETHER.
IT MUST HAVE BEEN SO MUCH FUN FOR FREUD AND HIS LITTLE PAL!!! Unfortunately, it wasn't as fun for the people they treated—for example, Freud's patient, Emma Eckstein. She made the mistake of telling Freud:
I have cramps.
M-hm
Freud discussed the case with his bestie, and they came up with a solution:
LET'S OPERATE ON HER NOSE!!!
DONE AND DONE! Fliess performed a half-assed nose job on Emma.
Almost Friday! Sweet.
KNA-KNACK
KNACK
KNA-CK-KNACK
THE EXTENT OF HIS HALFASSERY WOULD REVEAL ITSELF TWO WEEKS LATER

...when Emma's nose swelled up and started gushing blood!

IT TURNED OUT THAT FLIESS HAD LEFT A BIT OF GAUZE INSIDE EMMA'S NOSE — which caused several life-threatening hemorrhages!!!!

Emma was treated by a different doctor and her life was saved. In a letter to Fliess, Freud wrote:

I can give you a report on Miss Eckstein which will probably upset you as much as it did me.

But I hope you will get over it as quickly as I did!*

*Lupton, Mary Jane 22

Here's how Freud explained the cause of Emma's hemorrhages:

Her hemorrhages were hysterical, brought on by longing, probably at the "sexual period."*

*Lupton, Mary Jane 23

He elaborated in a longer letter to Fliess in 1896:

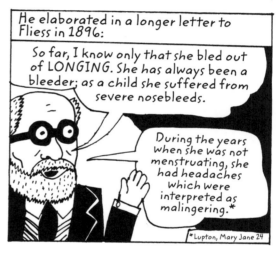

So far, I know only that she bled out of LONGING. She has always been a bleeder; as a child she suffered from severe nosebleeds.

During the years when she was not menstruating, she had headaches which were interpreted as malingering.*

*Lupton, Mary Jane 24

As far as the blood is concerned, you are completely without blame!*

*Lupton, Mary Jane 25

SO, ALL'S WELL THAT ENDS WELL!!

Except, of course, for Emma Eckstein's face, which had caved in on one side, leaving her permanently disfigured.

P.S. I still have cramps.

OK! Let's go back to a question I asked at the beginning of the chapter, i.e., why advertisements for pads and tampons so often use the word fresh

fresh
fresh
fresh
fresh
fresh
fresh
fresh
fresh
fresh
fresh
fresh
fresh
fresh
fresh
fresh
fresh
fresh
fresh
fresh
fresh
fresh
fresh
fresh
fresh
fresh
fresh
fresh
fresh
fresh
fresh
fresh fresh
fresh
fresh
fresh
fresh
fresh
fresh
fresh
fresh
fresh
fresh
fresh
fresh
fresh
fresh
fresh
fresh
fresh
fresh
fresh
fresh
fresh
fresh
fresh
fresh
fresh
fresh
fresh
fresh
fresh
fresh
fresh
fresh
fresh
fresh
fresh
fresh
fresh
fresh
fresh
fresh
fresh
fresh
fresh

That is, why these companies portray their products as "fresh" while portraying menstruation as the opposite of fresh—as something filthy, something **IN NEED OF** freshness. ➡

Of course, as we've seen, this is a product of our patriarchal history. But it's also clearly supported by (or goes hand in hand with) a strong desire in our society to sell single-use, disposable menstrual products.

Just like deodorant or lip balm, panty liners are a way to take care of yourself every day.

BUT BEHIND ALL THE TALK ABOUT "FRESH" AND "CLEAN," THERE'S A PRETTY GLARING PARADOX.

The material in sanitary pads is about 90% plastic—which stays in our environment forever and never breaks down.

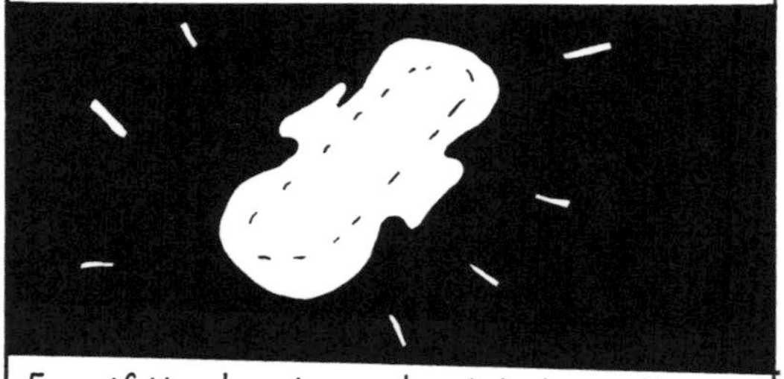

Even if they're chopped up into teeny tiny pieces, they'll continue to pollute our streams and the soil where we grow our food.

If plastic is burned, it releases dioxins into the air which end up contaminating bodies of water.

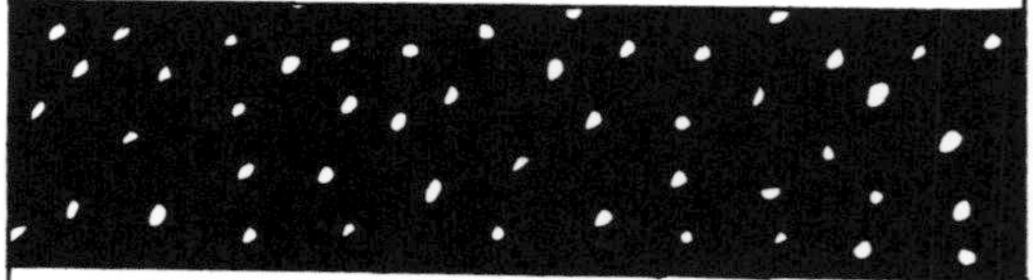

OVER 90 MILLION PADS AND PANTY LINERS ARE BURNED IN INCINERATORS OR BURIED IN LANDFILLS IN SCANDINAVIA EVERY YEAR. (www.ekohygien.se)

So instead of "A clean, fresh feeling every day," a more accurate slogan for these products might be:

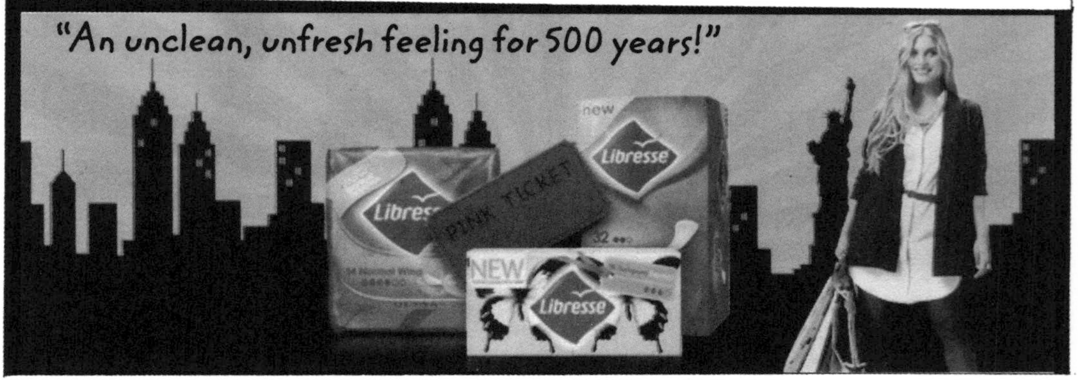
"An unclean, unfresh feeling for 500 years!"
Libresse
PINK TICKET
NEW

MAYBE THE UNRELENTING USE OF THE WORD "FRESH" TO DESCRIBE MENSTRUAL PRODUCTS CAN BE EXPLAINED BY THE PSYCHOLOGICAL THEORY OF PROJECTION.

Projection, as we all know, is a self-defense mechanism in which a person denies their own weaknesses and instead ascribes them to someone else in order to preserve their own self-image.

"IT'S YOUR PERIOD THAT'S UNFRESH! OUR PRODUCTS EMBODY FRESHNESS!" these companies insist—because in reality, the opposite is true.

Try a reusable option instead, e.g., a menstrual cup. Google for info.

OK!

JUST ONE MORE THING ABOUT MEN-STRUATION →

YOU MIGHT BE DISHEARTENED TO REALIZE THAT MENSTRUATION—AS A PHENOMENON, AN EXPERIENCE, AN EXISTENTIAL OR ARTISTIC THEME—IS ESSENTIALLY ERASED FROM OUR CULTURE, AND THAT EXPERIENCES OF MENSTRUATION ARE SELDOM REPRESENTED IN THE PUBLIC SPACE.

But psychoanalyst Bruno Bettelheim says there are tons of hidden, symbolic representations of menstruation in our culture!

Hello again!

There are tons of hidden, symbolic representations of menstruation in our culture!

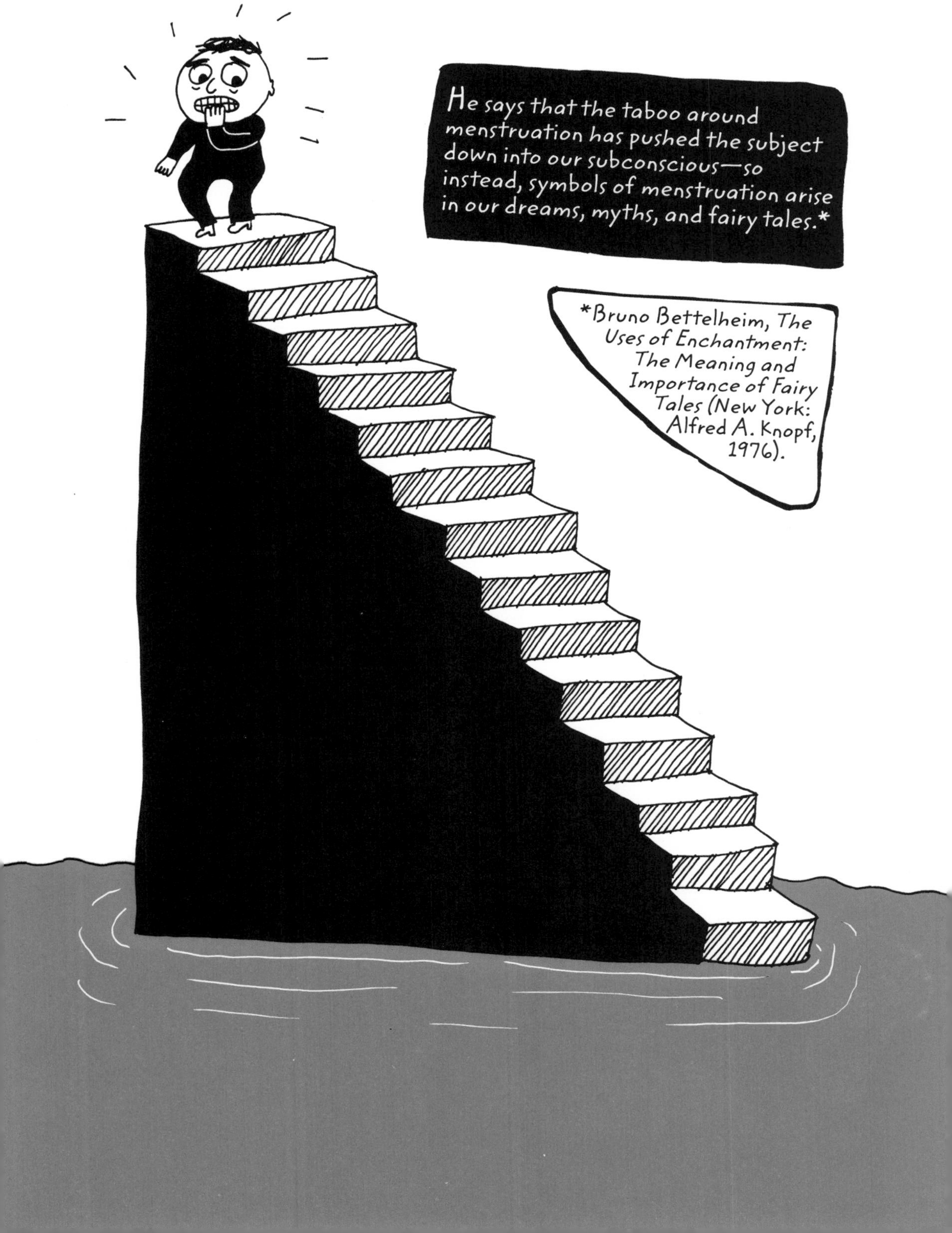
He says that the taboo around menstruation has pushed the subject down into our subconscious—so instead, symbols of menstruation arise in our dreams, myths, and fairy tales.*
*Bruno Bettelheim, The Uses of Enchantment: The Meaning and Importance of Fairy Tales (New York: Alfred A. Knopf, 1976).

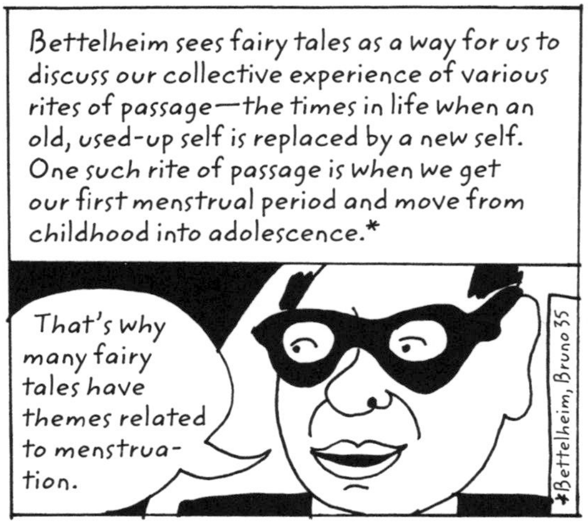
Bettelheim sees fairy tales as a way for us to discuss our collective experience of various rites of passage—the times in life when an old, used-up self is replaced by a new self. One such rite of passage is when we get our first menstrual period and move from childhood into adolescence.*
That's why many fairy tales have themes related to menstruation.
*Bettelheim, Bruno 35

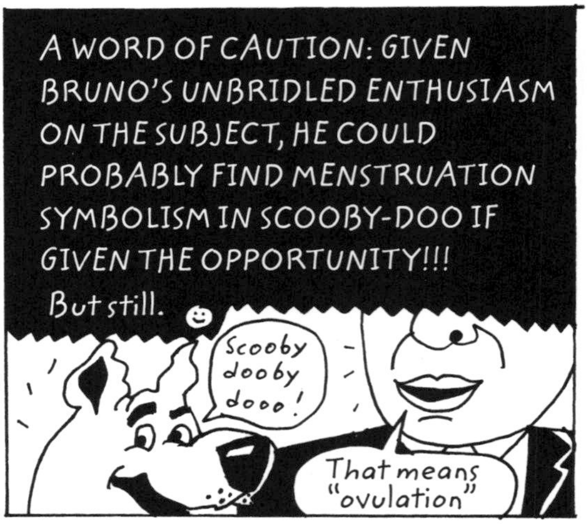
A WORD OF CAUTION: GIVEN BRUNO'S UNBRIDLED ENTHUSIASM ON THE SUBJECT, HE COULD PROBABLY FIND MENSTRUATION SYMBOLISM IN SCOOBY-DOO IF GIVEN THE OPPORTUNITY!!! But still.
Scooby dooby dooo!
That means "ovulation"

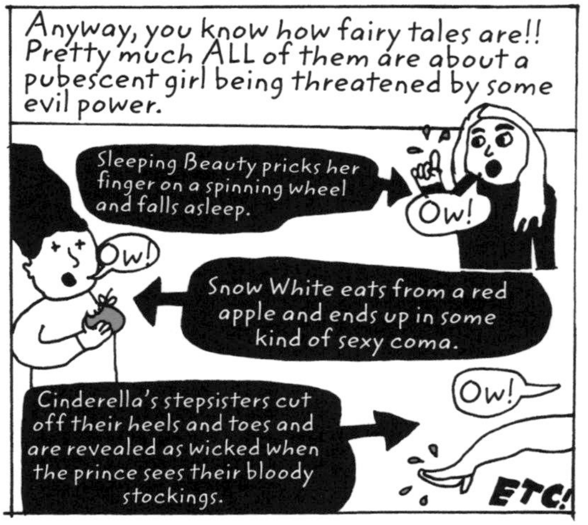
Anyway, you know how fairy tales are!! Pretty much ALL of them are about a pubescent girl being threatened by some evil power.
Sleeping Beauty pricks her finger on a spinning wheel and falls asleep.
Ow!
Ow!
Snow White eats from a red apple and ends up in some kind of sexy coma.
Cinderella's stepsisters cut off their heels and toes and are revealed as wicked when the prince sees their bloody stockings.
Ow!
ETC!

Now, personally, I'm most interested in the sexy-coma situation—and in what traditionally follows; i.e., a guy MAKING OUT with a girl who's in a sexy coma. Why is our culture so enamored with this Julian Assange motif?? SO ENAMORED THAT WE'VE KEPT IT ALIVE VIA ORAL TRADITION FOR HUNDREDS OF GENERATIONS???

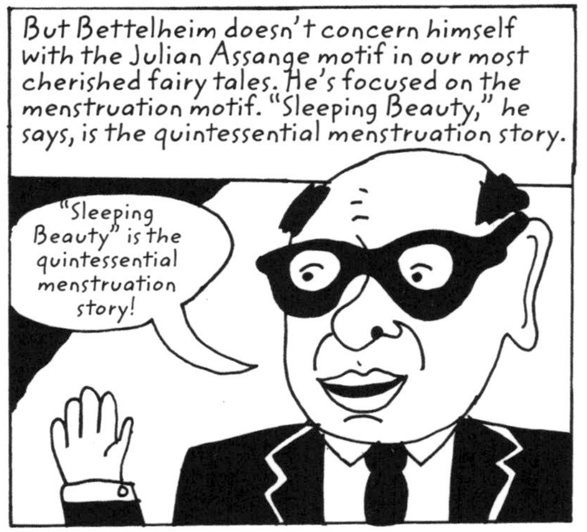
But Bettelheim doesn't concern himself with the Julian Assange motif in our most cherished fairy tales. He's focused on the menstruation motif. "Sleeping Beauty," he says, is the quintessential menstruation story.
"Sleeping Beauty" is the quintessential menstruation story!

BUT WHY IS SLEEPING BEAUTY THE QUINTESSENTIAL MENSTRUATION STORY ?????

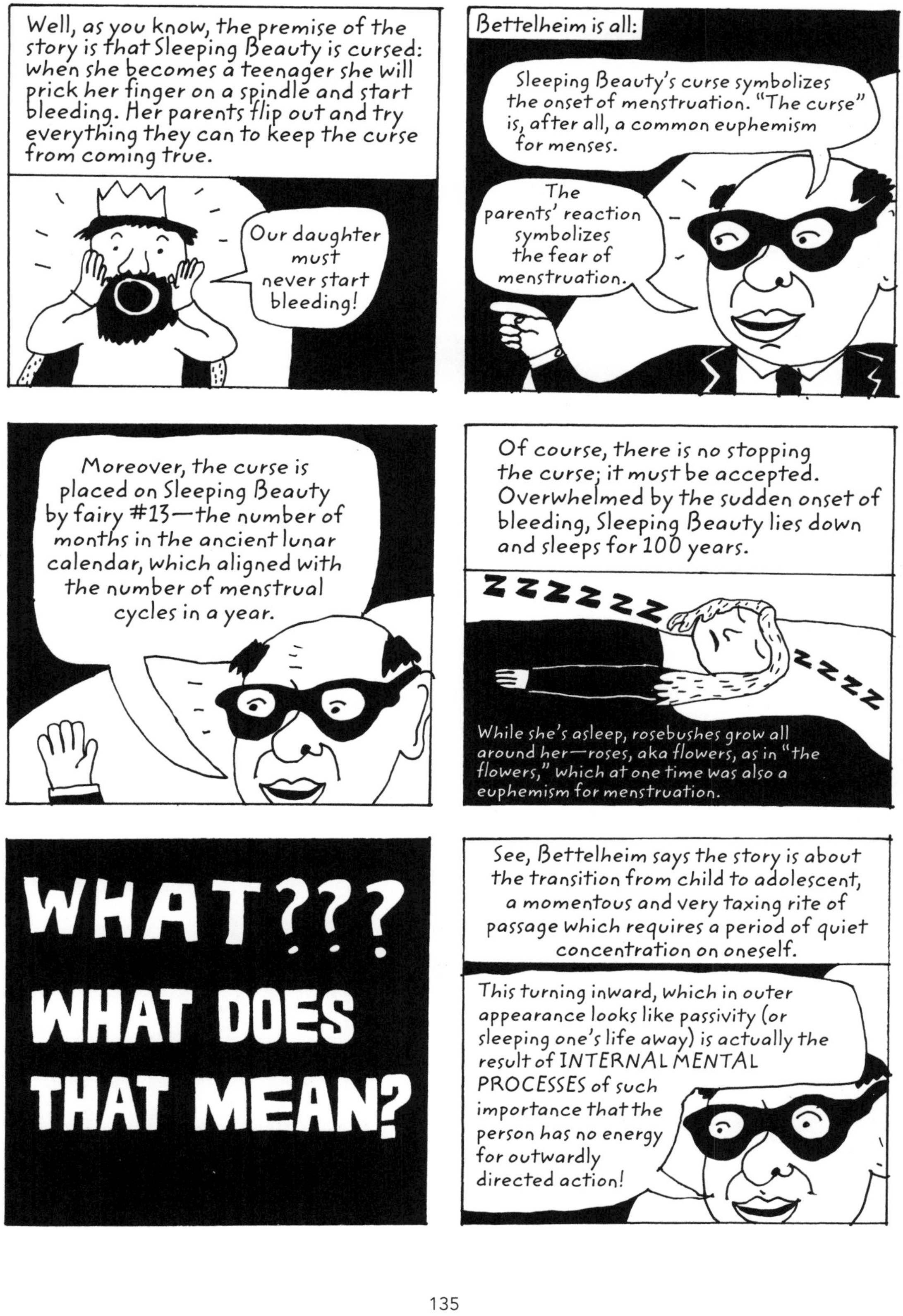
Well, as you know, the premise of the story is that Sleeping Beauty is cursed: when she becomes a teenager she will prick her finger on a spindle and start bleeding. Her parents flip out and try everything they can to keep the curse from coming true.
Our daughter must never start bleeding!
Bettelheim is all:
Sleeping Beauty's curse symbolizes the onset of menstruation. "The curse" is, after all, a common euphemism for menses.
The parents' reaction symbolizes the fear of menstruation.
Moreover, the curse is placed on Sleeping Beauty by fairy #13—the number of months in the ancient lunar calendar, which aligned with the number of menstrual cycles in a year.
Of course, there is no stopping the curse; it must be accepted. Overwhelmed by the sudden onset of bleeding, Sleeping Beauty lies down and sleeps for 100 years.
ZZZZZZZ
ZZZZ
While she's asleep, rosebushes grow all around her—roses, aka flowers, as in "the flowers," which at one time was also a euphemism for menstruation.
WHAT???
WHAT DOES THAT MEAN?
See, Bettelheim says the story is about the transition from child to adolescent, a momentous and very taxing rite of passage which requires a period of quiet concentration on oneself.
This turning inward, which in outer appearance looks like passivity (or sleeping one's life away) is actually the result of INTERNAL MENTAL PROCESSES of such importance that the person has no energy for outwardly directed action!

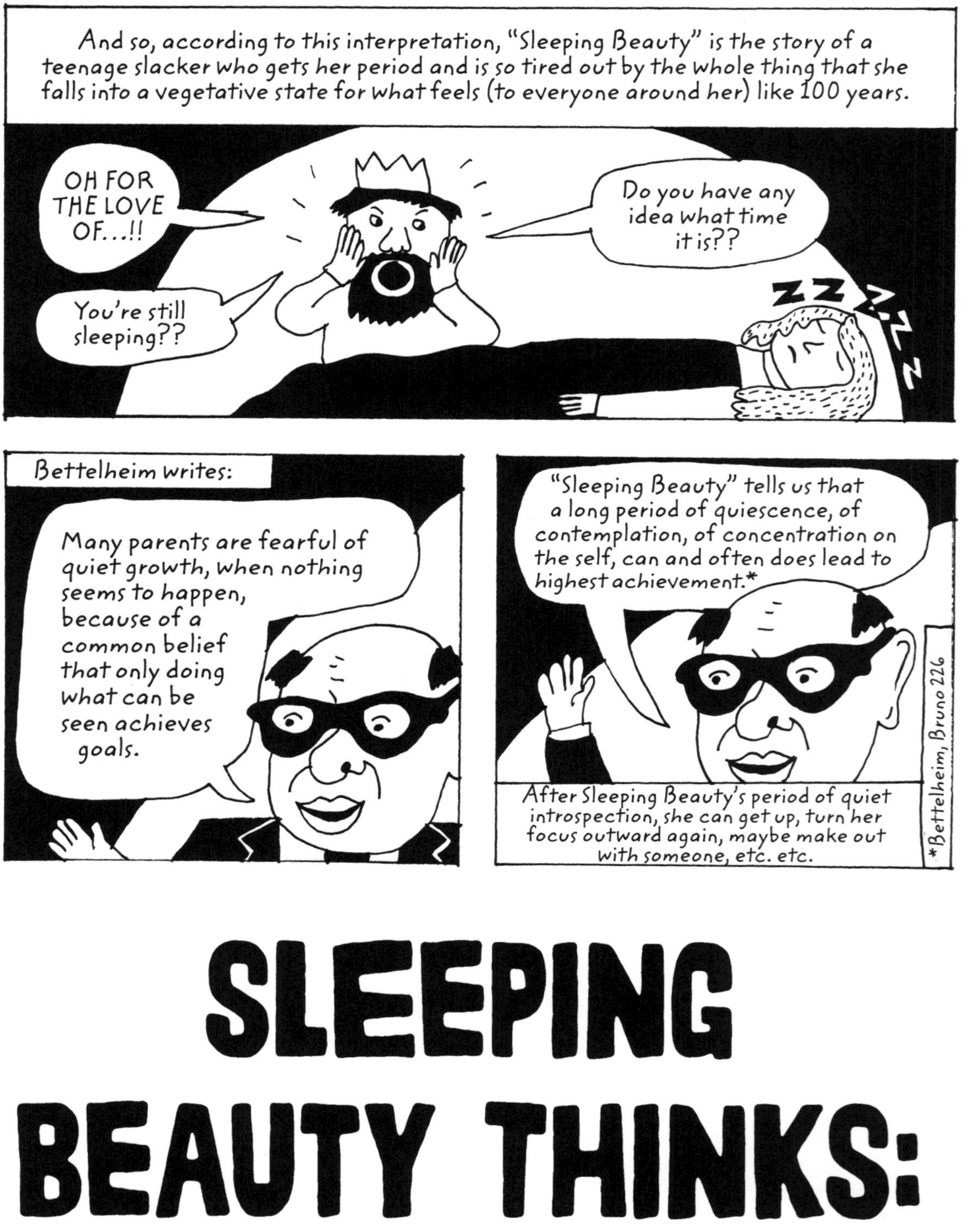
And so, according to this interpretation, "Sleeping Beauty" is the story of a teenage slacker who gets her period and is so tired out by the whole thing that she falls into a vegetative state for what feels (to everyone around her) like 100 years.
OH FOR THE LOVE OF...!!
You're still sleeping??
Do you have any idea what time it is??
ZZZZZZ
Bettelheim writes:
Many parents are fearful of quiet growth, when nothing seems to happen, because of a common belief that only doing what can be seen achieves goals.
"Sleeping Beauty" tells us that a long period of quiescence, of contemplation, of concentration on the self, can and often does lead to highest achievement.*
After Sleeping Beauty's period of quiet introspection, she can get up, turn her focus outward again, maybe make out with someone, etc. etc.
*Bettelheim, Bruno 226

SLEEPING BEAUTY THINKS:

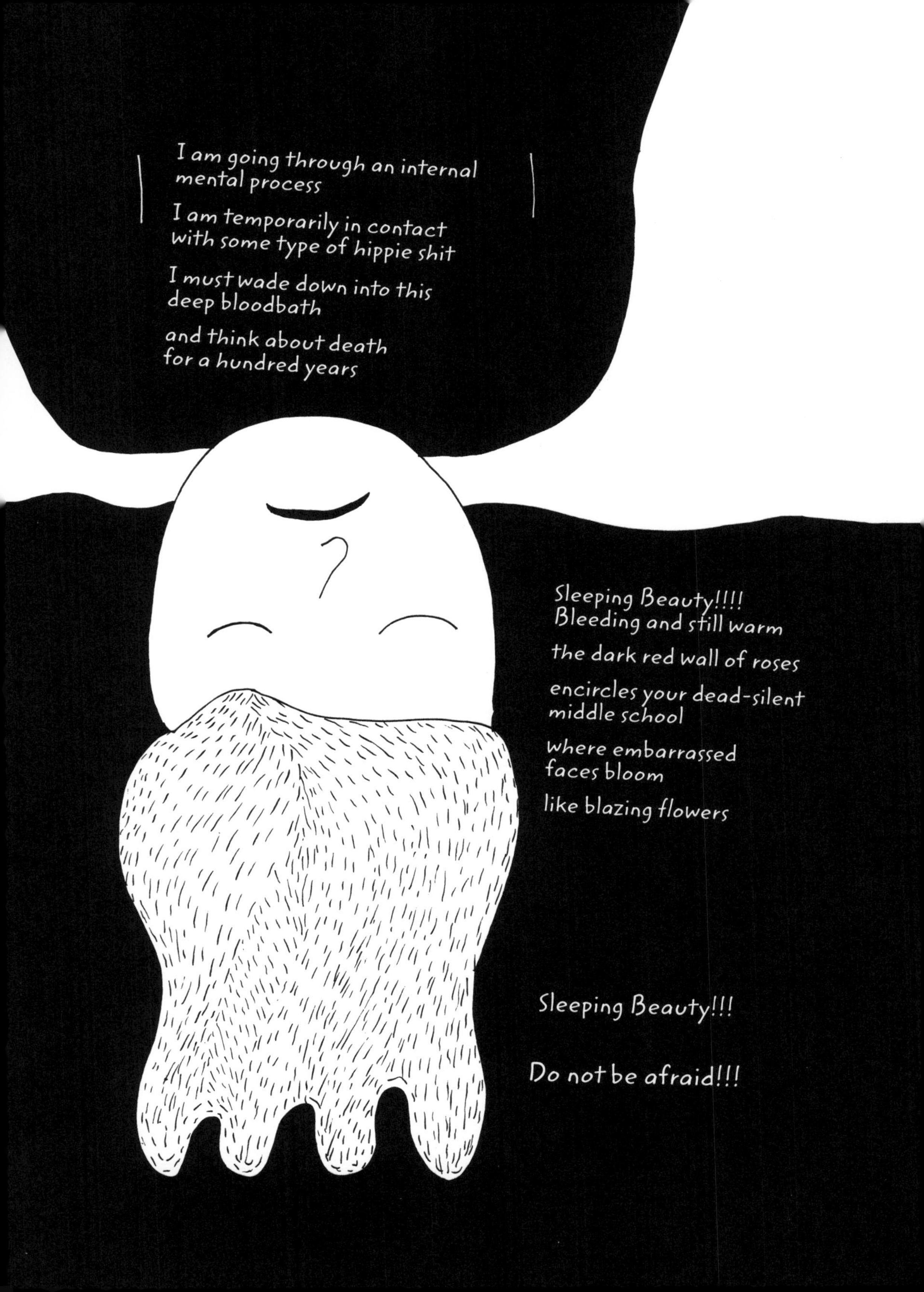
I am going through an internal mental process
I am temporarily in contact with some type of hippie shit
I must wade down into this deep bloodbath
and think about death for a hundred years
Sleeping Beauty!!!! Bleeding and still warm
the dark red wall of roses
encircles your dead-silent middle school
where embarrassed faces bloom
like blazing flowers
Sleeping Beauty!!!
Do not be afraid!!!

Sleep Take it Don't

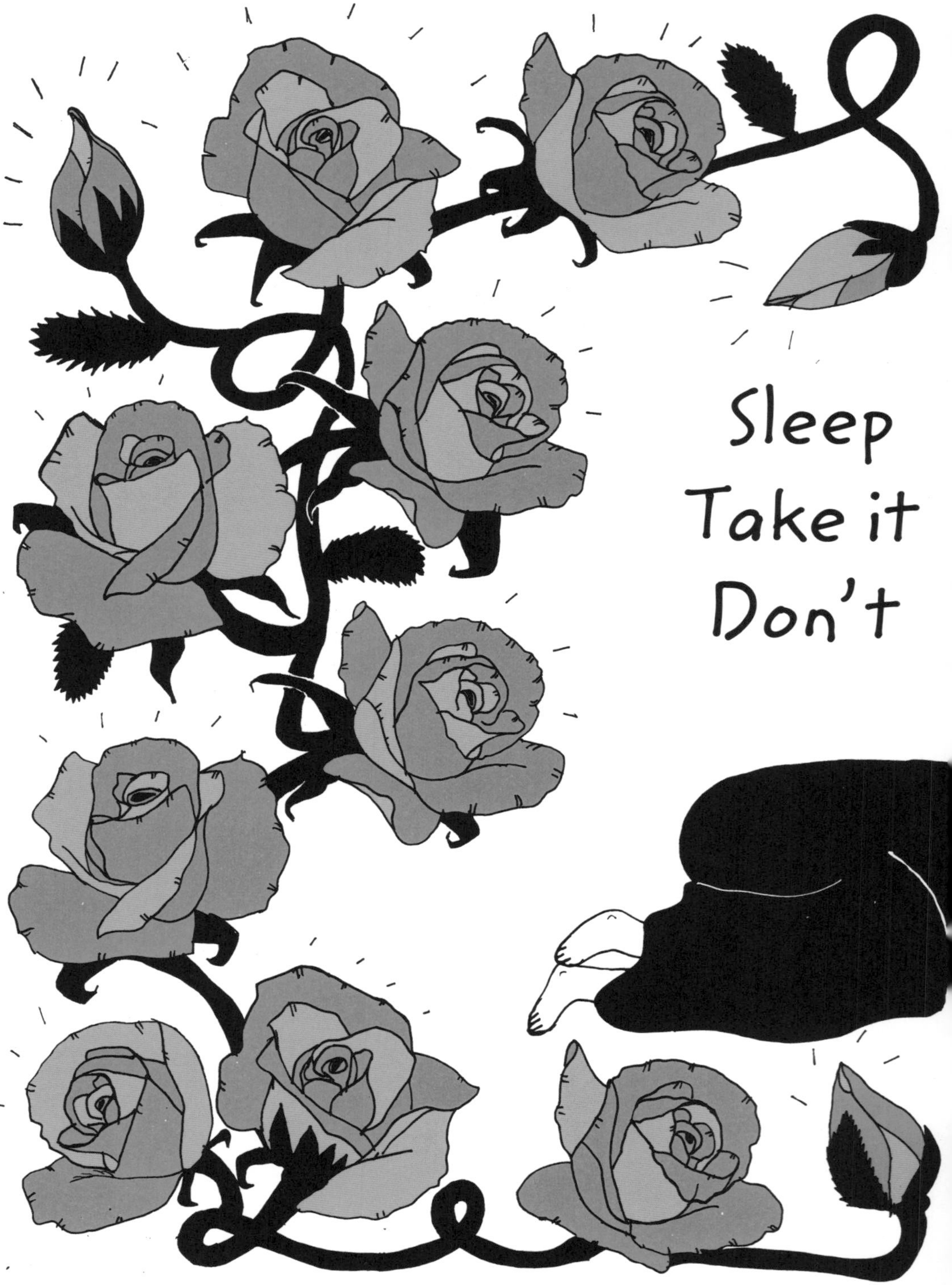

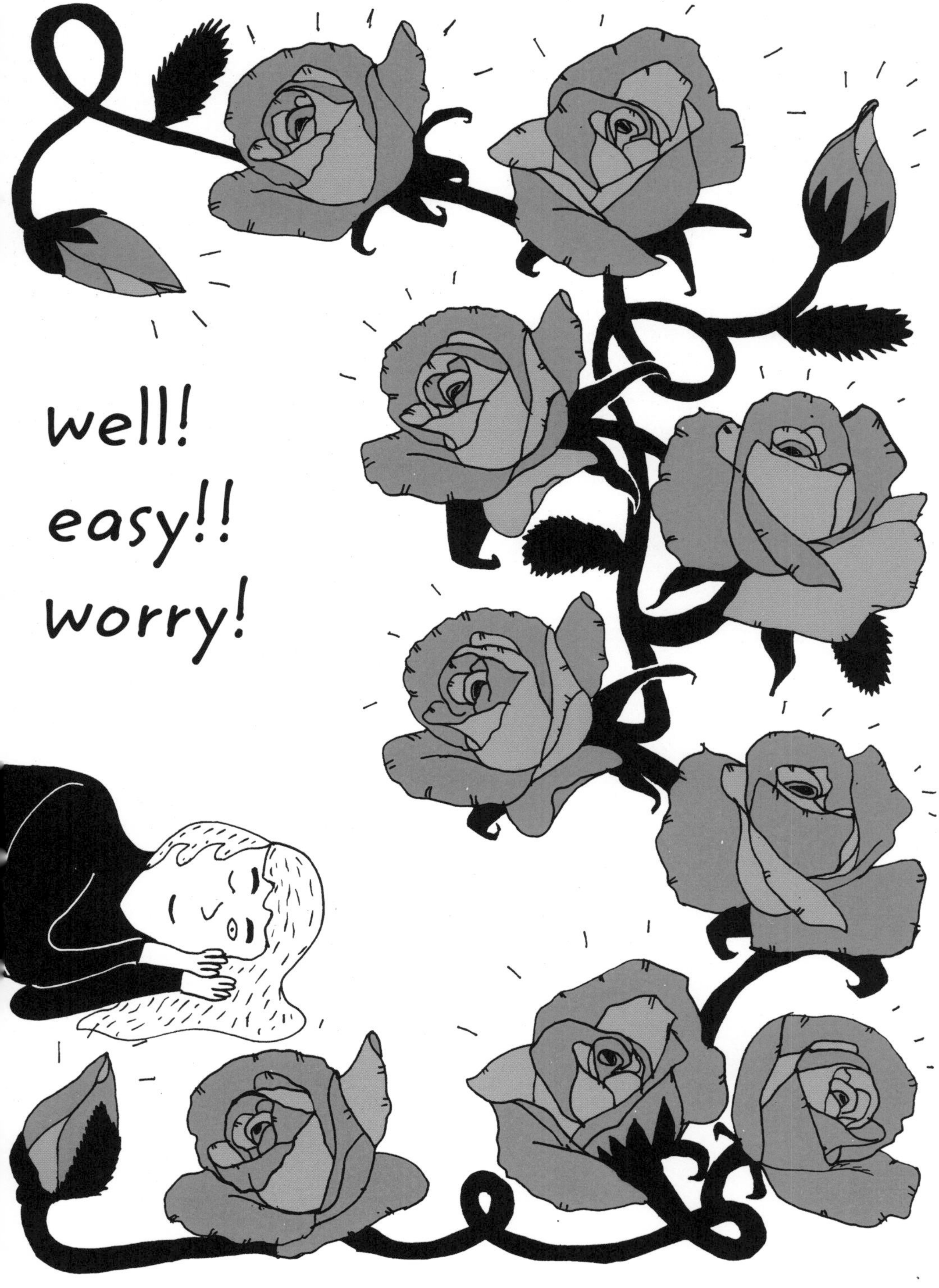
well!
easy!!
worry!

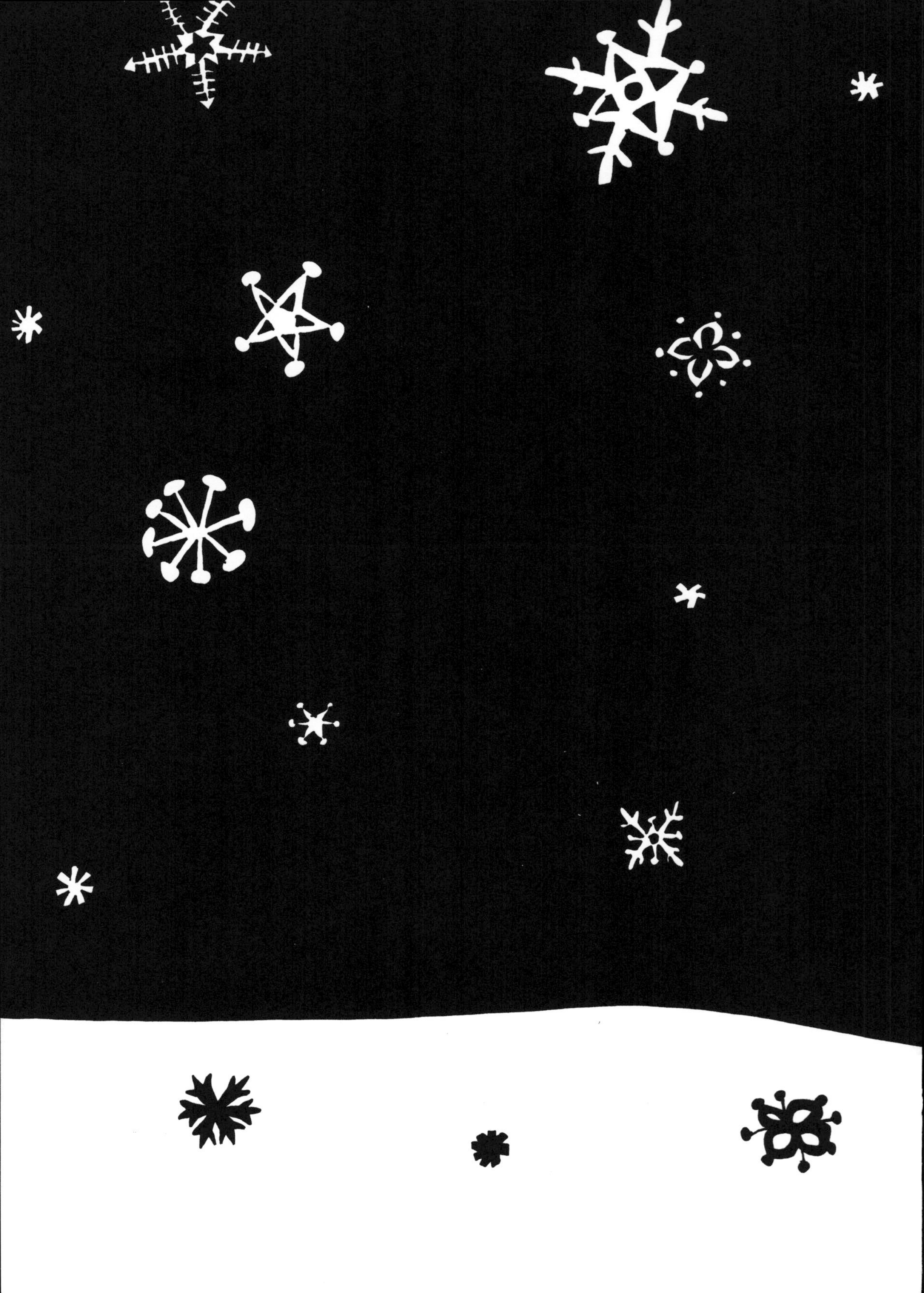

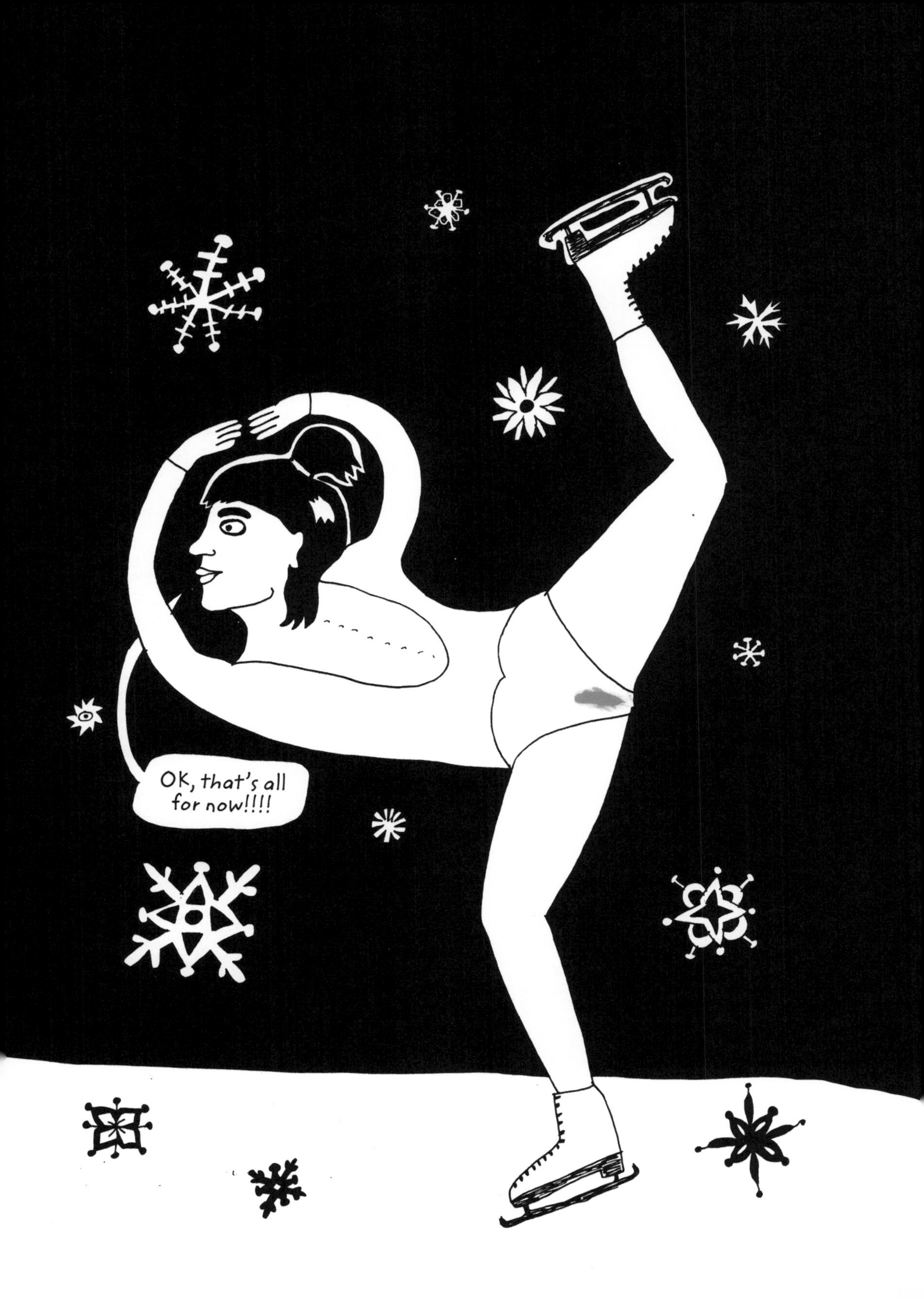
OK, that's all for now!!!!

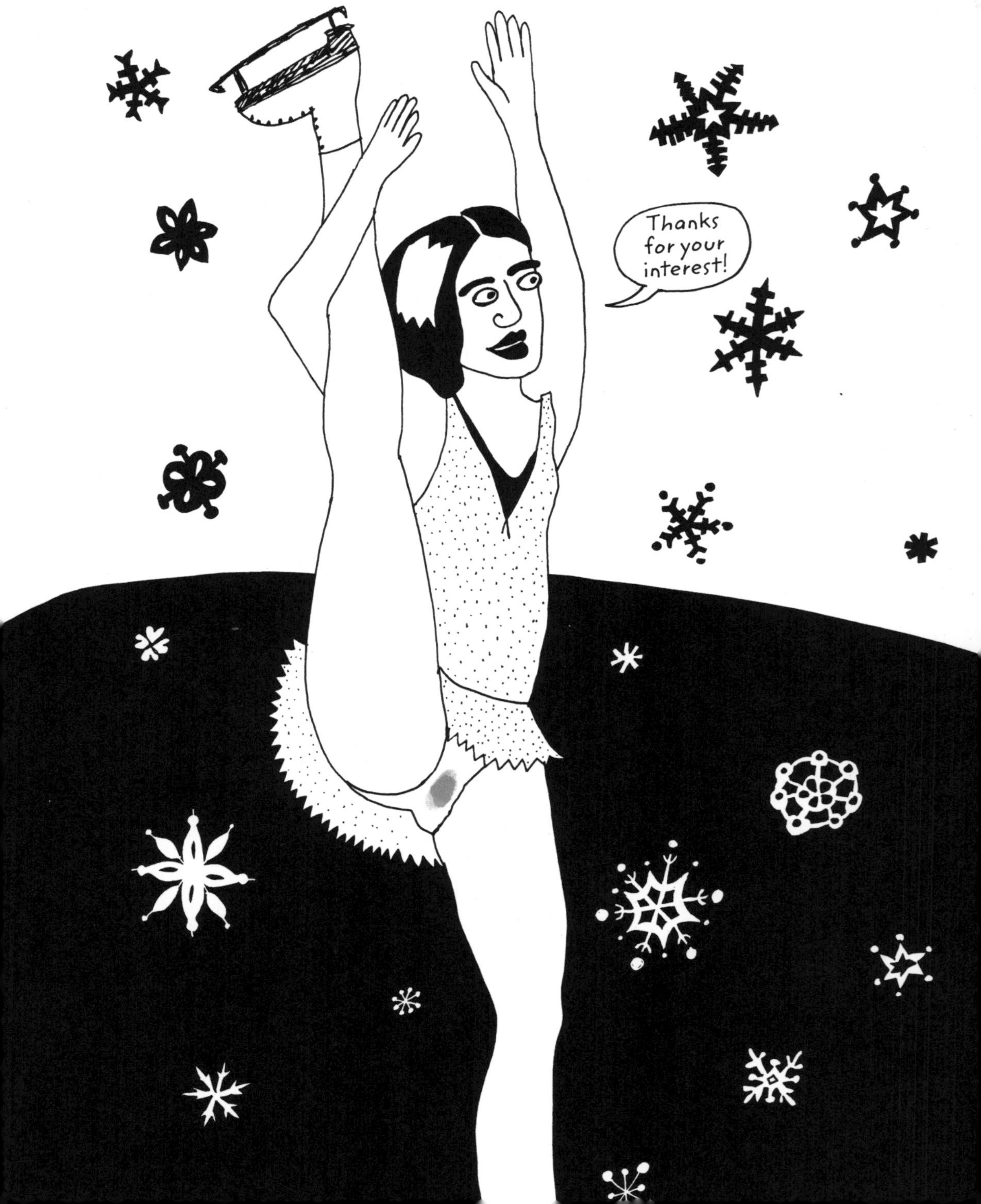
Thanks for your interest!

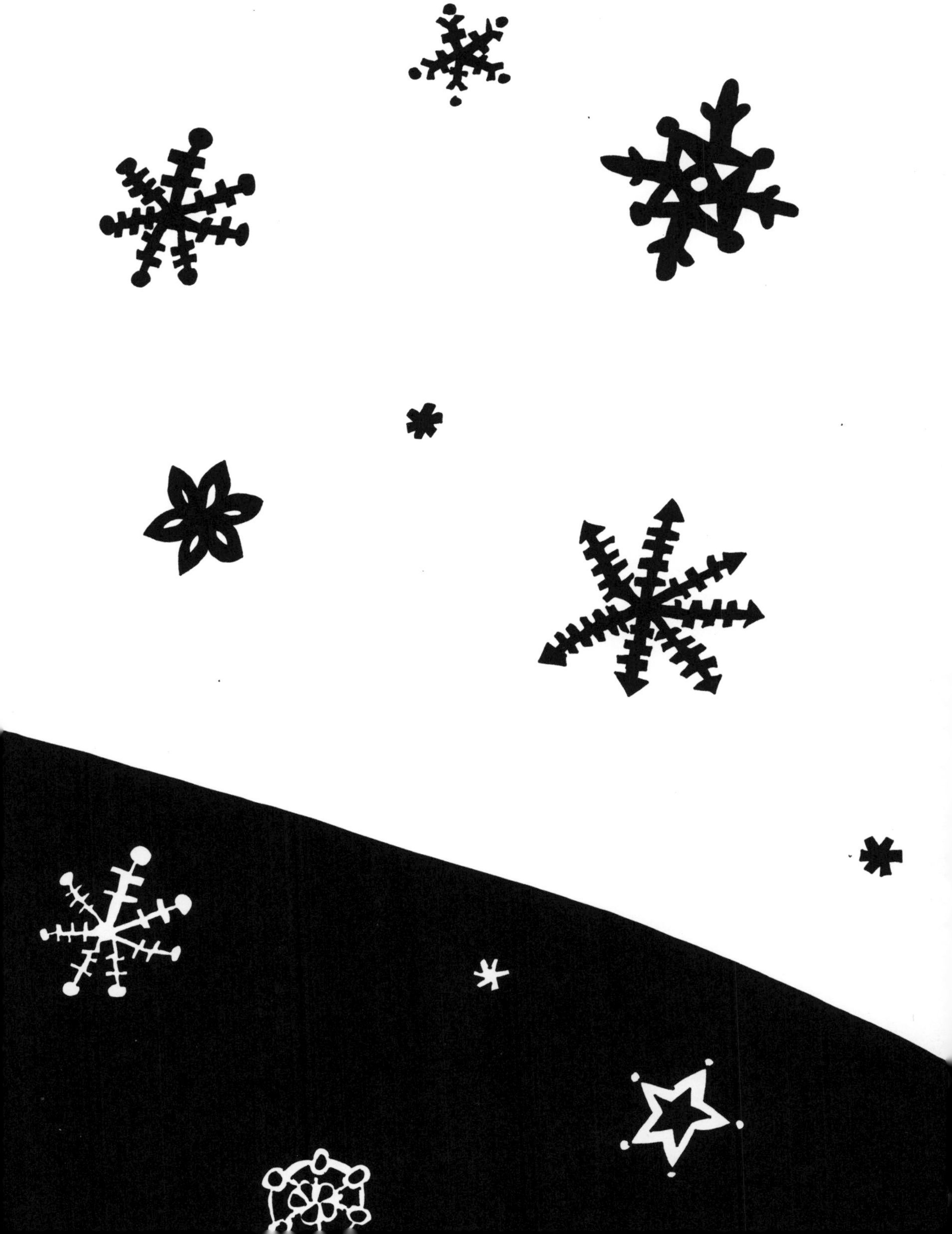